READING MARK STRAND

READING MARK STRAND
HIS COLLECTED WORKS, CAREER, AND THE POETICS OF THE PRIVATIVE

James F. Nicosia

READING MARK STRAND
© James F. Nicosia, 2007.

All citations from Harold Bloom's *The Anxiety of Influence* used by permission of Oxford University Press.

All David Kirby citations reprinted from *Mark Strand and the Poet's Place in Contemporary Culture* by David Kirby, by permission of the University of Missouri Press. Copyright © 1990 by the Curators of the University of Missouri.

A portion of chapter III originally appeared, in altered form, in *Bloom's Major Poets: Mark Strand*, edited by Harold Bloom. Used by permission of Chelsea House Publishers. Copyright © 2003 by James F. Nicosia.

All selections from *Selected Poems* by Mark Strand, copyright © 1979, 1980 by Mark Strand. Used by permission of Alfred A. Knopf, a division of Random House, Inc.

All selections from *The Continuous Life* by Mark Strand, copyright © 1990 by Mark Strand. Used by permission of Alfred A. Knopf, a division of Random House, Inc.

All selections from *Dark Harbor* by Mark Strand, copyright © 1993 by Mark Strand. Used by permission of Alfred A. Knopf, a division of Random House, Inc.

All selections from *The Weather of Words: Poetic Invention* by Mark Strand, copyright © 2000 by Mark Strand. Used by permission of Alfred A. Knopf, a division of Random House, Inc.

All selections from *Blizzard of One* by Mark Strand, copyright © 1998 by Mark Strand. Used by permission of Alfred A. Knopf, a division of Random House, Inc.

All selections from *Man and Camel* by Mark Strand, copyright © 2006 by Mark Strand. Used by permission of Alfred A. Knopf, a division of Random House, Inc.

First published in 2007 by
PALGRAVE MACMILLAN™
175 Fifth Avenue, New York, N.Y. 10010 and
Houndmills, Basingstoke, Hampshire, England RG21 6XS
Companies and representatives throughout the world.

PALGRAVE MACMILLAN is the global academic imprint of the Palgrave Macmillan division of St. Martin's Press, LLC and of Palgrave Macmillan Ltd. Macmillan® is a registered trademark in the United States, United Kingdom and other countries. Palgrave is a registered trademark in the European Union and other countries.

ISBN-13: 978–1–4039–7670–3
ISBN-10: 1–4039–7670–8

Library of Congress Cataloging-in-Publication Data

Nicosia, James F.
      Reading Mark Strand : his collected works, career, and the poetics of the privative / James F. Nicosia ; foreword by Harold Bloom.
            p. cm.
      Includes bibliographical references and index.
      ISBN 1–4039–7670–8 (alk. paper)
      1. Strand, Mark, 1934—Criticism and interpretation. I. Title.

PS3569.T69Z79 2007
791.43'682—dc22   2007061155

A catalogue record for this book is available from the British Library.

Design by Newgen Imaging Systems (P) Ltd., Chennai, India.

First edition: June 2007

10 9 8 7 6 5 4 3 2 1

Printed in the United States of America.

with Laura Nicosia
for Jake Nicosia

Contents

Foreword

Harold Bloom

I have known Mark Strand for a half century, and have read his poetry for rather more than 40 years. Like his major precursors, Walt Whitman and Wallace Stevens, Strand is a perpetual elegist of the self, not so much for himself as a person, but for himself as a poet, which is the mode of "always living, always dying," he has learned from Whitman and from Stevens.

If I had to name Strand's most representative poems, they might include "The Story of Our Lives," "The Way It Is," "Elegy for My Father," and the long poem or Stevensian sequence, *Dark Harbor*. I used to joke to Mark that his archetypal line was "The mirror was nothing without you," but as I have aged, I prefer a grand moment in the final canto of *Dark Harbor*, where someone speaks of poets wandering around who wished to be alive again, and says, "They were ready to say the words they were unable to say."

Even some four decades back, I always read each new poem and volume by Mark Strand in the happy expectation that he was ready to say the words he had been unable to say. Across the decades, it keeps puzzling me that really there are not any words he was unable to say. Though much sparser in output than Whitman, Stevens, and John Ashbery, Strand has developed a versatility that can rival theirs.

The elegy for the self may be the most American of all poetic genres, because our two greatest makers always will be Walt Whitman and Emily Dickinson, and they were always at home in that mode. Like Ashbery, Strand is a legitimate descendant of Whitman and Stevens. As a literary critic, I am a kind of archaic survival, a dinosaur, and I particularly favor the brontosaurus, an amiable enough monster. I do not believe that poetry has anything to do with cultural politics. I ask of a poem three things: aesthetic splendor, cognitive power, and wisdom. I find all three in the work of Mark Strand.

One of Strand's unique achievements is to raise the self's poignant confrontation with mortality to an aesthetic dignity that astonishes me.

His earlier volume *Darker* moves upon the heights in its final poems,
"Not Dying" and the longer "The Way It Is," the first work in which
Strand ventures out from his eye's first circle, toward a larger art.
"Not Dying" opens in narcissistic desperation, and reaches no resolu-
tion, but its passion for survival is prodigiously convincing. "I am
driven by innocence," the poet protests, even as like a Beckett crea-
ture he crawls from bed to chair and back again, until he finds the
obduracy to proclaim a grotesque version of natural supernaturalism:

> I shall not die.
> The grave result
> and token of my birth, my body
> remembers and holds fast.

"The Way It Is" takes its tone from Stevens at his darkest ("The
world is ugly / And the people are sad") and quietly edges out a private phantasmagoria until this merges with the public phantasmagoria
all of us now inhabit. The consequence is a poem more surprising and
profound than the late Robert Lowell's justly celebrated "For the
Union Dead," a juxtaposition made unavoidable by Strand's audacity
in appropriating the same visionary area:

> I see myself in the park
> on horseback, surrounded by dark,
> leading the armies of peace.
> The iron legs of the horse do not bend.
>
> I drop the reins. Where will the turmoil end?
> Fleets of taxis stall in the fog, passengers fall
> asleep. Gas pours
>
> from a tri-colored stack.
> Locking their doors,
> people from offices huddle together,
> telling the same story over and over.
>
> Everyone who has sold himself wants to buy himself back.
> Nothing is done. The night
> eats into their limbs
> like a blight.
>
> Everything dims.
> The future is not what it used to be.
> The graves are ready. The dead
> shall inherit the dead.

Strand's gift is harbored rather than sparse: that is my interpretation of
his major work to date, *Dark Harbor: A Poem* (1993). The poem
constitutes a "Proem" and 45 cantos or sections.
Dark Harbor, like some earlier poems by Strand, is an overt
homage to Wallace Stevens. It is as though casting aside anxieties of
influences Strand wishes reconcilement with his crucial precursor. The
"Proem" sets forth vigorously: "The burning / Will of weather,
blowing overhead, would be his muse." But, by Canto IV, we all of us
now are in the world of Stevens:

> There is a certain triviality in living here,
> A lightness, a comic monotony that one tries
> To undermine with shows of energy, a devotion
>
> To the vagaries of desire, whereas over there
> Is a seriousness, a stiff, inflexible gloom
> That shrouds the disappearing soul, a weight
>
> That shames our lightness. Just look
> Across the river and you will discover
> How unworthy you are as you describe what you see,
>
> Which is bound by what is available.
> On the other side, no one is looking this way.
> They are committed to obstacles,
>
> To the textures and levels of darkness,
> To the tedious enactment of duration.
> And they labor not for bread or love
>
> But to perpetuate the balance between the past
> And the future. They are the future as it
> Extends itself, just as we are the past
>
> Coming to terms with itself. Which is why
> The napkins are pressed, and the cookies have come
> On time, and why the glass of milk, looking so chic
>
> In its whiteness, begs us to sip. None of this happens
> Over there. Relief from anything is seen
> As timid, a sign of shallowness or worse.

This is the voice of the master, particularly in *An Ordinary Evening
in New Haven*. Strand shrewdly undoes Stevens to the glass of milk,
setting aside any more metaphysical concerns. An effort is made, for
15 cantos, to domesticate Stevens, but the great voice, of Stevens and

Strand fused together, returns in Canto XVI:

It is true, as someone has said, that in
A world without heaven all is farewell.
Whether you wave your hand or not,

It is farewell, and if no tears come to your eyes
It is still farewell, and if you pretend not to notice,
Hating what passes, it is still farewell.

Farewell no matter what. And the palms as they lean
Over the green, bright lagoon, and the pelicans
Diving, and the listening bodies of bathers resting,

Are stages in an ultimate stillness, and the movement
Of sand, and of wind, and the secret moves of the body
Are part of the same, a simplicity that turns being

Into an occasion for mourning, or into an occasion
Worth celebrating, for what else does one do,
Feeling the weight of the pelicans' wings,

The density of the palms' shadows, the cells that darken
The backs of bathers? These are beyond the distortions
Of chance, beyond the evasions of music. The end

Is enacted again and again. And we feel it
In the temptations of sleep, in the moon's ripening,
In the wine as it waits in the glass.

It is Stevens who tells us that, without heaven, all farewells are final.
What enchants me here are the Strandian variations on farewell. Waves
and tears yield to very Stevensian palms, and to the pelicans of Florida,
venereal soil. A greater meditation, suitable to Strand and Stevens as
seers of the weather, arrives in Canto XXIV:

Now think of the weather and how it is rarely the same
For any two people, how when it is small, precision is needed
To say when it is really an aura or odor or even an air

Of certainty, or how, as the hours go by, it could be thought of
As large because of the number of people it touches.
Its strength is something else: tornados are small

But strong and cloudless summer days seem infinite
But tend to be weak since we don't mind being out in them.
Excuse me, is this the story of another exciting day,

The sort of thing that accompanies preparations for dinner?
Then what say we talk about the inaudible-the shape it assumes,
And what social implications it holds,

Or the somber flourishes of autumn-the bright
Or blighted leaves falling, the clicking of cold branches,
The new color of the sky, its random blue.

Is that final tercet Strand or Stevens? As the sequence strengthens, deliberate echoes of Josh Ashbery, Octavio Paz, and Wordworth are evoked by Strand, until he achieves a grand apotheosis in his final canto:

I am sure you would find it misty here,
With lots of stone cottages badly needing repair.
Groups of souls, wrapped in cloaks, sit in the fields

Or stroll the winding unpaved roads. They are polite,
And oblivious to their bodies, which the wind passes through,
Making a shushing sound. Not long ago,

I stopped to rest in a place where an especially
Thick mist swirled up from the river. Someone,
Who claimed to have known me years before,

Approached, saying there were many poets
Wandering around who wished to be alive again.
They were ready to say the words they had been unable to say-

Words whose absence had been the silence of love,
Of pain, and even of pleasure. Then he joined a small group,
Gathered beside a fire. I believe I recognized

Some of the faces, but as I approached they tucked
Their heads under their wings. I looked away to the hills
Above the river, where the golden lights of sunset

And sunrise are one and the same, and saw something flying
Back and forth, fluttering its wings. Then it stopped in mid-air.
It was an angel, one of the good ones, about to sing.

The aura is Dante's, and we are in a spooky place—paradise of poets or purgatory of poets. If one line above all others in *Dark Harbor* reverberates within me, it is "They were ready to say the words they had been unable to say." The accent remains late Stevens, but with a difference that is Mark Strand's.

I commend James Nicosia's *Reading Mark Strand* as a superb guide for all readers.

Acknowledgments

Thanks to Harold Bloom, who has inspired me to be a better, stronger, more thoughtful reader; to James Tuttleton, for his thoughtfulness and direction; to Josephine Hendin, for her encouragement; to Cyrus Patell, for asserting boldness.

Thanks to Dan Bronson for encouraging originality; Lee Cullen Khanna for recognizing sincerity; Jim Nash for his cool confidence; Alyce Miller for her enthusiasm; and Naomi Liebler, for her genuine interest.

Thanks to Lisa, Steve, Aimee, Janette, Jessica and Helen, for their constancy.

Thanks to Mark Strand, for creating poetry that one can get excited about in these creatively challenged times.

Thanks to my father, for his faith.

"Between Two Great Darks":
How to Read Poetry

In "chapter" 9 of *The Monument*, Mark Strand reveals his nihilistic
view of the state of human affairs when he says, "Nothing is the destiny of everyone," yet also provides the foundation for poetry within
this nothingness by saying, "It has been necessary to submit to
vacancy in order to begin again, to clear ground, to make space"
(9). Readers and critics must, says the poet, provide space for the
poems themselves. No critical preconceptions or personal expecta-
tions should control their reading process. Yes, intimate knowledge of
this poet, and perhaps all the poets *that* poet has ever read, is essential
to developing a more profound poetic experience. But the *experience*
of a poem, Strand's or otherwise, is something that only can happen
in real time, that is, the time during which the reader reads the poem.
Other mental links to previous poems and poets may—and should—
be made by the individual reader, à la J. Hillis Miller's *Ariadne's
Thread*. But what fascinates the forthright reader of poetry is what
happens during the reading of the poem.

It is this active area in which Strand excels in transcending mere
tropes, and which concerns this study: what happens between the
bookends of darkness, the absences of poem in the moment right
before the reader engages the poem, and the moment after he/she has
read the last word. Strand dictates that this, in fact, is the way one
must engage the poem, both as writer and reader. To accomplish such
an "honest reading," this study commences with a phenomenological
approach. Without stubbornly clinging to Georges Poulet—or his
onetime proponent, J. Hillis Miller—this study esteems Poulet's position that one should pursue the mind of the author. While I do not go

so far as to assert, as Poulet does, that the reader must "reach . . . the mind of the author and nothing beyond that" (Miller 474), I do contend that, in this time of critical flavors of the month, there are less noble tasks than achieving oneness with the mind of the poet as manifested in the speaker. Also, while I do not *precisely* concur that, after reading, the reader is *completely* "empty, ready to be invaded and possessed by another book, another mind" (Miller 475), for a brief moment after a text is consumed, there *is* a necessary blank period where the reader must make a transformation from I-as-reader to I-as-self. Indeed, in the precise moment *after* reading, he/she no longer *is* a reader at all, and must endure a transition, however short, into mere being. The poet is, of course, also only I-as-poet when engaged in the writing process; we will recognize the realms before and after the ostensible writing of the poem as Strand's "two great darks." Thus, both I-as-poet and I-as-reader exist between two darknesses.

One can learn much about reading poetry if one pursues each poet on his/her own ground. Thus, this study chooses first to become keenly aware of the sound, sentiment, and lexicon of the Mark Strand poem, and hopes to inspire readers to read all poets with this kind of dexterity. Rigorous close reading of the poems allows a familiarity with them that, with sensitivity to "the mind of the poet," yields what we assert is the ultimate goal of any reader: poetic intimacy. Mark Strand is noteworthy as one of the latest in a long line of modern poets partaking in an imaginative poetic dialogue. If Strand is an essential poet as a bevy of critics—and a throng of readers—believe he is, learning how to read a Strand poem is learning how to read poetry.

THE CUMULATIVE EFFECT OF STRAND'S POETRY

This monograph's initial goal is to identify the recognizable elements of the Strand poem—the expressions of fear toward a malignant world, expressed as a privative darkness; the value of poetry in the face of apathetic nature; the necessity of absence or a primitive darkness as the genesis of temporary redemption; the value of indulgence in poetic activity; and the desire to revel in the "perfect moment." In doing so, we cultivate a vocabulary for discussing the crucial moments of evolution in a poetic career, which assists in answering the question that the poet himself attempts to answer: "What can a poem do?"

Readers recognize Strand's perception of the natural world as a volatile place—either malevolent or apathetic toward humanity— within which one can only hope to find short-term shelter. Although

Strand's speaker has frequent doubts about the imagination's capacity to sustain, he does recognize that poetry has value at least as solace, if not as a wholly developed artistic counterlife. Strand provides that shelter for himself and his reader, invoking the imagination; both "forget the world" when engrossed in the imaginative act, and the loss leaves room for a great acquisition—access to a poetic cosmos. The artistic creation becomes a haven within the natural world of destruction: when all that is natural erases one's grandest achievements, the only choice is to flee the rules of nature and present an artificial construct that will suffice, even if it does not evolve into a full-fledged imaginative counterlife.

The Strand speaker never desires *full* retreat from the physical world, however, because he knows it is not possible. He is renewed by finding temporary sanctuaries while fully engaged in creative moments of pure imagination. Within these sanctuaries, elements from the natural world are selected, recombined, and breathed into new existence—troped—by its new Creator, the Strand speaker. These natural-world objects are little more than big, mute mountains that loom ominously and obstruct light—or moons that merely reflect the light from some other generative source—giving little back to the world. Imaginative souls—poetry's readers and writers—must take from the world the items required to construct something more sustaining. As Strand says of a cloud's arrival on the scene in *Dark Harbor*, "its purpose / We would have to decipher and apply / To our own ends, so *we could say* that it came / For further clarification, some heavy editing" (XII, 15–18, italics mine). Through such "editing," Strand's mountains move and his moons shine.

Strand and his readers need to begin at a blank. By extracting—sometimes even himself—from the "real" world, Strand provides a sturdier foundation for the poetic world[1] that replaces it. Absence is a mode likened in many poems to "a place / beyond, / beyond love, / where nothing, / everything, / wants to be born" ("My Son" 23–28).[2] J. Hillis Miller defines this imaginative birthing place inside us as the *Cogito* (480–84). While the world presents a darkness of horror, or a privative darkness representing the removal of what was once there, Strand's desired poetic darkness is a primitive one, that promising state before things are. From this genesis begins the poem, in which man, disconnected from the cosmos, becomes the creative force in the absence of a benevolent God.

Once begun, the poetic process must be engaged in wholly. In "Eating Poetry," Strand expresses that poetry is a participatory act that must be immersed in fully, unselfconsciously, as a dog does while eating. The sense one gets of Strand's poetic theory is that each poem has been written in real time, and must be read in one sitting, within the fervor—the Transport, if you will—of imaginative projection. Action in the Strand poem therefore frequently takes place in present tense, ostensibly during the writing of the poem. Thus, we should read the Strand poem as an imaginative creation that takes place concurrent with our reading of it.

Our equation then reads as follows: By subtracting the world and even one's self from the poem as one begins (a privative action), all possibilities exist (a primitive condition). Once our worldly baggage is dropped from our shoulders and we assume a nearly tabula rasa state, we can go wherever the poem takes us. While participating in the poem, the imagination is engaged completely, effectively drowning out the cacophony of the natural world, thereby affirming the virtues of the poetic endeavor between two vast darknesses.

Strand engages the stuff of his fears and—particularly in the later, stronger part of his career—the poem momentarily alleviates them. And moments are an important qualification for Strand. That is, the poem—as the precise spot in time wherein the personal universe is fashioned—is the perfect moment for writer and reader, even if that moment is, by definition, fleeting. As Strand reminds us,

> Lyric poetry . . . celebrates or recognizes moods, ideas, events only as they exist in passing. . . . Even when poetry celebrates something joyful, it bears the news that the particular joy is over. It is a long memorial, a valedictory to each discrete moment on earth. But its power is at variance with what it celebrates. For it is not just that we mourn the passage of time but that we are somehow isolated from the weight of time. . . . [W]hen we read poems, during those brief moments of absorption, the thought of death seems painless, even beautiful.
>
> (*The Weather of Words* 5)

Even at its most potent, though, the instant the poetic effort ends—with the final words of the poem—poet and reader return to darkness. Furthermore, the instant the imagination ceases to be engaged fully—that is, the instant the speaker even becomes *conscious* that the imagination is engaged, the imagination becomes object instead of subject, and the intimate poetic linkage is severed. As Strand has quoted of Stevens, "As long as we ourselves are caught up in the process of creation, we neither see nor understand; indeed we ought not to understand, for nothing is more injurious to immediate experience than cognition" (*The Weather* 71).

Charting the Poet's Course

How do we recognize a poet's graduation into a "mature" stage? How can we assess a poetic career in the midst of its happening? These questions challenge us to carefully pursue a poet's unfolding as a writer. Only through doing so are we able to identify those crucial moments of imaginative evolution, and hope to say to ourselves and those who wish to learn about poetry, "I *know* the poetry of this writer."

Strand's most frequently anthologized poems—"Keeping Things Whole," "Eating Poetry," "The Marriage," "The Dead," "The Tunnel," "The Dreadful Has Already Happened," and "Pot Roast"—have been culled primarily from the early part of his career. While certainly attractive, clever, and memorable in their frightful expression of a nightmarish world, these poems are merely excellent prefigurations to the mature imaginative expressions that evolve from Strand, which, beginning with his *The Late* Hour (1978), reach genuine heights in *The Continuous Life*, and find their ultimate form in his magnum opus, *Dark Harbor*.

Perhaps Strand's early work is the most accessible—and anthologists are only doing what is necessary for their projects in choosing such poetic sound bites—yet sound bites are distinctly *not* what Strand is about. Magazine verse—the attractive memorable poem that evokes Stevens, Bishop, or any precursors that we may easily recognize—is something Strand has grown beyond. Indeed, the mature poet *must* grow beyond this stage of seeming like someone else. The 46-part poem *Dark Harbor* is the masterpiece of his career, and yet no single part is its quintessence. Like Strand's career, *Dark Harbor* is the sum of its parts, and thus essentially indivisible. To know this poem requires a confident knowledge of the history of Strand's use of the imagination. Thus, we need to engage in his work as a whole to recognize the great work, to engage in his entire career to recognize the lifelong process of becoming an accomplished poet.

Familiarity with other poets is an initial lead-in to the young poet's work. This neophyte's work incorporates an intriguing stylistics, a uniqueness of vision, and a resonance with a master poet. These three elements are not enough to qualify a poet for greatness, however, though they may be enough to garner great attention. Presenting the world as it appears to the poet in a compelling manner is one thing. But it is an altogether different thing to be able to map out new ground, to do something productive in the face of the terrors of the natural world, and to say something to the page that eats up his words—all of which only the stronger poet can do.

The use of terms like "precursor" and "strong poet" advances us, of course, into territory well established by Harold Bloom. Although diligently applying Bloom's model to Strand's career would be a worthwhile task, it would seem to be work better left for another project. However, this study does use Bloom's antithetical criticism as a touchstone as it charts Strand's growth into an astonishing poet who can affect the reader's universe within the confines of the poem and, ultimately, confront the anxiety of his own influence in *Blizzard of One*.

The poetry of which we speak begins as a voice that compellingly describes modern existence. At some point, however, the poet must do more than generate a compendium of motifs as he compellingly relates his humours. Strand remarks this in "The History of Poetry," sadly reporting of those weak poets who "do nothing but count the trees, the clouds, / The few birds left" (19–20). With this, Strand defines a significant qualification for an important poet, one with which this study also concurs. The strong poet goes beyond chronicling his world. He is generative in the face of perpetual annihilation. He is able to do something in the face of the world's whirlwinds, to provide an alternative *within the poem* to the banalities of the world *external* to the poem. The strong poet can take the reader along for the ride.

How can we identify this transformation in Strand from chronicler of a terrorizing world to creator of worlds? The discussion of this transformation not only limns the career of this poet, but also provides a viable methodology for assessing other poetic careers. On the surface, Strand may not appear to be a startlingly original poet—in that his poems are initially familiar, almost comfortable. His tongue-in-cheek tones, classic motifs, and ordered cadences enchant, before they ultimately discomfit the reader with the inseparable juxtaposition of starkness and humor, of joy and severity, and absence and promise. We are lured into a kind of inattentiveness by the familiar elements of the poem and do not immediately realize the profundity of the horrors contained therein, or the quality of the humor that so deftly masks such terrors. Thus, the uniqueness of Strand's application of common poetic tools both merits careful consideration and helps us learn how to read other contemporary poets, as well. His tone, his lexicon, and most of his stylistics are inherited from his American poetic forebears, and yet perhaps because of his *apparent* facility, only a percentage of the legion of his readers plumbs the depths of his work. However, *because* Strand evolves from many other prominent poets, incursions into his verses will also proffer paradigms to apply elsewhere in the contemporary poetic world.

In an interview with Cristine Bacchilega, Strand has said of his own poetry, "I'm really less interested in writing magazine verse or individual poems than in creating a literary spectacle . . . a little like *Barthes on Barthes*" (59). Attempting to provide consistent rules for the reader would bear out Strand's statement; he is, after all, a poet of intentionally contradictory means, one with a multiplicity of personae. No definitive criticism yet has been agreed upon to lend satisfactory insight into Strand's career, and thus far, the thoughtful close readings of his work have done little to provide a framework for understanding Strand's poetic philosophy, or recognizing the nuances of a career as it has unfolded.

"So deeply does the speaker feel the ugliness of reality . . .," says Peter Stitt, "that he attempts to retreat farther and farther from it. Through his death-consciousness, he diminishes the world until it virtually disappears into nothingness. . . . The closer reality draws to nothingness, the greater looms the power of the mind and the world it creates for itself" ("Stages" 202). In *The Weather of Words*, Strand expresses in prose the nihilism he practices in his poetry when he says, "Life . . . prepares us for nothing, and leaves us nowhere to go. It stops" (5). However, he also acknowledges that nothingness as the footing for poetry; take a privative blank, he contends, and turn it into a primitive one from which all things sprout:

> S is for something that supplies a vacancy, which I [as poet] might fill. It has a verbal presence that my own immediate appetite of ambition subverts, misreads, or makes into an appealing void, a space only I can elaborate on. I begin with something as if it were nothing (or nothing as if it were something) . . . (12–13)

Strand's view of the world is perhaps no better expressed—or placed—than in the concluding poem of *Selected Poems*, "Leopardi." In it, he feels the pain of an "old wound" (7), and leaves his wife in bed to "pay my late respects / to the sky that seems so gentle / and to the world that is not and that says to me: / 'I do not give you any hope. Not even hope' " (8–11). Despite the natural world's perpetual portentousness, the Strand speaker never desires full retreat from this world, because he knows it is not possible. Robert Frost's speaker acknowledges that "Earth's the right place for love" ("Birches" 52), and while Strand is not nearly as hopeful, he does find temporary sanctuaries and partial successes while fully engaged in glimmering moments of poetic creation and instants of replete indulgence in other creative activities. For Strand, the poetry created in this sanctuary contrasts with the volatile world outside his door. The images created in this poetic harbor are often stark, carefully selected to stand out against an empty black or white background. As Laurence Lieberman says, for

Strand, "The process of writing is an act of heroic struggle to stay alive in the spirit against terrible odds, to maintain the life of a beleaguered sensibility. Thus, the stripping away of all but the most subtle artifice, and the divesting of all stylistic flourish, all superfluities" (282).

While not trying to belabor any coupling of Strand and Frost,[3] Frost's acknowledgment in his preface to the 1954 collection, *Aforesaid*, that "A poem is best read in the light of all the other poems ever written," reasonably applies to the well-read Strand (Quoted in Barry). Indeed, in an attempt to establish a glossary to Strand, most of the rules one would establish regarding symbolism, style, and tone would be easily contradicted by a careful reader. As such a studied poet, Strand's range of experience and of allusion is broad. Nonetheless, reading Strand in toto does provide an unwavering strain of poetic philosophy revealed in a rather recognizable lyrical voice. Though he uses contradictory images to create similar effects—or the same image to achieve different ends—his vision is consistent: the world is inscrutable. To confront such a master of conflation, it is best to proceed in unadorned terms: he has his good days and his bad days; at times he is playful, at times desperate; at times he has answers for us, his readers; at others he does not have answers even for himself. Regardless of this inconsistency, we do comprehend (as opposed to merely apprehend) a poet's creative universe when we indulge in the poetry with an eye toward recognizing key transitional moments in his evolution. And we understand his attempts to escape the world's horrors (even if this means sometimes fully experiencing them) and to provide for himself and his reader a shelter from the world's storms in poetic participation.

David Kirby addresses this issue in optimistic terms:

> At the height of prowess, the artist is in a state of perfect health, perfect integration, using language that is as close as can ever be to the perfect language of Eden. At the moment of total absorption in the act of reading or writing, the poet becomes oblivious to himself, to his self, becomes no one, No One at all. (82–83)

While Kirby may sound a bit hyperbolic when he asserts that poetry has the power to bring the artist to "perfect" Edenic health, the poet—and, I assert, the reader—*do* leave the world behind when immersed in the imaginative act, and the loss leaves room for a valuable acquisition—the poetic creation.

Though less of a Strand fan, Robert Pinsky also has insight that can work as a springboard for this study. He asserts that Strand's poetry "is not of the kind that surprises the reader, by forcing us to revise our idea of what poetry is. . . . Strand is an original writer, but not of the kind who challenges our idea of poetry. He confirms that idea, rather than enlarging it" (300–301). On the one hand, Pinsky undervalues Strand in his belief that Strand's poetics do not augment our idea of poetry—ignoring, perhaps, what Kirby accurately identifies as an astonishing reductionism. Yet, on the other hand, in acknowledging Strand's place as a "confirmer" of the vital if vanishing poetic dialogue, Pinsky does recognize that part of Strand's appeal lies in a sense of familiarity that his work conveys: beneath the chaotic representation of the world, the shifting perspectives, the line-blurring between victim and victimization, between the world and the self, there is a poet chiefly concerned with the potential of poetry to vivify the self in the face of an apathetic world.

Undoubtedly, Mark Strand is a poet difficult to classify, explicate and, often, to read meaningfully. A perusal of the criticism can attest to this, as a great majority of critics addresses his work in terms of complacent generalizations, permitting large gaps between their facile words and his taut poetic creations. "Mark Strand's hallmarks are precise language, surreal imagery, and the recurring theme of absence and negation," says Cornelia A. Pernik without ardent effort. Other critics point to his use of dreams as a sign of his being a writer of the fantastic. His themes of absence naturally entice deconstructionists to claim him as one of their own. Poems such as "Pot Roast" and "The Thing Itself" lead Linda Gregerson to enlist him as a Romantic, and yet others, astoundingly, call him a confessionalist.

Much criticism of Strand has so far failed to engage itself in his poetry in meaningful ways. As a result of attempting poetic classification before poetic understanding, a large number of Strand's critics have put the cart before the horse, forcing Strand into preexisting molds without discovering first *what Strand does* in his poetry. There are, of course, some critics who have taken the opposite tack and have engaged themselves in the poems for the sake of summation, but they all too often arrive at unsophisticated conclusions. They provide generalizations about individual elements, but do little to connect the poems, or to provide any comprehension of Strand's poetic theory in context. Ultimately, there are too few of the Kirbys to help critically anchor Strand in the place he deserves in the poetic pantheon.

In identifying the evolution of Strand's predominant themes and motifs, it is important to note that, thematically and stylistically, the work evolves into a gradually stronger *tour de force*. Early in his career, Strand is that clever, remarkable poet who describes disturbing events and paints frightening places, but can do little more than lie in his bed, cowering. Hence, the title poem of his first, and most anxiety-ridden, collection, *Sleeping with One Eye Open*. In this 1964 publication, Strand establishes his sentiments about the natural and social worlds as indeterminate and chaotic places from which one must find solace. It also provides material for claiming that Strand is a fantasist, for the images presented within dreamlike states are often unreal.

Reasons for Moving, published in 1968, contains his most anthologized poem, "Keeping Things Whole," and although this poem was originally part of *Sleeping*, the work in this volume often is considered the quintessential Strand. In reality, the elements of absence; blurred lines of perspective (one never knows whether the speaker is speaking to us, a projection of himself, or whether he is being spoken to by someone else), disturbing imagery couched in stark, austere language, and symbolism that doubles back and contradicts itself are all present in larger quantities here than in other volumes. Strand's description of the frightful world is less overwhelmingly the topic of poetic rhetoric in this collection than in his first. Though tonally this is Strand at his most recognizable, this marks the beginning of Strand's consideration of the expanding role of the poet, the possibilities of sheltering oneself from the storms that he conjures up so menacingly in *Sleeping with One Eye Open*.

In *Darker*, Strand's poetic philosophy continues to come to the foreground and becomes more a topic of the poems. Strand seems at this stage to be learning how to conjure up at will the poetic imagination and knowing to what ends the imagination can be used. Ironically, *Darker* is the most hopeful—and, as a few critics recognize, the most consequential—of his first three volumes. But his view of darkness (and its corollary, absence) is an unfamiliar one. Strand elucidates here a primitive darkness from which all possibilities sprout—including the imaginative endeavor that is his work, and a primary motif in his work. The reason for his writing, in other words, is to write; the imaginative activity that one chooses to engage oneself in is not as consequential as the *engagement* of the imagination. In this collection, the poem is, for reader and speaker, a valuable, if temporarily redeeming action. It only begins, however, from a blankness, a darkness, of perfect wordlessness. Like his immediate precursor Stevens, Strand proceeds from the conviction that the use of too many words interferes with the ability to relate "the thing itself." Strand also seems more at home in his poetic world at this stage. His line lengths are growing; rhythmic patterns are smoothing out to more conversational pacing instead of the choppy, occasionally Hopkinsesque work of his first volume; stanzaic patterns are more regular; and the poems themselves generally fall within the range of 24–34 lines. The poetic form, it might be stated here, needs to become more transparent for the poetic ideals contained therein to shine, and this Strand recognizes and exhibits for the first time. It marks the initial major evolution in his career as a master.

It might be tempting to try to ignore personal events in the poet's life, in an attempt to evaluate the poetry in some objective way. But Strand's father's death in 1968 played too obvious a role in his poetic production to pretend that Strand the artist is distanced from Strand the person. Thus, the poetic voice that we will come to know as his did, in fact, develop as Strand the man encountered life crises. For almost two decades after his father's death, Strand's work embodied a reflective and reflexive reexamination of what poetry is and needs to be. *The Story of Our Lives*, published in 1973, arises as an interruption of the work that had been slowly evolving in his first three volumes. These eight poems are primarily elegiac, thematically complex, uncharacteristically long, and unavoidably personal. The Strand speaker known so well as someone we know so little is replaced by a more maskless speaker whose words on death, innocence, family and childhood are all too traceable to a Mark Strand that we *can* know, and that can be unsettling to the reader. What Strand says about being defined more by one's absence is no better realized than here, for we readers know Strand's persona more through the absence of personality in the first three volumes than we do in the overtly present Strand-as-son here. I do not believe Strand forgot this truth either, in the writing of the poems.

In *The Story of Our Lives*, poetry as a theme takes center stage as the poet self-consciously and painstakingly makes an attempt to use the poem to overcome his grief. It almost appears to be too great a stretch—the speaker is no longer solely in existence within the bounds of the poem. He is obviously a human being with a life far too complex to fully encapsulate within a poem, as the speaker of his previous volumes usually is. We recognize him as a man now, living outside the world of the poem and entering the poem in an attempt to replace his loss. We are for the first time wary of his presence outside the world of the poem as we read it. And by creating such a presence, the persona of the poem is in new ways elusive: he is suddenly more than the sum total of the poetic creation. As such, we are made aware of how little we are actually privy to. Furthermore, with each addition of Strand's self to the poetry, a subtraction, an erasure, a giving away of self occurs. *The Story of Our Lives* is certainly a grand undertaking of a poet undergoing enormous change (in the following year, he and his wife of 13 years would divorce), and using the poetry as a vehicle for renewal, ultimately concluding in a remaking of himself in the poem "The Untelling."

In 1978, Strand remarried—and one can place as much value on that as one likes—*The Late Hour* was published. This collection represents what may be considered a renaissance for Strand, although at the time it was considered a capstone. His work returns to its more characteristic lyrical qualities, shorter lengths, and self-enclosure. If a reader were to be ignorant of *The Story of Our Lives*, he, at first, would find little to suggest there was anything between *Darker* and these poems. Stylistically, Strand picks up where he left off in 1968. The anxiety that had characterized his earliest work, and had been retreating behind the gradual strengthening of Strand's poetic endeavor, is almost entirely replaced by this more secure speaker's voice. Still, the *world* has not changed; it is still an oppressive entity that must be pushed aside. Now resigned to this fact, the Strand speaker reflects upon it with melancholy instead of fear. He is secure because he now recognizes the elusive capacity of the creative act to at least address, if not replace, the world's chaos.

This poet has grown older, too; this fact apparently was made clear to him with the personally indulgent poems of *The Story of Our Lives*. He now confronts familial issues in several poems, even if he still relies upon motifs that have remained unchanged through his career. As such, Strand seems to be adding one more ingredient to his alchemical poetic recipe: personal elements, which he is now confident enough to include, where earlier poems simply would have broken down with such an inclusion. This is another recognizable quality of Strand's evolution into mastery—the ability not merely to re-create the self or recast oneself into a different form, but to add and subtract from one's form so as to move one step closer to perfecting the poetic vision. Thus, once again, darkness remains a necessary condition that one must establish before progressing with any worthwhile subjective endeavor. The world, which is still imposing, daunting and dreadfully unconcerned with human life, must be exorcised to establish a tabula rasa state. It is from this state—now referred to as a blank page as well as a darkness—that imagination can reign within the poem, within a dreamlike state and in fact within any wholly indulgent participatory action—if only for a moment.

There is, of course, a darkness at the end of these Strand poems. When the poem concludes, the imagination's reign ends and returns to the darkness from whence it sprang. *This* poet exhibits, and expresses, a confidence that the imagination goes there only to rise again phoenixlike from its ashes. In fact, this rebirth is a concern of the first poem in this collection, "The Coming of Light." In a moment of illumination and foresight, in fact, the poet recognizes that *tomorrow's* dust flares into breath. And so, Strand stakes his own claim to the ancient motif of breath, one that will recur as a trope for the imaginative act that exists between two darknesses. In this collection, Strand addresses the same concerns he has attended to for 15 years, yet he approaches these subjects from new perspectives as he grows older, and as he grows more experienced in and confident of his own creative endeavors. New images may arise to express familiar matters. *This* imaginative act may differ greatly in sound, structure, and sentiment from *that* one, but they both are performed for the same purposes and address the same concerns: they are redeeming acts engaged in for the purposes of establishing a temporarily fulfilling universe.

Strand's *Selected Poems*, issued in 1980, contained five new poems in a vein similar to that of *The Late Hour*, but mostly occasional and anomalous to the corpus in their rather frank—for Strand—reminiscences of actual places and events. For the most part—but for the marvelous and poignant quasi-translation poem, "Leopardi"—this publication was noteworthy as the definitive collection of Strand's previous best works. Then, nearly a decade passed before Strand released a new collection, primarily because he stopped writing poetry almost altogether. In the interim, he experimented with prose poetry and art criticism (he is, of course, a student of art and an active practitioner), wrote three children's books, and translated other virtuoso poets in outward-looking attempts to find answers to the question, "What can a poem do?" Though his poetic voice was silenced at this time, Strand has not related it as an entirely frustrating period. Instead, he was fully engaged in a variety of lofty ideals tangential to poetry. This decade of poet's block was in fact a fruitful rite of passage—a liminal zone, a period of trial that the poet must endure to emerge on the other side as a master of his craft.

Having confronted paternal death, divorce, a remaking of his own family, and now the blank page, Strand is now able to say confidently, "I have endured." The poetry is no longer tenuous but capable, no longer helpless, but effectual. It is now informed by something greater than abstract fears, that is, by the import of survival, and the ideas of the masters. With this ballast, he is able to chart his journey into the community of poets. The inclusion of the intimate and the weight of his poetic forerunners have only subtly recognizable effects on his work, but they transform him from a talented poet to a master. The evolution of Strand from champion of indeterminacy to director of his artistic fate is the process by which we recognize a truly luminary poet. "What makes a poet mature?" is a question of some magnitude. Vital if subtle transitions such as these help identify a poetic growth spurt that continues unabated through his most award-winning years.

Concerned with translation and the power of the word to have lasting redeeming effect, *The Continuous Life* (1990) shows a poet growing increasingly introspective and concerned with poetic principles. It reveals a poet who has just completed a long battle with writer's block, and reconsiders the life of the poet from within the poem and from without. Several of the works in this collection are prose poems. Ultimately, though the poems are concerned with lateness—time's marching on, the process of aging, and the search for something enduring in the face of time—Strand reasserts the value of the poetic undertaking in "Always," "Itself Now" and "Reading in Place." These poems address the broader philosophical issues of fate and chance, as well as authorship and uncertainty, while hinting at themes of interrelationships and inclusion. The poet, after adding the personal to his regimen, now looks outward into the larger community—of poets, of artists, and of society in general—to inform his work in more expansive ways. While his *The Story of Our Lives* was a stylistic contraction into the self, these poems are an opening into wider circles. For such broad-reaching efforts throughout what was still the early part of his career, Strand was named United States Poet Laureate in 1990.

In 1993, the 48-page poem *Dark Harbor* readdresses the poet's place in today's culture and, as such, carves out its own niche. As Christopher Benfey in *The New Republic* says clearly, "The overarching plot of *Dark Harbor* is the poet's counterlife in art, from his initial departure from the enclosure of family and home, to his journey through a place of . . . uncertainty, to his final sense of safe harbor within the community of other poets" ("Books Considered" 37). This poem is not thematically innovative, but condenses 30 years of Strand's writing into a sustained poetic masterwork. It is tighter in its strictures than any previous work of Strand's; the 46 parts are almost exclusively tercets, between 18 and 24 lines long, linguistically less clever, and consistently theoretical. Very little action occurs; the poem is more concerned with a reflection of things that *have* happened. It is a mostly serious work that contains engaging philosophical discourse focused on the fictional harbor that protects the poet from the storms with which the world has threatened him since 1964. As such, the poem deserves its own treatment, for it not only represents the longest sustained poetic endeavor of Strand's career and the fullest treatment of his poetic ideology, but also is his magnum opus. Most, if not all, of his hopes and fears, his concerns about and attitudes toward the power of the poem, and his shifting perspectives are troped anew, and nowhere is he at a greater height of his powers than he is here.

Subtly but unquestionably, Strand transforms himself from reporter of a terrifying natural world to *daemonic* creator of solipsistic harbors away from the world. As such, at the conclusion of *Dark Harbor*, Strand's speaker has chiseled his niche within the community of the great angel-poets, and seems at peace with existence. After such an accomplishment, Strand is left with a unique challenge. To continue precisely where *Dark Harbor* left off would be to become at best his own translator, at worst a caricature of himself. He cannot write another long poem in the vein of *Dark Harbor*; nor can he pretend to be nature's victim and write another *Sleeping with One Eye Open*. He has accomplished what few poets could hope to accomplish in a career. Thus, in facing this new blank page, in *Blizzard of One* (1998), he must ask himself what to do "Now that the great dog I worshipped for years / Has become none other than myself" ("Five Dogs" #2, 1–2). His anxiety of creation originates in himself, in his own success.

His solution is to take the molds created by the Mark Strand who wrote before and recognize that in his own new distress he shall find the potency to create obliquely from his previous self. Although the poems seem to contain more humor and playfulness, Strand has not suddenly become a nonsense poet. In fact, there are sadder moments here, too. Coming on the heels of the dissolution of his second marriage, this is a poetry addressing "the weather of leavetaking," and as such, abandonment is a prevalent theme. To attend to this new kind of aloneness, Strand frequently reverts to the shorter, starker formal presentation of his early work, yet the themes of *Blizzard of One* are more approachable than his self-conscious earlier works. In his desire to reach the perfect imaginative moment, Strand seeks the least conspicuous form. In doing so, he approaches perfect formlessness.

Between Two Great Darks

Throughout his career, Strand reveals a single persona who sees himself as two versions of himself, as someone else, or as no one at all. Strand's voice and figurations evolve, but his attitudes toward the world do not change. His faith in poetry fluctuates, but poetry remains the central redeeming force in his poetic life. This monograph focuses on the evolving poetic philosophy of Strand. The attitudes of

the poet toward the world, toward poetry, and toward the act of com-
posing are the primary focal points. The darknesses that Strand sub-
mits to are a necessary starting point for the poem—so necessary, in
fact, that in one poem he literally erases the world. In others, he
absents himself from the poem. In yet others he creates two selves. So
very often early in his career, he is not sure how or where to find
proper perspective—is he speaking now, he wonders, or is he being
spoken to by someone else? Later on, Strand will no longer exhibit
such doubts about his status as creator. Throughout, there is a
Strandian poetics to be known, and the unearthing of those poetics
can prove fertile for future projects on other poets' corpora.

Important to understanding Strand is the fact that "understanding" does not matter. The "real" world, he says, does not provide us
with any clarity. Indeterminacy and confusion rule. To seek a fixed
truth within such a world is a futile endeavor. Instead, one must erase
the need to discover one's self in the real world. That world should be
erased by full imaginative participation—in any event, in a dream, in
writing or reading a poem, in becoming someone other than oneself,
in translating others' works. Remove the chaos of the world and one
can find the world. Remove the chaos of self and one will find oneself.
Thus, examination of the concepts of primitive and privative absences
will yield insight into this central Strandian theme.

Strand's act of erasing or negating the world by application of the
active imagination creates a system of *ex nihilo*, where the privative
rather than the primitive dominates. Concerning the privative, when
something is removed—creating an absence—there is a palpable presence. Hence, a book with a missing page is defined by the absence of
that page. This presence is neither inherently evil nor unknowable; it
is simply unknown. This privative quality of Strand's poetry of absence
yields a terrifying yet elegiac weight—a frozen fear and blank stare
into the heart of nothing and a profound epiphanic knowledge that
something is gone. That epiphany is the solace within the *nihilo*;
the recognition of self comes through the removal of self. Privation
then yields consolation, and in this birthing, privation creates and is
now no longer solely privative in nature. It is primitive—a project of
genesis—the nothing from which something is born. Hence, it is the
slippery yet definitive presence established by the removal of the self
from nature in poems such as "Keeping Things Whole," and other
similar applications that we will confront later.

As a precept to these concepts of darkness, it is important to
recognize that things get their form from what is removed. What is
not the thing helps us understand what the thing *is*. What defines my

parameters is what is not me. Put another way, my perimeter is defined as the place where I end. The day has shape and meaning only because it is surrounded by two nights. Strand's recognition that the night will be followed by another day, that this poem's ending will be replaced by a new poem, grows throughout his career. It is in his early works that he is more plagued by doubt than in later ones, but the motif of day and night fits snugly with the concept of the poetic act as existing between two great darknesses, thus providing familiar, comfortable boundaries to existence. Whether the two darknesses are those places before and after poetic creation, or more readily recognizable as night and death, the necessity of confronting them is clear. As Strand explains in his outstanding poem, "The Continuous Life," we "live between two great darks, the first / With an ending, the second without one" (13–14). Sometimes he expresses delight in that fact "that the luckiest / Thing is having been born" ("The Continuous Life" 14–15). Other times, this place between darknesses is a blur

> Of hours and days, months and years, and [we] believe
> It has meaning, despite the occasional fear
> [We] are slipping away with nothing completed, nothing
> To prove [we] existed.
>   ("The Continuous Life" 15–19)

While Strand's speaker in "Keeping Things Whole" may profess to keep things intact by moving through space and time, the fact is he becomes conspicuous by his absence. He does "disturb the universe," and his imagination perpetually labels and categorizes the objects and events that occur within the poem's realm. The world may not exist for us or care about us, he recognizes, but it does contain useful objects with which we can parent our own private universe. When life becomes too much like Frost's branch that lashes one's eye open, we can erase it and start with our own tree. When we are absorbed in this creative act, that world is blotted out—we *have* staved off the final darkness—if only for a moment. Erecting an imaginative world is a life- and poetry-affirming task. One has temporary emancipation while indulging in this creation. However fleeting that may be, one may console oneself that it is worth the effort—even if the endeavor "has [only] been said for me" (*Dark Harbor* VIII 24).

Creating a subjective world within the imagination is a vital task. Erase the real world, says Strand, and from the darkness of possibility erect a new one. Immerse yourself in this creation and, for the moment, you have redemption. As Stitt says, the goal of the poetry is "to strip away the outer world so as to make the subject of poetry the act of perception in the mind, the creation of the poem on the page" ("Stages" 205). But if we keep in mind Strand's threat to create "a literary spectacle," it seems that engaging his poetry is vastly preferable to providing extratextual maxims.

CHAPTER 1

STAVING OFF THE WORLD:
THE EARLY YEARS

It is important to remember that Mark Strand does not intend his poetry to be studied in sound bites. If we take the *American Heritage Dictionary's* definition of holism, "The theory that living matter or reality is made up of organic or unified wholes that are greater than the simple sum of their parts," we can perhaps better find a starting point for the consideration of Strand's poetic cosmology. From his first volume, *Sleeping with One Eye Open*, to his 2006 collection, *Man and Camel*, transformations abound; confidence waxes and wanes. Nonetheless, Strand's poetic evolution progresses rather consistently. Strand's development as a poet reflects changes in Strand's own life (e.g., *The Story of Our Lives*, dedicated to the memory of his late father, is understandably the most recognizably divergent and personal of his volumes), and in his confidence in the *practice* of poetry. The poetic *theory*, however, remains intact. In fact, the poems themselves often are reconsiderations of themes from previous poems, or reapplications of theories to new situations. With few exceptions, Strand's work does not reveal a huge development of the craft of poetry, but rather the honing of a master craftsman. His maturation as a poet seems to have already occurred by the time he released *Darker* in 1970. Since then, his poetry appears to reveal not so much an improvement of his poetic craft as a reconsideration of ideas and poetics from different moments in a career and life.

To be sure, *Sleeping with One Eye Open*, first published in 1964, already exhibits much of Strand's artistic characteristics, and the poetry often succeeds. Here, Strand is preoccupied with the power of the malevolent world to insinuate itself between himself and his goals, whether the latter be unity with nature, communication, friendship, love, or even sleep. In the title poem, Strand's speaker lies half-awake listening nervously to the frightening silence of a storm as its eye passes over his house. Nature is as frightening in its quietude as it is when it is roaring. In this middle ground, lying with one eye open under the half-moon, expressing himself in half-rhymes, the Strand speaker ultimately claims he is a victim of nature—"Moonhandled," to be precise (30). In this early stage of his career, the alliteration and assonance sometimes seem forced and the short line lengths will not take him far as a poet. Tonally and topically in his early work, he is more likely to be "handled" by tropes such as the moon. The mature poet, we will assert for Strand in particular and poets in general, possesses the lyrical authority to handle the moon.

Early on, controlled by the moon, Strand's speaker remains intriguingly liminal at the poem's conclusion, caught between the fear of everything and the fear of nothing, "sleeping with one eye open, / Hoping / That nothing, nothing will happen" (35–37). Kirby is right in asserting that this poem is indicative of Strand's poetic voice and that it is "intoning the poems that define him" (9), but as Strand's career proceeds, increasingly fewer poems remain tonally concordant with this one. This poem's primary function is, however, to establish the environment within which the poet writes. This is the world, Strand seems to say, and this is my condition. Insecurity—about life in general, about the speaker's life in particular, about the poet's role as creator—reigns in a great majority of his early poems, in fact. To begin this study of Strand with this poem is not to identify it as most indicative of his poetry—and it is probably not among his very best work—but rather to provide a setting in which the rest of the poetry blooms.

The establishment of the world as a malignant force is reinforced in "Violent Storm." The night is expressed as having "dubious plans, and the rain / Beats down in gales / Against the roof" (25–27). The wind outside the doors is "loose, untidy" (30). But more vitally, this poem introduces the role of the poet, albeit an insecure poet, in providing refuge from the storm. In doing so, Strand presents a dualistic view of people as being either awake or asleep. Later, he will expand this view to include the active and the passive, the alert and the inert. Invariably, it is the former of each group that ends up in danger. However, it is also the awake, the active, and the alert who have a greater capacity to weather their storms, for this group includes the poets.

In "Violent Storm," the sleeping group has spent the night "[e]ntertaining friends" (2), and does not fear the change in weather. Meanwhile, the "wide-awake," of whom this speaker counts himself, are world-wary, world-weary, and

> tend
> To believe the worst is always waiting
> Around the next corner or hiding in the dry,
> Unsteady branch of a sick tree, debating
> Whether or not to fell the passerby.
>
> (13–17)

In this case, nature *does* have a consciousness, and it is a malevolent one.

The poet yearns for "a world of familiar views / And fixed conditions" (20–21), but the reality is far more sinister and indeterminate. And at this stage the poet finds no protection behind the walls of his poem or in what we will come to know as one of Strand's favorite tropes, mirrors:

> nor can we hide
> Before the duplicating presence
> Of their mirrors, pretending we are the ones who stare
> From the other side, collected
> In the glassy air.
>
> (41–45)

In the speaker's desire for continuity, the poem resonates with another of Strand's, "Eating Poetry." In this case, the speaker can be likened to the latter poem's librarian, the one who desires order, "a world of familiar views / And fixed conditions." In fact, the poet does not claim to *not* desire that. At this stage, he merely wishes he *could* achieve it. Later, in "Eating Poetry," he seems reconciled to the untidiness of the world and revels in it. Here, he sits cowering in his room, the poem a feeble attempt to stave off the eponymous storm. When he says:

> We cannot take ourselves or what belongs
> To us for granted. . . .
> We do not feel protected
> By the walls, nor can we hide
> Before the duplicating presence
> Of their mirrors . . .
>
> (33–43)

he is ready to learn the lesson of mortality, and is prepared to take that lesson to the next level, as it exists in "Eating Poetry." That is, if one cannot "feel protected," perhaps one should no longer spend one's life *seeking* protection.

The poem concludes with the dark becoming preeminent, and the concept of even any ensuing days seeming "unthinkable" (51). It is here where darkness and its partner, absence, first make their presences felt in the Strand corpus. Although the world is threatened by this privative darkness, darkness *later* is shown to be the primitive birthplace of the poem; it is both the resting place of the poem and the starting place from which the redeeming creative act proceeds. That darkness is redemptive and hopeful: "The blaze of promise everywhere" ("Always," *The Continuous Life* 30).

At this stage, however, the poet does not have the power to insert a strong poetic creation between the darknesses at the beginning and at the end of the world. Instead, he is left to flounder in fighting off the impending night that menaces him. The poetic creation in this collection serves only to stave off the complete darkness of imagination for a while. As the poem nears its end, the blackness grows: "Already now the lights / That shared our wakefulness are dimming" (52–53). In the final line, "the dark brushes against our eyes" (54); with the completion of the poem, darkness (i.e., the lack of poetry) is all that remains. In *Sleeping with One Eye Open*, Strand fears the dark place of the external world—i.e., the poem's external world—where his poem disappears after its completion. Within the poem, however, Strand has some solace against the darkness. There is a resonance of ego involved in the artistic consciousness that the world is "out to get him." That resonance is at least partially soothing. Ego is all the poet projects against the void that is the unredeemed world.

Throughout Strand's career, the poem becomes a progressively more potent action against the world's intrusions. Linda Gregerson argues in "Negative Capability" that "when Mark Strand reinvented the poem, he began by leaving out the world" (90). The sentence may not be her thesis, but it should not go unexamined. For the first part, Mark Strand's poetry does not appear to be a "reinvention" of any sort. Critics such as Denis Donoghue, who considers that Strand's early poems "sound as if they were written on the principle: take a cliché and wring its neck" (28), or Robert Pinsky, who has said that Strand confirms our idea of what poetry is, are more lucid. As for "leaving out the world," Gregerson's statement seems to be a bit flippant for such densely compacted poetry as Strand's. Indeed, Strand does not merely—or simply—leave out the world. On the contrary, the world is omnipresent in most of his work; when it is not, the process of obliterating the world from Strand's poem is a painstaking one, not one to be undertaken lightly. This act, in fact, is one of the *goals* of the poetry, and not performed extratextually. True, Strand wants to silence the world's shouts, but his success is partial and tenuous. It requires more than a pre-poetic "leaving out," and even the tiresome act of silencing the world calls attention to it. So we begin again by recognizing what is and what is not in the poems, for Strand, though a modernist in the Romantic tradition, is not able to construct stable realities in a void. His poems are instead havens, or to use his own term, harbors against the world's maelstroms.

Over the years, Strand's world becomes a place cluttered with more and varied dangers. He therefore transforms darkness into a necessary state—a blanking out of the world—that must be achieved in order for the poem to begin. As Mexican Poet Octavio Paz says, "Mark Strand has chosen the negative path, with loss as the first step towards fullness: it is also the opening to a transparent verbal perfection" (Quoted in Hamilton 525). For now, this poetic voice is not nearly powerful enough to create an alternate reality within which the poet can thrive. Neither does Strand yet have the confidence in the imagination to create on demand, as he is later able to instruct his readers to do. At this point, he can only hold on tightly to the poem and hope. Likewise, in roughly the first half of his career, Strand's poetry is at its most sparse. The only things that seem to exist in this world are those he creates in his poem—all else is a void. Lieberman likens the work in the first three collections to a Magritte painting: "[T]he objects in Strand's poem are so bare and plain and unembellished by ornament, a reader is dumbfounded by any effort to locate the source of the fierce supernatural energy that surrounds them" (23).

"Old People On the Nursing Home Porch" returns us to the darkness, this time as an expression of the inability of "the elders" who inhabit the nursing home to imagine their past. At the poem's outset, the "faded light / Of afternoon carr[ies] them off" (5–6). Faded though it is, it *is* light, and it *does* provide the elders with the ability to "recall the days it took / To get them here" (2–3). The poem begins in a darkness of imagination, yet sheds its own light for illumination. As the day—and the poem—comes to a close, the darkness threatens to cancel out the day's sunlight, the elders' imaginative act of memory and the poet's poem. For the second time we see the poem's end coincide with the onset of darkness, here where the elders "lie alone / In the deep and sheepless / Pastures of a long sleep" (28–30). Yes, this world is uninhabited by others; it is deep, long and, humorously enough, without sheep. The isolation and incommunicability of humanity are ultimately the most specific primary obstacles to the Strand persona in his first two collections, and although the speaker of "Taking a Walk with You" speaks of a "we," the connection made is not between himself and another in so much as between himself and his double—or perhaps himself and the reader.

While "Taking a Walk with You" projects a less intentionally malicious world, Strand makes it clear that the world is at best apathetic to human concerns, and that if there were a creative energy behind its creation, that force did not create it for us as the Creator of Genesis did. As Sophocles suggested, man is not made in the image of God, and we are not meant to recognize ourselves or God in the world. Punning as is his inclination, Strand tells us:

> The tree we lean against
> Was never made to stand
> For something else,
> Let alone ourselves.
> Nor were these fields
> And gullies planned
> With us in mind.
>   (10–16)

Nonetheless, Strand also celebrates for the first time the power of poetic imagination, for he declares that nature lacks "the wit and depth / That inform our dreams' / Bright landscapes" (1–3). This dreamlike state of poetic creation has had few transcendent moments thus far. Strand recognizes that nature is still "no less beautiful / For being only what it seems" (6–7), and thus sets up another dualism. Although our imagination has "wit and depth," Strand assails the authority of troping in his declarations against trees "standing for" something else, and in a later assertion that "clouds . . . Are cloudy without / Resembling us" (21–24). He also pays tribute to nature's dark regenerative powers, expressing the tree as "Rising from the dyed / Pool of its shade" (8–9). Just as the poem arises from darkness, its own lack of poetry, the tree rises from its shade, its own lack of being. Yet, in trying to note humankind's—and in particular, the poet's— separation from the indifferent world of nature, the Strand speaker likens the actions of nature to the actions of poetry, and compels communion in the very expression of disunity. Make no mistake about it: the unity comes only from an artificial act of imagination. Nature's trees do not rise from pools of shade. The human imagination, however, can *interpret* that it is "rising" from what we can *call* a "pool"—one that is unnaturally "dyed." That ability to trope nature, despite its distancing effect, is the way the poet can at least *approach* communion with nature. As Pinsky says, the poetry "is held together by what can be called Strand's remarkable sense of the poetic: the voice is alone, and what it is alone with is poetry itself" (300). By the time the speaker parallels "Keeping Things Whole" with the lines, "We live unsettled lives / And stay in a place / Only long enough to find / We don't belong" (17–20), he has firmly established that nature has an existence of its own and that it neither needs us nor resembles us. We are neither pilgrims nor visitors, just liminals in constant motion, desiring unity but finding a sense of "nearness" to nature as that which will, sometimes, suffice.

"Taking a Walk with You" continues to echo the turbulent theme of this collection, as clouds begin "storming / The vacant air" and "Don't take into account / Our present loneliness" (24–26). The lines that set this poem apart from those previous are the concluding ones:

> And yet, why should we care?
> Already we are walking off,
> As if to say,
> We are not here,
> We've always been away.
>   (27–31)

These are a challenging five lines. Unlike as in "Violent Storm," the poetic world is a place where we—the poet and the reader—are safe from the storm front. In fact, for the duration of this poem so far, we have not been "in nature." Indeed, we have been within the preternatural protective world of the poem. As Stitt says,

> The world of the mind is clearly predominant in the early poems of Mark Strand; reality is capricious, not to be trusted, even unknowable in any certain sense. . . . In his later poems, Strand will write with a good deal of confidence about the world of outward reality; in the early poems his trust is placed instead in the world of the mind. Thus these poems reproduce not images perceived "out there" so much as the images imagined "in here." Strand's major subject, then, becomes the question of human perception and how this can result in poetry.   ("Stages" 204)

While Kirby argues that "'Keeping Things Whole' itself is a major departure from what might be called typical early Strand," and complains that "[It] is too much like the poetry of other writers to provide a satisfying response to problems unique to Strand's speakers" (13), the poem has its Strandian prefigurations (e.g., "Taking a Walk with You") and many successors, and is an important stepping stone to Strand's poetry. It reveals one of the central concepts Strand carries with him throughout his career, that of the disequilibrium between man and nature. Sven Birkerts is equally off the mark—or at least unnecessarily reductionist—in his reading of "Keeping Things Whole": "These lines distill [Strand's] metaphysics, a kind of reversed Cartesianism wherein to be is not to be and thinking throws existing into question" (36). Birkerts seems to misread the concept of presence in absence, viewing Strand's every word literally. In fact, Strand places immense importance on his ability to think, and here does not doubt his own existence, but his own place within the *rest* of existence.

"Keeping Things Whole" and "The Whole Story" provide the first sounds of Strand's early mature voice and pose the problem of finding proper perspective within the world. While the speaker of the former poem claims that he is what is "missing from the world," he is, in fact, like Stevens' jar in Tennessee. Just as the jar gives order to the slovenly wilderness in "Anecdote of a Jar," so too does this human, subjective (hence unnatural) projection of self "part the air" (9), dividing the world. While the speaker may profess moving "to keep things whole," the speaker and the world are irredeemably estranged. Strand's emphasis is on the dichotomous nature between the poet and the world: "Wherever I am / I am what is missing" (6–7). But he also makes it clear that there is no order in the world; order is an act of the imagination. By (imaginatively) walking through the world, Strand (dis)organizes it.

Jane Candida Coleman concurs, noting that Strand's purported absence "is certainly not removal of self but the poet as an integral, almost godlike part of the universe, attempting to write the mystical, the unsayable from the inside out, battling with a world that may (or may not, always Strand's stance) exist except in the experience of the seer" (178). Indeed, as in "Taking a Walk with You," the world external to the speaker is the same as the apathetic one of naturalist literature. Even as Strand's speaker cuts his way through the air, "always / the air moves in / to fill the spaces / where my body's been" (10–13). Ultimately, Strand establishes the poet's role in ordering nature, reminding us of Stevens while seemingly making a corrective movement of his own here. Strand will follow up on the motif numerous times in the future.

"Keeping Things Whole" is a reconsideration of Stevens' "Anecdote of the Jar," and a considerable *apophrades* at that. In it, Strand examines the juxtaposition of man in/with nature, and provides a startling philosophy. So divergent are man and nature, says Strand, that coexistence means the disintegration of one or the other. In this case, if the speaker even pauses for a moment to consider nature, very unlike Wordsworth, not only does he not become part of the environs, he actually causes the environs to disintegrate: "Wherever I am / I am what is missing." Furthermore, in performing the act of merely being, he himself loses his primary identity. Instead of being himself, he becomes *not-nature*: "In a field / I am the absence / of field."

In "Anecdote of the Jar," the jar alters its environs. Therefore, in preserving itself, it forces nature to adapt to it. In "Keeping Things Whole," to *prevent* nature from having to adapt to his presence, the speaker does the adapting. He is a liminal, a perpetual and constant outsider, and he moves to get out of nature's way, thus preserving nature's integrity.

Strand's speaker in "Keeping Things Whole" exists within the field. However, the place he occupies is a defiling of that field. Thus, instead of preserving his integrity at the expense of nature, he claims to preserve the surroundings by moving out of the scene. He recognizes that he is as separate from nature as is Stevens' jar; he is "what is missing." The concern of Strand's speaker is with preserving the unity of nature, not with preserving his individuality.

Like Strand's speaker, Stevens' jar "does not give of bird or bush" (11). It is, however, the un-natural focal point, and as such, nature is the force that must adapt. For Strand, nature is the focal point, and wherever and whenever he interjects himself, he becomes the nonnatural corrective jar. The speaker embodies the somewhat frightening notion that the poet must *always* move—must always write—to preserve *anything*. Not unlike a shark, should the poet stop moving, he would die; furthermore, should he stop, the world will be irreparably blemished.

Stevens' jar creates order within a disorderly wilderness; by creating a new environment, the jar has kept itself whole at the expense of nature. Strand makes a corrective movement against Stevens' poem by going one step further than simply placing that jar (i.e., himself) in a field. He places it in the field, identifies it as the thing that does not give of bird or bush, and then moves it out of the field to reestablish harmony.

"The Whole Story" confronts the Strand motif of speaker-severing as a way of further amplifying our inability to find clear perspectives within the world. Before the poem even begins, Strand has an external narrator addressing the poem's speaker:

> —*I'd rather you didn't feel it neces-*
> *sary to tell him, "That's a fire. And*
> *what's more, we can't do anything*
> *about it, because we're on this*
> *train, see?"* (epigraph)

When the poem proper does commence, the second speaker, who is in no better position to evaluate events than the reader is, relays a story in second-person voice of a fire he sees outside the train. Strand's "you" is frequently addressed to such a double, a mirror image of his own self created to examine his own situation "objectively." Quite often, however, as in this poem, it is equally likely that he is addressing his reader.

In the second stanza, the poem's speaker declares what the epigraph's narrator prefers him not to do. In doing so, he further muddies the waters of perspective by saying that *we* give *him* "an odd look / As though I had said too much" (11–12). Are we readers then placed in the position of the narrator who wished he would not say this? Or is his address to the "you" really himself, and therefore he himself takes on a slippery dual role? Both appear plausible, for in the third stanza the perspective blurs further. The fires he speaks of can reasonably be interpreted as poetic fires; he tells himself/us that he "travel[s] by train to keep / From having to put them out. / It may be that trains / Can kindle a love of fire" (15–18).

The speaker challenges perspective once more by wondering if "you [the double or reader] are a fireman / In disguise" (20–21), before shifting again to consider if "You are the one / Who loves a good fire. Who knows?" (23–24). The "Who knows?" utterance is familiar in Strand's work, for when trying to place oneself in context with the world, one does not fit; as in "Keeping Things Whole," one merely "parts the air" and becomes "what is missing." The Strand persona, and we, as we read along, have no place in reality. But the "Who knows?" is not an expression of despair, for what follows is always a commemoration of the capacity of the imagination to create a gratifying subjective reality. After all, as Stevens says, "What the poet has in mind . . . is that poetic value is an intrinsic value. It is not the value of knowledge. It is not the value of faith. It is the value of the imagination" (*Necessary* 149).

As we return to the final stanza of "The Whole Story," we discover a last twist:

> Perhaps you are elsewhere,
> Deciding that with no place

To go you should not
Take a train. And I,
Seeing my own face in the window,
May have lied about the fire.

(25–30)

Tracing the poem's literal progression becomes increasingly difficult, until, in this stanza, the contradictions appear to negate all meaning. However, the poem is an imaginative creation in which we partake from the outset. We may be the "you" of the poem, or we may not be. Regardless, we *are* present in the poem, and on the train with the speaker. In fact, if we double back to the epigraph, we may realize that perhaps it is not the speaker to whom the narrator speaks, but to us. In this, we are even further entrenched in the poem's life and the poem's creation, for the poem does, in essence, both live and create as it progresses. Thus, the reader is a sort of co-creator of the landscape, because Strand has brought the reader into the imagining process. Strand frequently instructs his readers, "Imagine this" or "Think of that"—often using those very words. In doing so, he invokes a Pouletian symmetry between reader and writer. The poet calls us into his consciousness; the very making of the poems is up to us, coincidentally as it is up to him. Further study of Georges Poulet perhaps is worth pursuing in this respect, for there are many instances where Strand specifically seeks a unity of vision with the reader. As J. Hillis Miller relates, "The plunge into a book is achieved only in the perfect *coincidence* of the reader's mind with the '*intimité indescriptible*' of the author's mind" (472). In Strand's directive poems, the speaker commands the reader to read precisely. The intimacy Poulet demands, however, comes not from a trained Pouletian reader, but from a Strandian speaker who commands precise attention from word to word, line to line, in order to satisfy the poem's literal and figurative requirements.

In the final stanza, "Perhaps you are elsewhere" presents the possibility that the events of the poem may have been lied about/imagined—which, of course, they have. Neither the poet, nor his speaker-narrator, nor the "you" as poet's mirror or as reader, has to be on the train. The participatory imaginative indulgence—of envisioning the train Strand tells us to envision—is what matters. The poem, as the mind's creation, reflects upon a person engaged in a very similar creative act, thus presenting a mirror between poet and poem. Irvin Ehrenpreis provides insight into this uncertain sense of perspective when he says:

Strand does not open the lyric to the world but makes it a self-sustaining enterprise. His forms tend toward the infinite regress of a mirror watching a mirror. In his realm you can realize your own self only by imagining another self which in turn is imagining you. That other may be a lover, a wife, a child. It may be your own old self which the new one has destroyed and replaced—after, of course, being imagined in advance. But the movement of all the profound self-awareness is toward decoration rather than abundance. Caught up in the subject-object relation, Strand sees the world as what the perceived is not, and the perceiver as what the world is not. (47)

ABSENTING THE SELF,
REACHING ACROSS THE VOID

Reasons for Moving represents Strand's full arrival onto the literary scene and into full maturity as a poet. The stormy world of *Sleeping with One Eye Open* still looms ominously, but at times it subsides and the speaker is more able to successfully contemplate his state of being. He is now able to project stronger defenses against the natural world's incursions. Although poems like "The Mailman," "The Accident" and "The Man in the Tree" are placed prominently at the fore to reveal the malevolent world as the canvas for his painting, Strand ultimately celebrates the imagination as that which provides a temporary haven.

"The Mailman" finds the lines between the roles of victim and victimizer blurred. The titular character brings the speaker a letter containing "terrible personal news" (8), and, wracked with guilt, pleads for forgiveness for having to be the bearer of bad tidings. The speaker then invites the courier inside, where he falls asleep, becoming "an inkstain / on my crimson couch" (14–15). Meanwhile, the speaker reveals that he has been sending the letters himself, letters that mirror the distorted perspective that we see in "The Whole Story" and "The Tunnel" from *Sleeping with One Eye Open:* "You shall live / by inflicting pain. / You shall forgive" (20–22).

What to make of such a line? How, we might ask, can one be in the position to forgive when it is we who have been doing the assailing? It is fertile ground for observation. The figure of writing—itself a quasi-violent act—factors greatly into this poem. Therefore, we may wonder if this mailman is yet another imaginative projection of the speaker's self upon whom he inflicts and is inflicted. In that sense, the speaker is at odds with even himself. "What is my role?" the speaker asks in this poem. He absents himself from the world to resurrect himself in the poem, only to wonder and doubt if the pain of the transformation is worth it. Indeed, at this stage, the writing of the poem is painful, but as Strand will later say, "Still, we feel better for trying" (*Dark Harbor* XXVIII 18). So, he forgives—himself, his other self, and the world.

As Robert Pack says, "If what a man does and what happens to him are . . . the same, then compassion and pity are the same, and so too are responsibility and innocence. Thus the speaker and his other self are as much the victims of what they do as they are victims of what happens to them, and their identities have no fixed center" ("To Be Loved" 39–40). By removing his personality from the poem and replacing it with two projections of himself, Strand has the ability to consider himself from two disparate angles, reconsidering his place in the world. If the mailman represents the external world, we also recognize that the figure of poetry as represented in the letter-writer takes prominence as the external world/mailman *sleeps*. Even though at this stage the poetic philosophy is not fully elaborated, Strand's presentation of dichotomous relations between the chaotic—even dangerous—world of nature and the private world of self is present. It is not coincidental that the letter writer is most satisfied as he *writes*. And as he writes, the world goes dormant.

"The Accident," an equally compelling lyric, restates these concepts. Once again the speaker is the victim—and another train figures into his condition. This time, the train engineer—who again may be the speaker's double—runs over the speaker and then carries the victim home to nurse him. But first we are given an intriguing passage in which someone with a flashlight frightens the engineer away from the tracks, leaving the speaker bleeding. In the sixth stanza, the injured speaker, still lying on the tracks, remarkably is able to see the engineer at his home, sitting "in the kitchen / staring at the dark. / His face is flushed, / his hands are pressed / between his knees" (32–36).

Whatever challenging logic the events of the poem provide, the primary assertion in the poem is the potency of imagination. Why the poet is endangered is ambiguous. The train may represent the chaotic world that perpetually torments him. Yet, the speaker pities the engineer who has led him to such a state. Once the speaker is left alone, his own imaginative creation comes to the foreground. Dissevered from the world by the train, he now is able to envision the engineer's home and thoughts. But before the engineer abandons the speaker, *his* glasses cloud, as he, too, is drawn/written into the private universe. This motif is resurrected as synonymous with darkness in later poems. When one's glasses cloud, and one's vision is obscured from the real world, one is better able to imagine his/her own *personal* world more clearly. It is not merely coincidence that the moment his vision of the world is clouded by the steam of the speaker's blood, he is able to speak his own story:

> the details of his life—
> he has a wife
> and a child he loves,
> he's always been
> an engineer.
>   (14–18)

It is also not coincidence that he stops speaking when the world intrudes with light from a flashlight.

The speaker, imaginatively engaged for the duration of the poem, sees more clearly than ever the thoughts and actions of the man in the kitchen. If the latter is himself, he fears the silencing of his other half's breath—that power to speak the imagination in a poem. Indeed, that power *is* important, for it *does* bloom, and, as the breath fades, the world is in flux:

> the fields bend
> under the heavy sheets
> of the wind
> and birds scatter
> into the rafters
> of the trees.
>   (43–48)

In this precarious position, reality bends, and the world—though affected by the poet—cannot be troped effectively. The poet's voice is becoming silenced. So the engineer returns to join his victim (himself a victim of guilt). But he is probably too late to save this imaginative projection—or himself. This poem must end. The speaker's final words are "The end of my life begins" (66).

As Strand will repeat frequently, the end of the poem necessarily coincides with the end of the imaginative undertaking. That is, any value or redemption found in the poetic act is obliterated as the words end; there is little residual hope for next time that lasts beyond this poetic encounter. Here in "The Accident," as both characters are imaginative projections, when the poem ends the "life" of the character also will end. The troubles of the world still plague him, and the speaker *still* cannot find lasting peace even within the poem, yet Strand has found a way to keep the world at bay. It is a tenuous grip on his own personality, and he may be insecure in this place, but while the poem runs its course, he *is* alive.

"The Man in the Tree" is a valuable poem to examine for its poetic imagery. It is meaningful that the speaker here is naked while conversing with someone below who is wearing a heavy coat. The dualism of the previous poems in *Reasons for Moving* is repeated here, and readers recognize the speaker as representative of the poet. Although darkness and absence are not ominous in these poems, and the motif of clouded vision has appeared earlier, here the concept of clothing will be found as equally synonymous with (Wordsworthian) worldliness. Strand links the throwing off of clothing with the act of clearing ground for the poem to begin. When the world is present, the poetic act is endangered. If the poet can bestow a darkness, or cloud someone's glasses, or cast off a character's clothing, that person is now primed to begin the imaginative act that is the poem.

It is not surprising to find the words of the person with the heavy coat falling silently to the ground, or to discover that inside his coat are white moths, like so many white pieces of paper. The speaker questions, "why / our lives took a turn for the worse," but knows he will not find an answer in this indeterminate world (13–14). But while answers to the natural world will not come, for him, the imaginative soul, astonishing things can occur in his private universe:

> Clouds sank into my arms and my arms rose.
> They are rising now.
>
> I sway in the white air of winter
> And the starling's cry lies down on my skin.
> A field of ferns covers my glasses; I wipe them away
> in order to see you.
>
> (15–20)

In this poem, the *speaker's* sight is obscured—but in antithetical fashion to the imagery of "The Accident." The natural world again clouds the poet's imaginative vision. Once he clears away this world, however, his imagination returns, and the magic returns: "I turn and the tree turns with me. / Things are not only themselves in this light" (21–22). Strand inherits the Whitmanian tradition of the word "turn" here. When he turns, that is *tropes*, the tree transforms with him. Also noteworthy here is Strand's inheritance of the Stevensian attention to prepositions; his tree turns *with* him, not the more obvious *for* him. There is a unity in this troping act, for though the poet cannot achieve unity with a natural tree, he *can* unite with a created tree. Furthermore, if the poet imaginatively can transform the world, he also reveals the possibilities for his listener: "You close your eyes and your coat / falls from your shoulders, / the tree withdraws like a hand" (23–25). Lines such as these, which do appear regularly, provide metaphoric guidelines for the process of accessing the imagination. When emptied of one's clothing and turning one's eyes from the world and into the self, the self is pregnant with possibility. Yet here, as is also revealed many times in Strand's body of work, the poetic imagination has an unstable advantage over the real world. The speaker struggles not only to understand the world, but also to maintain the poetic endeavor; he knows the poem is coming to a close, and careful readers must recognize the same. All he *can* ascertain is that "nothing is certain" (26). When he says, "The poem that has stolen these words from my mouth / may not be this poem" it is *not* that poem anymore (27–28). The poem completed is a not-poem, Strand articulates, for it is no longer capturing the full attention of the poet's imagination. However, by giving away himself, his poem, his life, he communicates; and by this act the poem is no longer just for him.

After positioning himself in such an uncertain stance at the outset of this volume, *Reasons for Moving* ends with some of the strongest assertions of the imagination's potential to date. "The Ghost Ship" exerts a pure imaginative vision that floats through the crowded city unseeing and unseen by the world. Its power is complete and its direction is unswerving, "vague" though the ship may be (3). It "floats" through streets (1–2), "glides / through the sadness / Of slums" (5–7), and sails through "outlying fields" by two other figures of power, an ox and a Quixotic windmill (8–11). Like any other Strand figure of imaginative creation, the shipmates are single-mindedly focused, blind to the peripheries of their vision, as well: "Their eyes / Do not / Turn or close" (22–24). While Linda Gregerson may assert that the ship appears to be a passive vehicle—"the sentence is almost drawn to 'it is moved' instead of 'it moves' "—Strand does utilize active verbs (99). Indeed, the ship is a vehicle for the imagination, and as such it keenly pursues its own ends. The ship cuts through the world by choice every bit as much as the speaker of "Keeping Things Whole" does, displacing water and creating a wake as it does. It is vital to recognize that it does this—and is present in the first place—as a direct result of an *action* by the projecting poet.

"The Kite" is the same breed of imaginative projection, even more powerfully elucidated. It is supported by—not unlike water to a boat—and sometimes buffeted by, what it is not: air. As the kite slices through the air, it focuses the reader's attention and brings new perspective to the world that forms its backdrop. It has Strand's "blind and blackening" powers (4), of course, and as expected "the wren, the vireo, the thrush / make way" (5–6). Like so many imaginative projections of Strand's before and after, this one is focused and focusing, darkening peripheries and spotlighting the poet's chosen tropes. In this poem, Strand's speaker is not the poetic force. Here, the figure of imagination is launched by a man who "runs by / Holding the kite string" (31–32). And like the crew of the ghost ship, he does not see the viewers of the kite—of which Strand's speaker counts himself (and the reader, in the elusive "we" construction that we have seen before). Most significant is the reader's attention to the kite flyer. The poet has the power to order the world by placing himself outside of that world, and the reader recognizes the poet's troping powers—and his insecurity over the poem's lasting value—in the following lines:

> Leaves fall
> As he moves by them.
> His breath blooms in the chill
> And for a time it seems that small
> White roses fill the air,
> Although we are not sure.
>
> (35–40)

To further complicate matters, it turns out that all the events of the poem up until the last dozen or so lines occur in the imagination of a man asleep in a chair, dreaming.

Furthermore, as with Strand's other speaker-creators, he does not see the world outside. Instead, he continues to create in his subjective dream world. And, in case we forget that the kite will not exist—the effect of the poem will not last—after his dream poem and the Strand poem end, the kite "disappears" exactly as the man awakens at the poem's conclusion (59–61). The visions created by poet Strand, for the sleeping poet, for the kite-flying poet, for the interested speaker who speaks for us readers, all unravel when the poem is no more. As Strand states in a plainspoken manner in *The Late Hour*, "after the story, / their voices were gone" ("Exiles" 45–46).

The assertive speakers of "What to Think Of" and "Eating Poetry" further elaborate the capacities of poetry. Even though there may be worry for the future of poetry, as expressed by the marching, suit-wearing, screaming babies locked in a warehouse in "The Babies," or the stagnant, unimaginative couple who float with the wind in "The Marriage," "What to Think Of" provides a how-to guide to the imagination. One of the earlier instances of what I have termed a directive poem, it is simple in its theme, yet packed with some of Strand's most fantastic images. "Think of the jungle, / The green steam rising," is his opening advice, quickly followed in the third line by "It is yours" (3). What we imagine, Strand says, is there due to our ability to think it. Like a magician unafraid to share his tricks with his audience, Strand lucidly expresses part of his poetic theory here. In our imagined world, we have all the powers that his speakers, dreamers, ship-builders, and kite flyers wield. *We* become "the prince of Paraguay" (4), *our* "minions kneel / Deep in the shade of giant leaves / While [we] drive by / Benevolent as gold" (5–8), and *we* cut through the world and reorder it. When we think of ourselves again, we become "almost a god" (13). And our kingdom is in the dark, where our hair provides the light by being "on fire" (14). One might say that Strand had forced the reader into Poulet's "perfect *coincidence* of the reader's mind with the '*intimité indescriptible*' of the author's mind. . . . Having abandoned all particular commitments, the reader becomes a kind of neutral power of comprehension" (Miller 472).

Kirby focuses on the negative artificiality of the "cold confetti of paradise" in the concluding line, and experienced Strand readers already recognize that concluding lines repeatedly reveal the inevitable end of the subjective vision. Kirby likens the poem to "a studio shot complete with cheap effects," and concludes that "success is intoxicating, but temporary" (19). However, it would seem that a subtle but vital shift in his syntax would bring about an alternatively insightful reading. That is, he might say, "Success is temporary, but intoxicating." Though the imagination cannot be sustained forever, it *is* still "the cold confetti of *paradise*" (28, italics mine).

"Eating Poetry" is equally celebratory, further illuminating the idealism of primitive darkness. In the poem, Strand recognizes the value of *reading* poetry. The imaginative energy required to write *or* read is similar, and this poem also would well lead further Pouletian forays into Strand's work. Indeed, as J. Hillis Miller says, Poulet "wants to reach through his '*critique de pure identification*' the mind of the author and nothing beyond that. . . . If there is for Poulet anything beyond consciousness, or other than consciousness, it is to be found not outside consciousness, but within it, at its inmost center" (474). "Eating Poetry" celebrates the kind of primal indulgence that poetry inspires in writers and readers, with the speaker gradually regressing to a canine state, while the reserved, studied librarian hides in the light "with her hands in her dress" (6).

By this juncture, readers should recognize that those who are clothed, and those bathed in natural light are incapable of accessing the joys contained within the imagination. Meanwhile, the other dogs—the poets whose work the speaker is reading—are on fire with inspiration, lighting up the world from the darkness of the basement. They partake in a wild abandonment, the fire motif returning as "their blond legs burn like brush" (11). Even though the speaker tries to convince the librarian that poetry will not necessarily harm her—or at least to assuage her fears—by licking her hand in a friendly gesture, she screams in alarm. The dog-speaker then gets angry at her—or perhaps gives up on her in disgust—and snarls at her and barks. The speaker thus leaves the reader with a decision to make. He is "a new man. . . . I romp with joy in the bookish dark" (16–18). The reader can join him with the other dogs, or be left behind with the librarian. The poem thus ends unequivocally asserting the utter delight of emotional indulgence that poetry can offer to those who are willing to disrobe for it.

THE TENUOUS OPTIMISM OF *DARKER*

I'm not a hopeful man—I don't have much good to say about my fellow human being—but I think I'm an optimist. I wouldn't write anything if I were a pessimist. I may have a bleak view of the world, but I wake up every morning ready to go.

—*Mark Strand*, Interview, Jan. 26, 2002

Midway through his career, David Kirby asserts, Strand discovers that "Poetry can now be curative as well as expressive" (26). While Kirby correctly identifies this development as a significant one in Strand's evolution, his choice of "The New Poetry Handbook" as a contemplative, philosophical work is puzzling: "A true anatomy is conducted. Here poetry is treated in greater detail, with greater seriousness and awe" (25). In this clever collection of epithets formulated in conditional statements, poetry is asserted in many ways—some serious, some comic, some with awe and some with mischievousness. The less serious maxims can be found in several statements like "If a man publicly denounces poetry, / his shoes will fill with urine" (19–20). Nonetheless, there are sentiments in the poem that reveal much about Strand's poetic sensibilities.

The importance of complete imaginative engagement is asserted in commandment three: "If a man lives with two poems, / he shall be unfaithful to one." As Strand begins in this stage of his career to focus on the search for the perfect moment of subjective paradise achieved outside the world's presence, he also recognizes that the "moment" of the poem is valuable only while one is fully immersed *in* the poem. Full engagement of the senses darkens the participant's peripheral world; all that remains within the field of imaginative vision is the poetic world. For a poet to be engaged in two poems, therefore, is an impossibility. While indulging in one poetic creation, the other, even if the ink is still wet, becomes part of the world external to *this* poem.

> If a man conceives of a poem,
>   he shall have one less child.
>
> If a man conceives of two poems,
>   he shall have two children less.
>   (7–10)

The notion of a poem being an offspring of the poet, and that has its own life after it is fathered, is an ancient one. In rules four and five, Strand proclaims his embrace of this conceit, and bears out Pinsky's assertion about Strand's confirming our ideas about poetry. The lines need little elaboration other than to state that, like children, the poem is no longer part of the poet once it is completed. Although many poets have celebrated this fact, Strand takes the opposite tack; for him, art is not the goal, the process of *creating* art is. Where the poem goes after it is completed may be a concern of Strand's, but he has not yet found an answer more satisfying than the statement from "Exiles": "after the story, / their voices were gone." Faced with the possibility that the poem is merely a self-contained effort, with no lasting value except for the poet's—and reader's—own engagement, he ultimately decides that it is worth the effort nonetheless.

In rules 11 and 15, Strand unsurprisingly equates poetry with power and then illustrates that power by granting the poet "a beautiful mistress" (30). Whether the mistress is some recondite reward for his work is arguable. What is more likely is that the mistress *is* the poem with whom he has his affair, just as it is his child earlier. Here again Strand uses contradictory images to assert parallel points. In rule 16 of the "Handbook," he warns of "praising the poem of a fellow overly," for it will "drive his mistress away." In this case, the mistress figure is repeated to produce an alternate postulation. Strand continues to aver that that poetic pleasure is sustaining for the reader as well as the writer, so long as there is complete immersion in the poem. On the overzealous attention to another poem, Strand warns, affectation is impotence. One must be sincere in one's indulgences; the imagination requires it.

Ultimately, this poem ends in the recognizable Strandian territory of absence. "If a man finishes a poem, / he shall bathe in the blank wake of his passion / and be kissed by white paper" (41–43). The "blank wake," which manifests itself as "white paper" is the same void we have seen several times before. That it is white paper instead of some darkness is not troublesome. Strand is merely continuing to find new figures to represent now-familiar ideas. In this case, the whiteness of the paper makes clearer the Strandian motif of perfection in absence, but in remarkably affirmative tones. There is always a white paper confronting the poet after his undertaking is completed; it is the paper of the *next* poem, the potential perfect poem that provides the perfect moment, both of which by definition never can be achieved in practice. In *theory*, with a white paper staring the poet in the face, the potential is unspoiled by words. It is pure idea; even the contemplation of this poem is pure imaginative bliss. Strand continues in this collection practicing his "white paper" theories in poems like "Tomorrow," where, in successive imaginative endeavors, the speaker's friends "will come back and you / will invent an ending that comes out right" (11–12). Contained in the repetitive failures is a continued and recurring sense of promise.

"The Dress" puts into practice Strand's guidelines. The speaker advises the listener—the librarian from "Eating Poetry"?—to free herself from her clothing, for when one's flesh is "deep in the white folds of your dress, / . . . you will not hear . . . / . . . the poem / filling your pillow with its blue feathers" (3–8). But if one empties oneself of worldly concerns (embodied in the clothing that conceals our "purity"), the passionate mole, the systematizing owl and the transcendent poem "will find you . . . / and you will fall into another darkness, one you will find / yourself making and remaking until it is perfect" (10–12). As Miller says of Poulet, "Reading reaches, beyond words, an ineffable presence of one's consciousness within another. When this reading is over, this presence vanishes, leaving the mind of the reader once more empty, ready to be invaded and possessed by another book, another mind" (475). This casting off of the world—and subsequent "putting on" of the poem—enables the listener to indulge in his/her passions, conform the subjective world to his/her standards, and take him/herself to imaginative heights time after time. Though Poulet's "possession" may be a bit severe terminology for Strand, this poem is, to date, Strand at his most optimistic, and poetry—with its unnatural Whitmanian-Stevensian blue feathers—at its most omnipotent.

"The Dance" is another poem that exalts the pure imagination. The speaker confronts his long-familiar fears about the world in general and death in particular: "And who doesn't have one foot in the grave?" (4). Knowing better than to challenge nature head-on, he shrugs his shoulders in the face of the world's threats and recognizes the poem's fleeting nature. "What else can we do?" he asks (3). The world drags him down, just as the trees are weighted with Stevensian "shaggy" leaves (5), and "light falls like an anchor through the branches" (7). In the speaker's imagination, however—in his mind's ability to create a temporary alternate reality—he is happy and transcendent: "My mind floats in the purple air of my skull. / I see myself dancing. I smile at everybody" (9–10). Ultimately, the same repeatedly accessible creative abilities are engendered as the speaker is "borne again and again into heaven" (12). For a poet earlier seen cowering in his bed, the exaltation that he now exhibits in the face of life's ordeals is striking.

Still, for all the playfulness and confidence exhibited in the first half of *Darker*, it would be incorrect to say Strand is entirely celebratory in this volume. "Black Maps" may teach us how to be our own creators, starting from the dark promise of potential that will be expressed in "Always" as "the blaze of promise everywhere" (30). However, "The Guardian" wallows in the reminder that there is no everlasting peace available to the poet. Indeed, to love anything, says the speaker, means to love "what fades" (3). To be "borne again and again into heaven" implies by its converse that one is also continually cast out of heaven. It is this negative half of the notion that concerns Strand in the latter stages of *Darker*. The nature of dualities plays largely in Strand, and *Darker* often *requires* the ability to hold two diametrically opposed concepts in one's mind concurrently. Strand has mastered Stevens, of course, and one of the latter's maxims would seem to apply here: "[T]he imagination is the power that enables us to perceive the normal in the abnormal, the opposite of chaos in chaos" (*Necessary* 153).

"The Guardian" presents such a set of circumstances. In it, Strand establishes the coming of night as a synonym for the onset of poetic inspiration, yet also wistfully mourns the passing of the day, and mourns the dead. Most problematic is the conclusion, addressed to the "Guardian of my death" (6). If the Guardian is he who preserves his absence from the "death world" (one could not in all good conscience allude to religious afterworlds for Strand), then the final three words—"I am alive"—are moot. If, however, we recall Strand's poetics, we will recognize that he is absent from the *poem*. In fact, just as day fades into night, the redeeming poetic endeavor is replaced by a poem. The *act* is replaced by the *thing*. The poet identifies himself with those things that pass, those people who left and who are leaving—for he is most alive when he is "dead to the world," that is, participating in the poem. Similarly, he is absent from the poem once it is completed. The logic is intricate, yet the point is clear: although the joy received from the act of writing a poem is fleeting, it *is* what the poet loves—and needs. But where the lastingness of such endeavors is highlighted in previous poems in this volume, here the question, "Why do I love what fades?" resonates.

In the face of such troubles staving off death, Strand gives us another advisory poem in a vein different from that of "The New Poetry Handbook." "The Hill" expresses the philosophy of a rather tired-sounding speaker who walks away from the world, and grows more lighthearted the farther he travels. Again readers recognize the familiar elevation of the process over the result. Although "the colors of arrival fade" (11) and perfect moments slip into oblivion, the goal is to continue to put "One foot in front of the other" in the exercising of one's imagination (3, 9, 10). In this metaphor for poetry, the walking can be done no more precisely—or quickly—than by taking a single step at a time. In doing so, one is fulfilling each moment's potential, and in fulfilling each moment's potential ("The hours pass" [9]), one fulfills one's life ("The years pass" [10]), and all the while the world spins unconcernedly. One can almost hear this speaker issue a Frostian sigh when he ends his anecdote, "That is the way I do it" (12).

"Breath," one of Strand's candidly articulate poems, is valuable in its presentation of the speaker as a horizon—present by his absence. For indeed, a horizon is nonexistent but for the *concept* of a horizon. Again, the speaker is confident within his poem: he knows that "as the sun rises and sets I know my place, / that breath is what saves me, / that even the forced syllables of decline are breath" (9–10). These are quite potent phrases for Strand, who recognizes at least partial salvation in his ability to create poetry, even if the poetry is banal ("forced syllables of decline"). And once again in this collection, when the poem ends, he trusts that tomorrow he will have another poem to create, another step to take away from the world. As he says, "breath is the beginning again" (17). In this poem, Strand also proves himself a proponent—via Emerson—of Plato's theory of ideas. Things and ideas—especially imaginative ones—are greater than the words we use to describe them: "breath is a mirror clouded by words, / . . . breath is all that survives the cry for help / as it enters the stranger's ear / and stays long after the word is gone" (13–16). This is one explanation for Strand's frequent allusions to the tenuous condition of, and *not-ness* in, his poetry. The words of the completed poem are valueless but for their capacity to engage and inspire by their *ideas*, which come from a purer source, and for their power to project an imaginative vision strong enough to obscure the world. When the breath is expired—or rather, inspired into someone else (the poem, the reader), "all resistance falls away, as meaning falls / away from life, or darkness falls from light" (18–19).

As Pinsky says, Strand "remind[s] us that in its isolation, the imagination does not only speak to the world across the void: what it speaks is a poem" (301). For once, Strand has an answer to the question, *Where does the poem go after it is completed?* In "Breath," it goes to the listener, and Strand's ultimate gift is breath—life, if you will—to the listener himself: "breath is what I give them when I send my love" (20).

The insecurity of the poet concerned with his ability to produce poetry, however, becomes the fretful consideration of the concluding poems of *Darker*. In "My Life By Somebody Else," the speaker makes various quasi-disturbing, quasi-humorous efforts to lure the poetic muse back to him. He tries bribery with a bowl of milk (a life-giving drink), placed prominently on his desk. Yet "You never came" (4). Following his "Handbook" rules, he remakes his metaphor and sits naked at his typewriter. *This* has no effect. He uses sexual imagery to entice his muse. But neither the offer of himself or his wife produces the desired effect. Instead, he says, "I waited" (8). This is significant in its inversion of the active, walking figure of "The Hill," for here the days do not fly by, they "drag on" (9). The light of the natural world, however "exhausted" it may be (9), continues to shine in the imagination's stead. "It is pointless to slash my wrists. My hands / would fall off. And then what hope would I have?" (11–12) is a shockingly horrid relation that directly addresses the writing act. Despite his wooing attempts, "Why do you never come?" he asks (13).

The forlorn figure that arises in this poem does so because of a frustrating lack of imaginative power. In its stead, Strand absents himself and considers the figure of other poets whose style he can emulate. Significantly, at this period Strand begins undertaking major translation projects and begins rewriting poems of the style of those he admires. He seems to say at this point, *If I cannot write from my own imagination, I will write from someone else's.*

An alternate reading of the "you" addressed by the reader is, of course, available. It is plausible that he is addressing his readers. Strand has grappled with the unknowability of his creation's power, and here he may be doubting his ability to reach the reader as he so desires. Again we find him not knowing whether his poetry will last beyond the moments of its creation, or whether he will reach "communion" with his reader—or within the community of poets—as he achieves in "The Dance."

"Elegy 1969" continues the downward spiral of this volume. Modeled after Carlos Drummond de Andrade, it too struggles with the imagination. Can the poem last, it asks. Is this act worthwhile? While unconcerned with the answers earlier in *Darker*, now the Strand speaker fears the answers are negative. Instead of a useful, life-affirming activity, "You slave away into your old age / and nothing you do adds up to much" (1–2). You "go through the same motions" (3), engage in fitful sleep (14), "hard light falls on your shoulders" (12), and perhaps worst of all, the speaker decides, "literature wasted your best hours of love-making" (15). The poem ultimately ends in a rejection of personal power, for "you can't, all by yourself, blow up Manhattan island" (20). Whereas this volume began in confidence, it ends in confusion, as the figure of imaginative stagnation looms large, and the speaker is holding on for dear life. "Courtship" finds the poetic "you" struggling to re-create himself as he prescribed earlier in his "Handbook," yet the key word here is "struggle." His reinvention is a "confused" one (14), and "you curse the day you were born" (15). He does take the woman "by storm" in the end, but the tone achieved is not one of success; although they will "marry," there is no unity, no "marriage." "The world is ugly. / And the people are sad," Strand quotes from Stevens in "The Way It Is." This epigraph proves to be the final word on the poems of *Darker*, which toys with promise but cannot yet sustain itself in the manner the poet desires perhaps too desperately at this phase of his career.

CHAPTER 2

"STILL WE FEEL BETTER FOR TRYING," OR WHY WRITE A POEM?: *THE STORY OF OUR LIVES, THE LATE HOUR*, "NEW POEMS," *THE CONTINUOUS LIFE*

Written after his father's death, and dedicated to Strand's father, the poems of *The Story of Our Lives* could have been Strand's most cynical, disturbing creations to date. Curiously, they are not. Instead, this volume is Strand's furthest foray into the imaginative world, and, upon further reflection, this is not such a surprise. The elegiac form, after all, has been invoked throughout history by masters during personally trying circumstances because of its potential to replace loss. Poems such as "The Story of Our Lives" contain the same suspicions about poetry's ultimate capabilities, but in fact end up celebrating the subjective world. In fact, this collection creates, until *Dark Harbor* in 1993, Strand's longest sustained alternate universe. Therefore, many critics consider it one of his finest works. The characters of "The Story of Our Lives" become part of the book discussed in the poem, and the perspectives and intertextuality wind themselves around so tightly that the only thing that is certain is "the book" created in the poem that creates the poet who writes by the book. The book, being a Mark Strand construct, does not last, of course. But for the moment one is engaged in the textual whirl-wind, one's loss is repaired. The nature of the elegiac form utilized in several moments in this collection allows for the loss to be replaced by the poem itself, and as such, the poem becomes both the most intimate and impersonal memorial construction a poet can formulate.

"Elegy for My Father" is a sensitive poem in six parts that draws for the first time a picture of an actual Mark Strand, subject to the same worldly trials as any other mortal being. This introduces a new period of poetry for Strand. The extended length of the vision, and the extended vision itself, mark departures for Strand. But the ultimate sincerity of the poem leaves some with a sense that Strand is not trying to create a "poetic spectacle" as he has claimed elsewhere. Although the poem deals with the most real despair yet encountered in Strand's world—*this* death is no mere conceptualization—it ends with a clear elucidation of part of his theory of absence.

In "The New Year," Strand repeatedly absents his father from the world. Each time he mentions his father's absence, his father becomes more present in the reader's imagination. Again, this is a desired consequence of the elegiac form. Few times in American literature has a person been so well eulogized as here. Although it is a new year, the sense of despair, the void left by his father's death that makes the absence such an immense presence, leaves this poem with a poignant silence that exists more like a conventional one than a Strandian silence of potential. There is no promise here:

> It is over and nobody knows you. . . .
> There is a shore and people are waiting.
> And nothing comes back.
> Because it is over.
> Because there is silence instead of a name.
> Because it is winter and the new year.
>   (18–25)

This despair is complete and, for the most part, antithetical to Strandian poetics. The rhythm of the final five lines is choppy, curt, tense, and abrupt; each line is end-stopped, portraying the sense of finality in these endings. Beginnings *are* mentioned in other poems in this collection, and overall, renewal is achieved at the conclusion. But this volume is too unlike most of Strand's career to treat and evaluate it as a typical Strandian endeavor. In general, the poems in *The Story of Our Lives* are less attentive to asserting the value of the artistic creation and merely are artistic creations.

Perhaps the only exception to this rule is "The Untelling." This poem makes some of the most robust observations of the need for poetry, and entertains a sustained poetic enterprise. As Ehrenpreis says:

> [W]hat seem to be people are sometimes characters waiting for a poet to invent them. Or his people may create themselves by writing the story in which they will appear. A self is the creation of one's memories. But since these cannot be verified, a poet may imagine a past and challenge recollection to oppose it. Indeed, since all memory is partly invention, we are constantly remaking ourselves. (46)

"Remaking ourselves" is, of course, a concept we have seen before. Strand explores it even more in depth in this volume, and quite successfully too. In "The Story of Our Lives," the faculties of artistic creation are muted. True, the figure of a book plays largely in the events of the poem, but ultimately the book represents humankind's fate. This book is a troublesome proposition, for the speaker is the one who writes it. Critics have contended that the poet therefore has the power to write fate. It seems more likely, however, that the self-determination of the poet is a pretense. In this chicken-or-egg scenario, the book has come first. The speaker may believe that he is choosing to write the book, but every time he puts pen to paper and consults the book, the words are already there. Even when he chooses his own destiny, this choice has been predetermined, as well. Such despair and resignation dominate the poem. Ultimately, we are prisoners of fate: "They are the book and they are / nothing else" (7: 22–23).

"The Untelling," which concludes this volume, pools all this intense despair and turns it into renewal. As Richard Howard states,

> Strand must untell the story so that he does not accumulate his experience but rather, by words, so that he rids himself of experience, empties himself out of memory and foreboding, lays waste to the past and the future so that there is that space about him in which the story—the life, the poem—may occur. (*Alone* 601)

As deep as Strand's despondency is, so powerful is this poem's renewal. When the reader encounters the opening lines, he sees Strand as a real man, for he has felt the pain of his loss in these poems. As such, the reader celebrates this revival of self as well. Experienced Strand readers issue a sigh of relief, for the familiar Mark Strand is back:

> He leaned forward over the paper
> and for a long time saw nothing.
> Then, slowly, the lake opened
> like a white eye

and he was a child
playing with his cousins . . .
                    (1–6)

Once again the figure of writing has the capacity to effect change. When this speaker/writer writes, "He wanted to move beyond his past" (p. 106), and when he picks up *his* pen, he *does* move beyond his past. He writes his future as he rewrites his past. Indeed, by writing, "He would be the man / he had become, the man / who would run across the lawn. / He began again" (p. 109). When he begins again, he successfully creates again. In elegiac form, Strand creates out of his misery, and in doing so, elucidates some of the themes that had been more difficult to comprehend in the less intimate volumes:

> He felt himself at that moment to be
> more than his need to survive,
> more than his losses,
> because he was less than anything. . . .
> The silence was in him
> and it rose like joy,
> like the beginning.
> When he opened his eyes,
> the silence had spread, the sheets
> of darkness seemed endless,
> the sheets he held in his hand. . . .
> He sat and began to write:

THE UNTELLING
To the Woman in the Yellow Dress

Mark Strand has resurrected himself in his poetry. From a loss more real than any figured before, he has arisen. And it is the same silence, the same darkness, the same beginnings wrapped up in endings that bring him back. They are the familiar themes and sensibilities he has always professed. Strand has used them to great advantage in this personally and poetically most challenging test. His poetic philosophy remains intact, and it redeems. Ultimately for the reader, the poems in *The Story of Our Lives* seem to remain too personal to become ours. They remain Strand's, especially because little of his later work attempts the stylistics or form let alone the intimate approach. Strand's poetry resumes instead in the vein that previously had been established.

"You Love What You Are":
The Late Hour

In fact, *The Late Hour* returns Strand to his career path almost as if *The Story of Our Lives* did not exist, though there are a few new twists. The poet himself has entered a new phase of his life—having experienced his father's death, his own divorce and remarriage—and his themes are now more inclusive of family past and present, one of the few lingering motifs from *The Story of Our Lives*. He can no longer completely disconnect himself from home and hearth as he had in the previous years' work. Perhaps the consideration of these elements of his life arises only after these life-changing events.

"The Coming of Light" breathes life into itself from the outset. Strand sounds rejuvenated by a promising future—surprised to be so, but rejuvenated nonetheless. "Even this late it happens: / the coming of love, the coming of light" (1–2). The images that follow are familiar and celebratory, with dreams pouring into the listener's pillows. Ultimately, poetic light is created out of the darkness of the world, and it sings despite the threat of "tomorrow's dust" (7).

"Another Place" confronts the question of fate that remains from *The Story of Our Lives*. It presents a situation in which there is minimal light; it is not quite the darkness of perfection, yet it is also not nearly bright enough to see "what is to come" (6). It is instead a liminal place of partial darkness. In returning to this insecure place, the speaker reveals something arising out of his imagination: "the water / the single boat / the man standing" (8–10). Neatly explained is this world of the imagination, the one that creates its own light, its own characters, and its own meaning out of the meaninglessness of the world: "what light there is / spreads like a net / over nothing" (13–15). Indeed, the light of Genesis was also able to shine on nothing, for God had not yet created anything else. Furthermore, when the speaker says, "what is to come / has come to this / before" (16–18), we recognize that he is talking about the beginning and ending points of darkness, out of which the imaginative creation grows, and into which it disappears. In between the privative and primitive darknesses, the man exists; the imagination projects itself, and makes itself available to take the boat across the water. In the final lines, Strand mourns the state of oblivion poetry has come to. Sadly, in his estimation, "this is the country / nobody visits" (21–22). Poems such as this make one wonder about statements such as Lance Olsen's, "The poems maintain a fragile awareness of the external universe" ("Entry" 95). As we have seen, the "external universe" is a factor to be confronted in numerous poems. Strand may imaginatively obstruct the vision of the world, but it is looming at the poem's outset and/or conclusion.

"Lines for Winter" falls into the directive subcategory of Strandian poetics, where the speaker directly addresses the reader, or as in this poem, more likely his own self. As in "The Hill," this speaker treads along in a type of poetic foraging mode. "Whatever we tell ourselves will be, *will* be," is the unadorned message. As a man thinketh in his mind, so is he, is the maxim, and here the speaker tries to remind himself of that. We must "go on / walking, hearing / the same tune no matter where / you find yourself" (3–6). These instructions on how to create and how to satisfy one's imaginative desires are quite lucid. Even though we may know "nothing" (12), we do know "the tune your bones play / as you keep going" (13–14). So long as we are engaging ourselves, Strand says, we are staving off the cold of winter. The ultimate meaning of the tune is immaterial; even if our tune is a delusion, it is the playing of the tune that gratifies. It is, in fact, nearly a Nietzschean philosophy Strand asserts here. If life is meaningless, one can at least submit to that meaninglessness and celebrate the action that personally suffices. Yet Strand draws the line at the poem, for the poem *is* a meaningful act that may be just for himself. Ultimately, in the face of a fateful end, the final act we must take, Strand says, is to yet again tell ourselves, no matter how hard it might be to convince ourselves, "that you love what you are" (23). One leaves this poem unsure of how successful the speaker has been in his attempts. The poem that follows adopts an altogether new tack.

"White," is a reconsideration of Strand's poetic imagery, and achieves a new buoyancy. "Now in the middle of my life," he begins, "all things are white." We sense not that he has changed his mind about the world, but that he requires a fresh metaphor. White replaces the darkness that he must make of the world before making a poem. But now the poem is hardy, able to reach out into the world and to reorder it. The union of all life in this whiteness, this new flavor of absence, is one of the most celebrated events of his poetic career. Here, the poem even reaches things that are "beyond the edge of sight" (35), a remarkable statement from a man whose only redemption comes in temporary private moments. From this light of absence comes the light of imagination, and this time it lasts. It exists in dreams, where the imagination runs free, and even lasts throughout the day. In a certain increasing number of efforts, then, it can be said, Strand emerges as an idealist.

Of course, this is not a permanent condition. In "For Jessica, My Daughter," Strand's worries about his insignificant placement in the universe resurface. A considerably matured poet with increasing familial responsibilities, Strand writes his growing daughter into his poetic world to absent her—save her—from the world. Howard contends, "Even the act of recording my terrors makes them no longer mine" (*Alone* 594), before going on to say, "Emptying, in fact, is the creative performance of these poems" (598) and considers each poem to be an act of purgation. In so writing, Strand thus protects daughter Jessica from the world. Still, Strand knows that this poetic cosmos will not endure, so he imagines a light—in a second reconsideration of this term—that becomes a poem that she can take with her in the privative dark that will exist when *he* is absented from *her* world—literally and figuratively. In this sense, his poem has, for the second time in the volume, the power to endure beyond its writing. And also for the second time, the personal elements that find their way into the poetry after *The Story of Our Lives* further enlarge its vitality and beauty. Though the tonal changes are subtle, it is obvious that in practice, Strand places increased faith in the poem's authority *after* it has been written.

Of course it is not coincidental that the speaker "goes away" in synchronization with the last words of the poem. However, now this light, this "sheet of paper" (43) is not only just for him. In his ability to "imagine" this light (40), he in fact *can* imagine his daughter carrying away the very poem he writes about her carrying away. Certainly this is a poet with exponentially growing faith in his endeavors. As he learned to re-create himself in "The Untelling," he so he learns to refigure a relationship with his daughter. The imaginative power that, until recently, could only temporarily obscure the world is now reconstructed to have some semblance of permanence. By imagining the poem permanent, it *is* permanent—as a man thinketh a *poem* is in his heart, so a poem is?

So confident has this speaker grown that he can now find answers in his poems. "Where Are the Waters of Childhood" instructs us, his readers, once again as to how to tap into the imagination, and how to access the necessary primitive state. The waters of childhood are where our lives began: in the kingdom of rot, where things have decayed. We must begin to reconstruct, reimagine, and reinvent from the darkness of our memory. Indeed, to return to familiar childhood places and find them alive would be to give them a different life from the one locked into our memory. The Romantics taught us enough about mutability than to think that the places of our childhood would exist in reality exactly as they exist in our mind. So, we must instead retrieve them in a place of stagnancy, where they have not changed from their past. Once we return to our own dark place before we were born, to our own nothingness, the visions will come flooding back, Strand says, in an image that perfectly reveals the imaginative act. When he says, "See the two dogs burst into sight," in our imagination, they have no choice but to burst into sight (20). Furthermore, "When you leave, they will cease, snuffed out in the glare of an earlier light" (20–21). The images burst from the purity of a primal darkness, and that is where they return. The final stanza begins, "Now you invent the boat of your flesh" (34). Strand clearly posits where our redemption is: in the self that is not our self—the water, the mirror, the projection of our self within a poem that is us by being not us. We are not, in fact, our flesh, but must invent ourselves *from* our flesh. And we again must celebrate, for "The waters of childhood are there" (36).

Finally, "The Garden" wonderfully epitomizes Strand's definition of the imagination, and is perhaps the best place for any student of Strand to begin. "It shines in the garden," the poem begins, recalling Stevens and Marianne Moore's real toads in imaginary gardens. "It" also re-creates the past in a vision of the world that is *not* the historical past. After all, an imagined scene is the most pure because it is found in the imagination, not in the imperfect world. In "The Garden," the scope is broad: the major themes of family and past and how we can reach back to both are repeated here. Again we find that the pure imagination can route back through all the years by not concerning itself with physical history. We go back in our imagination to places "suspended in time" (5), not located in 1947 or 1963. And as we have seen time and again, the imagination—itself absented and referred to solely as "it"—repeatedly shines—until the last line, in the moment before it vanishes, which is perfectly described by Strand with the words, "in the moment before it disappears" (18).

CLAIMING LEOPARDI'S NIGHT: "NEW POEMS"

The concept of the imagination as "it" returns in "A Morning," one of the five "New Poems" included in *Selected Poems*. "I have carried it with me each day," the speaker begins in an uncharacteristic nostalgic tone. More often than not, Strand has expressed himself in the present tense, to bring the reader into the imaginative process *as it occurs*. This sense of immediacy is vital to reaching communion with the reader, for, as J. Hillis Miller explains, "If nothing is prior to consciousness, . . . then consciousness is, from the point of view of human existence, the origin of everything else. . . . [T]he moment of the *Cogito* is the ground or foundation of everything else. Everything follows from it" (481). In this summary poem, and increasingly in the latter stages of his career, Strand takes a step back to achieve a broader perspective on his career.

Strand typically denotes darkness as his starting point, adding the current image of a family figure—an uncle—who provides the boat for him to discover the source of imagination as he rides the waves of reminiscence. He ostensibly marks the beginning of his career in this moment from the waters of his childhood; before his imagination had achieved maturity, so to speak, he moved "like a dark star, drifting over the drowned / other half of the world" (7–8). As we have come to expect, this darkened state has provided his imagination with creative opportunities.

Strand then offers the figure of a mirror—the body of water into which his image is reflected. This mirror does not reflect accurately, however, for although no mirror is true, water is even less reliable. The mirror, of course, is a favorite trope for Strand, for indeed it provides a reasonably dependable reflection of a person without *being* that person. Just like any good poetic trope, it defines a thing even as it is clearly not that thing at all. The trope of a mirror, therefore, is doubly potent, for it is troping a trope. In "A Morning," Strand holds up a water-mirror that projects the speaker for us even though it is, in fact, not the speaker at all. Therefore, even the self is a projection in the poem and can be remade and reborn time and again.

St. Bonaventure's view of the mirror is that we exist only as we look into it. The imagination is a vital element in the vision of a projected self. Nonetheless, by using water as his reflecting source, Strand establishes a mirror that has greater *depth* than reality has, because water's depth is greater than a mirror's. And Strand does note that in this water is "the one *clear* place given to us when we are alone" (11, italics mine). This is cause for celebration. It is clear in the sense of being uncluttered. But it is also clear in the sense of being transparent, and as such, it does not have to move to keep things whole.

Remarkably, then, "Leopardi" ends this collection where our discussion began. The world exists in a state of privative darkness from which Strand will create the poem that is, at the same time, not his poem, because of its offspring status as a moderately close but intentionally unfaithful translation of Giacomo Leopardi's "La Sera del Dì di Festa":

> Things pass and leave no trace, . . .
> and whatever our ancestors knew time has taken away.
> They are gone and their children are gone

and the great nations are gone.
And the armies are gone that sent clouds of dust and smoke
rolling across Europe. The world is still and we do not hear them.
                                                          (15–21)

Strand returns to melancholy and doubt, and to a larger acknowledgment of the world than the one found in the highly self-contained
poetry of his early career. The fact that he uses Leopardi as his
departure point is evidence alone of this outward-lookingness.
Recollecting the passing of an important moment from his childhood, the speaker indulges in a parallel important moment of imaginative creation during his walk within his poem. Yet it ends in the
same darkness as it begins, for he hears an "unrecognizable song"
sung by a drunk (12–13). This song is matched with the song he had
heard as a child in his bed one night, and both songs—that of the
Fool and of the wise ignorant—are certainly recognizable as parallels
to poetry. The passing of these songs into silence has "wounded"
him, as the ending of his poem has. The parallel of a birthday with
the creation of this poem returns Strand to the insecurity we have
seen so often in his work. Just as his birthday party had to come to an
end, so too does this poetic endeavor (and *Selected Poems* as a whole)
have to end. And with the world telling him, "I do not give you any
hope. Not even hope" (11), this poet again wonders, "What will
happen from here?"

"Still We Feel Better for Trying": *The Continuous Life*—A Turning Point

"Not every man knows what is waiting for him, or what he shall sing /
When the ship he is on slips into darkness, there at the end," are the
concluding lines of *The Continuous Life*, a collection that subtly but
distinctly marks a strengthening of Strand's poetic stance. It is not the
very first time that we have found Strand looking forward at the end
of a poem or collection of poems, yet the confidence we have seen
waxing and waning in preceding volumes culminates in this collection's certain show of conviction. For while "not every man knows,"
this man, the poet, knows the song he will sing in the face of his inde-
terministic fate; it is the song he has been singing in his white breath
of *The Late Hour;* the song he sends to daughter Jessica, the song of
the imaginative self.

The Continuous Life represents a transitional, sometimes experimental
volume that breaks some new ground while reasserting important

themes and revealing deeply held convictions about the place of poetry in modern society. The collection is careful to attend to past masters (overt references to Goethe, Kafka, Virgil, even Orpheus, among others) and genres (narrative poetry), as well as current considerations of Strand's (particularly the role of the translator, as evidenced by his reconsiderations of Leopardi and the aforementioned artists). It is a work that in many ways foreshadows his great work, *Dark Harbor*. It is also a work that ends Strand's writer's block of nearly a decade, and that reveals a writer coming out of a state of creative flux. At this time, he was teaching at the University of Utah, one of the more extraordinarily picturesque locales in which he had lived as a poet. Understandably, the landscape plays a prominent role in this volume. Strand has frequently related his love of city life, New York in particular, and Utah is as far as one can get from Manhattan in the continental United States. Thus, in many ways, Strand is writing from a liminal zone, and trying on potential selves in this eclectic collection. Noted anthropologist Victor Turner distinguishes such a liminal place as a "realm of pure possibility whence novel configurations of ideas and relations may arise" (Quoted in Alexander 33).

Certainly here, as well as in *The Story of Our Lives*, Strand is vigorously investigating the potentialities of the poetic self. He pays great attention to different forms, styles, and concerns in his experimentations, trying to decide which role he would like to play in the future. In pieces like "Grotesques," it is easy to recognize Strand trying on hats in his monologues and dialogues of various personae. Generally, *The Continuous Life* contains more vernacular language and more colloquialisms than Strand is apt to use. "So what" is the refrain of "Cento Virgilianus"; Orpheus is seen "pulling out all the stops" in "Orpheus Alone" (9); events occurring within the poems are twice referred to merely as "great" ("Luminism" 17; "Life in the Valley" 14); and "Danse d'hiver" speaks of "The old gang" (5). Meanwhile, promise unabashedly comes to the fore when the great forgetters of "Always" make a blank for him to create something anew as *The Continuous Life* comes to a close. Ultimately, Strand emerges from an uncertain place with a degree of poise and assertiveness that heretofore have been concealed. *The Continuous Life* is then both a turning point and the documentation of an emergence from a liminal place, one that has brought Strand world-class eminence.

The collection begins with "The Idea," which, like the first poem of his three preceding volumes, is a prelude. It expresses the desire to reach past this world to a purer one inside the self. Published soon after being named Poet Laureate in 1990, Strand continues to

succeed, for he achieves his required nothingness within the world
and erects a cabin amid that nothingness. It begins:

> For us, too, there was a wish to possess
> Something beyond the world we knew, beyond ourselves,
> Beyond our power to imagine, something nevertheless
> In which we might see ourselves . . .

Strand is now reaching further than ever before. Where in *The Late
Hour* he was pondering the lasting value of the imagination, now he
searches for something even *beyond* the power to imagine. It is the
same poetic theory, but applied more vigorously and exponentially.

Throughout "The Idea," Strand intimately includes the reader in
the endeavor by speaking of "we." By bringing the reader on this
journey, Strand makes this the latest of his directive poems. "Inevitably
a writer who shows us how he writes," Kirby says perceptively, "Mark
Strand also shows the reader how to read" (8). Threatened by the
natural world—a night wind that tells us to "Go back to the place you
belong" (12–13)—Strand conjures up a cabin, a haven amid the haz-
ardous universe. This cabin, he adds, must remain unoccupied for it to
remain transcendent, to be that "Something beyond the world we
knew" (2). Once entered, it would become part of the world we do
know. His concluding lines, "But that it was ours by not being ours,
/ And should remain empty. That was the idea" (19–20) reveal a
wonderful piece of intricate logic. He begins the poem desiring an
idea, then creates a cabin—the cabin amid the "false curves and hidden erasures of the world" (10), and then that cabin becomes the idea
he had searched for at the outset. What can be transcendent? The idea
can. When the idea of a cabin becomes a literal cabin, it is no longer
an idea, and therefore is no longer transcendent. Again, Strand has
vaulted the imagination to its venerated place.

Perhaps nowhere better does Strand prefigure *Dark Harbor* than in
"Velocity Meadows," which is, incidentally, one of the most appealing
titles in Strand's corpus. Here, the confident speaker looks back, in
much the same way the speaker of *Dark Harbor* does, with a sense of
calmness that comes from Wordsworthian reconsideration of an event
after it has been experienced: "I can say now . . . I knew that a train, /
Trailing a scarf of smoke, would arrive, that soon it would rain" (1–4).
When he says, "A frieze of clouds lowered a shadow over the town,"
readers who have already experienced *Dark Harbor* may expect that
speaker to say he was confident that "The turbulent sky would drop

the shadowy shapes / Of its song" ("Proem" 8–9). But this poem is populated by others who deserve their own attention. Time seems, ironically, to slow in these "Velocity Meadows," as Strand's brush carefully paints the landscape: "The air smelled sweet, and a girl was waving a stick / At some crows so far away they seemed like flies. / Her mother, wearing a cape and shawl, shielded her eyes" (8–10).

The poem then contemplates perception in a way that Strand has not done since earlier in his career. A second "speaker" enters and provides his own observations on the same scene. In this way, one might view the scene described as a painting that two people with differing viewpoints and experiences with art might interpret. "Look at those clouds forming a wall, those crows / Falling out of the sky, those fields, pale green, green-yellow, / Rolling away, and that girl and her mother, waving goodbye," the second man explains (12–14).

Immediately, the speaker accepts this new interpretation, and the poem quickly unravels into an apocalyptic scene. Ultimately, the artistry explained by the speaker's initial interpretation gives way to a more earthbound—"realistic," if you will—reality. If the speaker wanted to make the painting into a still life, or appreciate it as Keats' Grecian urn, this second figure neutralizes that desire before "running away" (16). When "The lights of the town were coming on, and I saw, dimly at first, / Close to the graveyard bound by rows of cypress bending down" (17–18), Strand recognizes the physical world's preeminence. It is, after all, the town's lights that are coming on, not the artificial lights of the poet's moon. And, of course, the graveyard figures prominently at the end of any poet's vision, waiting as the final place for him and his imagination. The cypress trees, then, also echo the theme of the death of a beloved, and Strand, at first, seems to reinforce this obliteration of imagination by painting "The girl and her mother, next to each other, / Smoking, grinding their heels into the ground" (19–20). At second glance, though, despite the shocking image of the pair "smoking," perhaps they are enacting their defiance by "grinding their heels into the ground." Such a definitive act of recalcitrance represents an ultimate personal victory in the face of an impersonal, unyielding nature. Whatever nature is going to do to the imaginative souls, Strand seems to say, perhaps an obstinate effort of any sort is the only valuable action we can take. If the world is going to burn us to cinders—as the mother and daughter are in this natural crematory act—then we can at least face the fire head-on. If Sisyphus is eternally condemned to roll that rock up the hill, at least he can curse the gods as he walks down to repeatedly chase it.

If the light of the imagination is easily and violently effaced in "Velocity Meadows," then the phoenixlike re-creation of light is equally pacific at the outset of Strand's homage to Andrew Marvell and Archibald Macleish, "A.M."[1] Here, Strand parallels the light of the poetic imagination with the morning light. Again, this is not the light of the natural world; it is the light of imagination reflecting upon now what is *not* a generic absence, but some specific, previously inflicted death: "How well the sun's rays probe / The rotting carcass of a skate, how well / They show the worms and swarming flies at work" (13–15). The poem begins *in medias res*, with an ellipsis and a surprisingly honest description of such a Macleish verb as: "the *dark* infinitive to feel" (1, italics mine). Strand is rarely as upfront in his portrayal of emotion, or willing to invoke pathetic fallacy. In a remarkably long sentence—one that readers should recognize as typically Strandian—it is not until the fifth line that Strand syntactically completes the independent clause with the easily overlooked words "must end." In between, Strand rails against feeling, saying it "would endure and have the earth be still / And the star-strewn night pour down the mountains / Into the hissing fields and silent towns until the last / Insomniac turned in" (2–5). If feeling, then, is a kind of darkness of privation, this speaker calls for that darkness, and "the damages of night" (10) to be quickly replaced by a primitive white. In a Whitmanian bestowal of democratic verve, "early risers" will then watch as this whiteness casts its light "so on down / To the smallest blade of grass and fallen leaf" (5–8). Like Whitman, Strand assigns this light to the insignificant and wounded. And as in Whitman, subtly hidden in the act is the truth that it is dispensed by the potent poet, who is brandishing his power for the good of others, not sharing what actually belongs to the "blade of grass and fallen leaf."

The imagination encompasses all, Strand's speaker says, celebrating in perfect rhyme at the conclusion of "A.M.," "How well they shine upon the fatal sprawl / Of everything on earth. How well they love us all" (16–17). Unlike his early poetry, Strand's later poetry exhibits that despite the death and darkness illuminated by the sun's rays, the imagination still reigns. In *this* reconsideration, the world can shine its light upon the miseries of the universe without gravely damaging the poet's psyche. In making such an uncharacteristic and in fact unusual effort, Strand clears more ground for his future. It is not the last of this collection.

"Orpheus Alone" represents the poet's bold attempt to consider the history of poetry—one of at least two such attempts in *The Continuous Life*. In it, Strand's principal concern is with denoting "[t]he third and greatest" poem the world had seen (40). Orpheus' own two songs—one an elegy for the lost Eurydice, the other an imaginative creation born from the primitive absence of pastoral retreat, "[c]ame into the world as the world" (41). This poem, unlike the previous two that were focused on creation, entered into existence to remind the world of its very impermanence: "it came / As things come that will perish, to be seen or heard / A while, like the coating of frost or the movement / Of wind, and then no more" (42–45).

As if Strand's poetry was not redolent with reminders of transience, was not already fraught with the promise of death, here Strand defines modern poetry as necessarily being by, for, and about that very privative darkness. Furthermore, Strand reminds us, even in light of such transience, poetry must seek the eternal, and as such, place itself between finite and infinite: "it came in the middle of sleep / Like a door to the infinite, and, circled by flame, / Came again at the moment of waking" (45–47). It is here where Miller, speaking of Poulet, can lend great insight:

> The supreme importance of the moment of self-awareness makes Poulet especially delighted by passages where an author describes his awaking from sleep. If the moment of waking is like a repetition of the creation of the world, so that the waker is seized with an astonishment before things comparable to that of Adam or Miranda, waking is also a daily repetition of the *Cogito*, and is a fresh re-enactment of the discovery of the self. (481)

This final poem of Orpheus, of course, refers to his exploits on the island of Lesbos, ending, necessarily, "[w]ith his severed head rolling under the waves" (52). Though, as for that, even Orpheus' head has power, "Breaking the shifting columns of light into a swirl / Of slivers and flecks" (53–54). This final great poetry, one may or may not be surprised, reveals itself not unlike Strand's own: "it came in a language / Untouched by pity, in lines, lavish and dark, / Where death is reborn and sent into the world as a gift" (54–56). Ultimately, Strand reveals the necessity of loss, death, and absence as the necessary starting point for all that follows. Without a voice to initiate poetic language, and without mutability and mortality to threaten us with a more potent silence, we have no need for poetry. Death's "gift" to us is the reminder to speak now. Orpheus' gift of himself is "So the future, with no voice of its own, nor hope / Of ever becoming more than it will be, might mourn" (57–58). Even if we can only borrow phrases long-since shopworn—because we have "no voice"—we can at least mourn. And in that mourning is the creation of something new for ourselves—our own poem of sorrow. So, tightly wrapped with beauty and sorrow—for, after all, Orpheus was made to suffer as a result of his songs—this poem achieves grand heights without really becoming a representative Strand poem. Though not very characteristic of Strand, "Orpheus Alone" possesses the ambition to define the role of poetry at its very foundation; to say that, even if all we have is grief, in having poetry we have two more things, too: the song that is the rebirth of that grief, and the recollection of a moment of solace.

Poems like "To Himself" and "Luminism" reconsider familiar themes in an attempt to re(de)fine Strand's poetic philosophy for future attempts. In the first poem, Strand "set[s] the writing of years / Against the writing of nothing" (4–5), while also setting the value of writing for oneself as a necessary solipsistic act against writing as being a selfish act:

> You were mine, all mine; who begged me to write, but always
> Of course to you, without ever saying what it was for
> Who used to whisper in my ear only the things
> You wanted to hear . . .
>
> (7–10)

The self to whom he writes here—the egoistic self that *desires* to write, perhaps as opposed to the self that *needs* to write—gets an upbraiding for demanding himself to write, "as if there were something / You wanted to know, but for years had forgotten to ask" (12–13). Not unlike so many other Strand poems, this one ends at the precise moment where there is some attempt to find an answer—or in this case define the question: "Something to do with sunlight slanting over a table, / An arm rising, a face turning, and far / In the distance a car disappearing over the hill" (14–16). That car necessarily represents the question that may have been asked, but by this time, of course, it is too late to ask. One could describe this poem as that of the poet's existential angst—or mid-life crisis, if you prefer. Even the outset of the poem, "[Y]ou've come to me now without knowing why" ends without any closure or insight into beginnings, middles, or endings (1). The speaker has provoked himself to write without having a reason for writing, and, when he attempts to seek a question about what to do now "[t]hat night will fall" (12), all he achieves is synecdoches ("An arm rising, a face turning") and a fading image.

The magnificent and aptly titled "Luminism" presents the converse view about poetry's potential, ending as it does with the self-assured one-line sentence: "I had no idea what it meant until now." Of course, like "To Himself," meaning is not revealed to the reader. This poem ends before the speaker discloses "what it meant"—though in this case the speaker probably has no intention of making any such revelation. "Luminism" may be, in essence, the answer to the question Strand could not find the words to express in "To Himself." "I remember it, / As if it had come from within, one of the scenes / The mind sets for itself, night after night, only / To part from, quickly and without warning" (2–5), Strand begins. The poem comes too hot on the heels of "To Himself" (two pages later) to forget the inner dialogue contained in the former poem. Here, however, the speaker is not annoyed with his own lack of rationale about writing. He has reached some understanding as an apparent result of his experience with the former poem, and now seems secure, even excited, about remembering one of the important moments that confirm poetry's value to self and society. Unlike Stevens' "Auroras of Autumn," this poem's speaker is delightedly overwhelmed—and incorporated into a natural whole—by a magnificent sunset:

> The streets shimmered like rivers,
> And trees, bushes, and clouds were caught in the spill,
> And nothing was spared, not the couch we sat on,
> Nor the rugs, nor our friends, staring off into space.
> Everything drowned in the golden fire. . . .
>
> (7–11)

This, however, is not the event that confirms poetry's value. Neither is Philip's declaration that "This hand is just one / In an infinite series of hands. Imagine" (13–14), though that phrase itself seemed to "master the night and portion out the sea," to employ a Stevens phrase from "The Idea of Order at Key West": the moment he speaks, the blinds on the sunset seems to close. The instant a human voice interferes with the perfect(ly) natural event of a sunset, the voice—as a not-sunset—denies the sunset any totality of the watchers' attention. Furthermore, the infinite series of hands serves to interlock humanity *against* the sunset, as it were. Finally, the sky becomes a purple bruise and the friends at this get-together stop to define and label the sunset: "everyone stood / And said what a great sunset it had been" (16–17). The phrasing here is necessarily inadequate. Since the only thing "everyone" has at their disposal to "capture" this natural event is language, they cannot ever hope to re-create the event adequately. All a trope can do is mimic, perhaps substitute, and as substitute for the thing itself, it is always a faint imitation, or at best a close approximation. Here they can do little more than call it "great."

The most important turn of events for the speaker, however, is "something else happened then—/ A cry, almost beyond our hearing, rose and rose, / As if across time, to touch us as nothing else would" (18–20). It is not insignificant that it was a "cry" that was uttered, and that it was "as if across time." This was a *new* utterance, not some vain attempt to capture nature as it is, but something to replace nature's action once the action is completed. As such, this cry is its own valuable event, its own best self and not a pale imitation of natural reality. Certainly it reconsiders Stevens' "The Course of a Particular," where "one holds off and merely hears the cry. / It is a busy cry, concerning someone else. / And though one says that one is part of everything / There is a conflict, there is a resistance involved" (4–7). There seems to be little resistance to the cry in Strand's poem. Stevens' penchant for downward movement is replaced by Strand's ascending cry, and while Stevens is able to hold off—or at least is desirous of holding off—Strand strains to hear the cry. Even *if* this cry is "concerning someone else," Strand intends to eavesdrop on its message. And finally, there is no resistance involved for Strand, for he already has been touched by Philip's utterance. Thus, the cry is able to rejuvenate him and provide him with momentary meaningfulness.

A sense of static peace then follows as a matter of course, with "Life in the Valley," the sister poem to "Luminism." Ostensibly written in and about the same Western locale, the poem concerns the Strand speaker—uncharacteristically speaking to a *we* that is not the reader but a companion—confronting frightfully majestic nature. Strand's commencement is seemingly designed merely to evoke a laugh: "Like many brilliant notions—easy to understand / But hard to believe—the one about our hating it here / Was put aside and then forgot" (1–3). Of course, humor has been a frequent strategy for Strand to couch more austere perceptions. He continues by cataloging the reasons why he and his companion forgot to hate their homestead. "Those freakish winds . . . were not enough to drive us out" (3–7), he recounts. "Nor were . . . heavy snows. We simply stayed indoors" (8–11). As in "Luminism," Strand remembers the input of "Our friends," who this time describe "the views—starlight over / The clustered domes and towers, the frigid moon / In the water's glass" as nothing more or less than "great" (12–14). Also as in "Luminism," Strand finds his mate and himself in accord with those friends: "And we agreed," he says (14).

When he jots down a list of his and his partner's favorite sights, however, one gets the sense that he now distances the pair from their friends by delineating a very different set of "great" sights from theirs. The natural light's play on the landscape is what attracted the friends' interest; this couple, however, favor the artificial—and thus temporally limited—creations of humankind and the promise of death. They, after all, "got to like the sight of iron horses rusting / In the fields, and birds with wings outspread, / Their silver bones glowing at the water's edge" (15–17). Strand has admitted that the birds are airplanes, inspired as it were, by the airport he lived near in Utah (Interview, Nov. 2, 2002). The final line, the couple's final amusement, "far away, huge banks of cloud motionless as lead" (18) necessarily sinks into conclusion, cutting off any resounding consideration of itself. Instead it suggests irony; after all, who would admire clouds ominously described as "motionless as lead?" That irony is what takes us back to the beginning of the poem to reconsider, *Is this opening sentence itself ironic? Is it possible the notion of their "hating it here" was put aside, forgot, but then remembered again? Or is it that the "agreement" of line 14, and the subsequent depictions of the portentous are dripping with sarcasm?*

Even if none of these cases is true, this is a speaker in Strandian tradition, who recognizes the importance of fate, of impending doom, and is in any case thankful for the reminder from nature of death's preeminence. The reader is left to determine which one provides a more frightful scenario though couched in lyrically pleasing tones.

A further irony that might arise is the title of the collection, and the poem that shares the title, which follows "Life in the Valley." Here, in one of his finest poems, the poet returns to images of childhood to discuss not reminders of death, but *some* sort of life-in-the-face-of-death. Though Strand dabbled in personal reminiscences in the new poems at the conclusion of *Selected Poems* in 1980, here, the imagery is more universal than personal. The poem begins with a delightful—if metaphorically terrifying—figure of "children crouched in the bushes," ostensibly hiding from their parents who have called them to dinner (2). After all, they are, in kid-perspective, "Watching the grown-ups for signs of surrender" (3). Strand then magnificently translates the meaning of signs of surrender into adultspeak: "Signs that the irregular pleasures of moving / From day to day, of being adrift on the swell of duty / Have run their course" (4–6).

Strand's first apostrophe comes across as a sarcastic swipe—in Whitmanian flourishes—at the everyday adult life of contemporary American culture, or the lack thereof:

> Oh parents, confess
> To your little ones the night is a long way off

> And your taste for the mundane grows; tell them
> Your worship of household chores has barely begun;
> Describe the beauty of shovels and rakes, brooms and mops;
> Say there will always be cooking and cleaning to do,
> That one thing leads to another, which leads to another;
>
> (6–12)

Of course, the magnificent use of irony and humor would only be *somewhat* effective if the poem were not metaphorically engaging as well. Certainly, "the night" is more than just one day's nightfall; it is death. And if these parents have convinced themselves that it is, indeed, "a long way off," they have all the more reasons for partaking in the mundane tasks that fill their days. These parents are telling themselves, to use an Eliot phrase, that "There will be time, there will be time" ("The Love Song of J. Alfred Prufrock" 26). When the list of confessions continues, however, the opposite lesson seems to be the one Strand wants the parents to focus on: "Explain that you live between two great darks, the first / With an ending, the second without one" (13–14). The first darkness is the privative one, out of which humans are born. The second is death, the final erasure of all that the parents can or will do. In poetic terms, the first darkness is that from which the poem is born, the second the silence that occurs after its final utterance is issued. One would think, thus, that this poem would be taking on *carpe diem* tones. But the litany of this deathwatch poem continues. Strand urges the parents to explain:

> that the luckiest
> Thing is having been born, that you live in a blur
> Of hours and days, months and years, and believe
> It has meaning, despite the occasional fear
> You are slipping away with nothing completed, nothing
> To prove you existed.
>
> (14–19)

Here, Strand's admonition is fairly unambiguous, the irony dropping away. But one must not forget that these words are somehow supposed to teach the *carpe diem* inversion, which is: *Seize the mundane. If you have completed nothing, done nothing to assert your existence, then strive that much harder to do nothing.*

The poem abandons irony altogether when the speaker begins his third sentence with:

> Tell the children to come inside,
> That your search goes on for something you lost—a name,

A family album that fell from its own small matter
Into another, a piece of the dark that might have been yours,
(19–22)

This admonition to the parents is the reverse of the first. Now, the
night is no longer "a long way off" (thus allowing the children to
remain outside); instead the speaker asks the parents to get the children inside. The speaker also now describes more specifically the
problem: these parents have lost their will to live, to make their mark.
Somewhere along the way, some "small matter" has changed their
destiny, and this poet of small things is the one to refocus the reader,
at least, on the immeasurable value in every miniscule act. In fact,
being "between two great darks" as we are, one might say that the
only way to gain "a piece of the dark that might have been yours" is
to indulge in that moment that the parents in this poem have allowed to
slip through their hands. And now they ask their children to help do
so for them, to go back in time and search for that lost moment. Of
course, in Strandian philosophy, that moment, though it can be
approximated, can never be recaptured. Furthermore, every moment
spent in search of that moment is the loss of this *present* moment. The
only potential for these parents, it appears, is in their children, for *they*
are their parents' mark, their piece of the dark that is theirs:

Say that each of you tries
To keep busy, learning to lean down close and hear
The careless breathing of earth and feel its available
Languor come over you, wave after wave, sending
Small tremors of love through your brief,
Undeniable selves, into your days, and beyond.
(23–28)

These "small tremors of love" are the minute moments that bring
some respite to their days. At its conclusion, the poem has been transformed lyrically and tonally into something beautifully haunting,
something not so mundane about small lives, small actions, or small
loves in the face of the second unending darkness. Sadly, with their
moment having passed, the parents seem to but wait for death. At
best, one could say they are listening to Mother Earth for answers.
But Strand's readers know that Earth is no mother for us, and if she
was, she has abandoned her children; she has no answers for us, and
no concern for us. That one candle to light in the darkness is for us
and us alone. Most remarkably, however, is the assertion that these

somehow lost parents have stumbled onto something that actually lasts into their days—and beyond! That assertion causes us to go back and reconsider just what that small something is.

Of course, the experienced Strand reader may recall a plethora of small sustaining moments that Strand has provided in the past. To discern precisely what will sustain in "The Continuous Life," we must reconsider Strand's admonition(s) to the parents. In what we originally analyzed as a string of appositives, Strand uses the words *confess, tell, describe, say, explain,* and *tell* and *say* one more time each, as directives to the parents. What seems more than likely, however, as the poem progresses, is that the advice is not in actuality appositional, despite the tone being presented as such. Because of the apparent contradictions between some instructions and others—and because of tonal differences from beginning to end—it becomes clear that these utterances are in *opposition* to each other. And, in typical Strand style, what one says is not so important as one's saying it. Therefore, what seems to be a buildup to a final, perfect instruction to the parents is really no more viable an answer to the children than any of the previous parental confessions. But let us take this part a bit more slowly.

Strand's first advice to the parents is to *confess* that their "taste for the mundane grows." While few parents would trumpet the merits of the mundane, if they revel in "the beauty of shovels and rakes, brooms and mops," their indulgence will satisfy them in ways similar to the satisfaction of the poet's indulgence in poetry. The second way to stave off death is, apparently, to ignore it and simply engage in the daily grind: "there will always be cooking and cleaning to do/ . . . one thing leads to another, which leads to another." The decision whether to view the next lines as one suggestion or as several is left to the individual reader; in any case, the reader must recognize that Strand has severely compressed the time between "two great darks" when he says, "the luckiest / Thing is having been born, that you live in a blur / Of hours and days . . . "

When the speaker next proffers, "Tell the children to come inside," it is the best proof of the oppositional status of his coaching. The previous three-to-five suggestions would each allow for the parents' "surrender"—i.e., allowing the kids to stay outside. Now, the speaker switches allegiances, if you will, and asks the parents to include the children in the previously discussed search for the lost "small matter." And of course, in this case, since the children are included in the search—and are also, presumably, small—it is also possible that the children themselves are now the small piece of the dark the parents can call their own piece of immortality.

Most implicating of Strand's primary lesson in the poem—i.e., say *anything*—is the enjambed, throw-up-your-hands-in-frustration conclusion to the first part of his harangue: "You don't really know." Though the last advice, again, sounds the most beautiful, and reveals a tender connection between humankind and a caring Nature, this too is but one of several possibilities for the parents to share with their children. Indeed, *say anything* is what Strand teaches, so long as the sayers commit to their utterance. In this way, Strand echoes Frost, who advises his reader to make a claim that he took some purported road less traveled. The truth of the choice matters very little. Bask in the mundane. Search for meaning in the universe. Listen to the earth share its wisdom. Whatever the preference, indulge. "They're not ready to give up," Strand says in praise of the parents. "They thrive on their dailyness. . . . It's one of my few positive poems, I think" (Interview, Nov. 2, 2002). Participation in the act—and the decision to value the act—makes all the difference in the face of privative darkness. "The Continuous Life," like all genuinely transcendent poetry, avoids satisfactory explication, and continually leaves critics—despite repeated returns to the poem—with a sense that there remains much more to plumb. This poem is one of those exquisitely layered American poetic creations that is both perplexing and familiar, intimate and odd, and Strand, bringing it at the close of a volume of wavering self-assurance, seems not only invigorated but also at the top of his game.

"Always" may be Strand's purest expression of the value of—and necessity for—primitive darkness. Returning to his starker style, erasing all traces of the world before writing this poem, he figures "The great forgetters," who do their own erasing (4). These forgetters, whom we may loosely term "poets"—yet who are also disturbing in their ruthlessness—gradually erase the world "down to the last stone . . . / And only the cold zero of perfection / Left for the imagination" (22–24). When they are done, gone are the miseries of the world, the "scars" left by boats running along the San Francisco Bay (11), and the "sulphur yellow streetlamps" that intrude upon the purity of the dark night (17). Then again, gone, too, are the Cranian "harps of beaded lights / That vault the rivers of New York" (13–14). Though many critics choose to view the forgetters as utterly destructive forces, the conclusion of the poem seems to suggest a different movement. It ends with "no grass, no trees . . . / The blaze of promise everywhere" (29–30, ellipsis Strand's). From this promise grows the imagination. This is a disturbingly simple declaration within a deceptively simple poem, which can surely shed light on Strand's own poetic process. For better or worse—or rather, for better *and* worse—all that can be accomplished can be erased. As such, all that can be accomplished *must* be erased in order to create anew.

Mostly, the world provides horrors for us to endure. Strand knows that to temporarily escape the world's horrors he must provide an imaginative shelter. The poet and reader redirect their consciousness away from their scars when immersed in the imaginative act; that loss immediately opens up space for the poetic cosmos to fill in the blanks. Strand will later describe this absence more optimistically as "the great space that he felt sure / Would open before him, a stark sea over which / The turbulent sky would drop the shadowy shapes / Of its song" (*Dark Harbor* "Proem" 6–9). Miller identifies this moment as

> a naked presence of consciousness to itself. . . . [C]onsciousness is, from the point of view of human existence, the origin of everything else. . . . [T]he moment of the *Cogito* is the ground or foundation of everything else. Everything follows from it, as a tiny square of paper unfolded may be a map of the world, or as a colorless button grows, in a glass of water, into a magic Japanese garden full of flowers, trees, and shrubs. (480–81)

Whether these "great spaces" that ensue are caves within a mountain, harbors within a city, breaks in a cloud, silences within a din, or great forgetters closing their eyes to the world, the Strand poem presents imaginative alternatives to modern existence.

While everything outside of the poetic imagination threatens a privative darkness (representing the removal of what was once there), Strand's desired dark space is a primitive one, that promising state *before* things were. Here, daemonic man, disconnected from the cosmos, indulges in his own creative force. Here, the poet selects elements from the natural world—the altered light of a sunset, the merely reflected light of frigid moons—and breathes them into new existence. Trope said sunset, and it lights lakes on fire; trope said moon and it shines of its own.

Fate returns to Strand's poetry in "Se la vita e sventura . . . ?" (Portuguese for "If life is a misfortune . . . ?"—certainly a question with which Strand has struggled for 40 years). Reminiscent of the omnipotent book of fate in *The Story of Our Lives*, the poem finds the poet asking, "Where was it written" time and again, wondering even if his fate is sealed, and considering how he can discover his future. Ultimately, he even considers the fate of his poetry:

> Was it written that I would be born into myself again and again,
> As I am even now, as everything is at this moment,
> And feel the fall of flesh into time, and feel it turn,

Soundlessly, slowly, as if righting itself, into line?

(29–32)

In "this moment," the speaker has achieved that elusive unity that he frequently seeks but infrequently gets glimpses of. Note the splendid pun of "righting itself, into line" (i.e., writing itself into lines [of poetry]). As is customary in a Strand poem, the darkness of night then spreads out everywhere. But as has been Strand's recent experience, the night is filled with both fairies and demons. Akin to the sun's rays that shone on Strand's "rotting carcass of a skate" in "A.M.," here the natural world does not only part for the poetic imagination, but also for "the blurred shape of the murderer / Fleeing the scene" (14–15). The faculties of the Strandian imagination continue to multiply, evidenced here in that one has the capacity to access them even as the ultimate victim—at the hands of the murderer. Even at the hour of one's death, as one is entering "Once more [into] the unreachable sphere of light" (20), the imagination functions well. As the victim is dying, we learn this new facet of the imagination's potential: He is

>   . . . sinking
> Into his wound like a fly or mote, becoming
> an infinitesimal part of the night, where the drift
> Of dreams and the ruins of stars, having the same fate,
> Obeying the same rules, in their descent, are alike.

(22–26)

The imagination's reign has spread to all phases of existence, even until the moment of death. In this poem, with its echoes of Dickinson's "I heard a fly buzz when I died," even the man with no power to stand or speak, let alone halt his own death, has one thing: the imagination that links him to the rest of the universe. A powerful thing, indeed, has Strand's imagination become, and in this he foreshadows the triumph that will be *Dark Harbor*. At this stage in Strand's career, the dichotomy between the worlds of nature and men versus the world of the subjective imagination has grown to its apogee. The natural world is more often at its ebb, and the imagination at its flow.

Note the condition of poetry in "The History of Poetry." "Our masters are gone," Strand begins, describing the poetic world as one in tatters. Furthermore, he says in this presaging of *Dark Harbor*, "and if they returned / Who among us would hear them [?]" (2). This entirely negative privative absence mourns presumably the great poets who have served as poetic inspiration for future masters—notably the

Romantics Keats and Wordsworth and modernists Stevens and Bishop. Too few poets of this era, Strand says, create, but merely document. Strand invokes his own angels—they will later become the great poets of the past in *Dark Harbor*—who seem to pity these lazy poets and try to reignite their poetic fires. Yet, Strand says, "[W]e have lost our will, / And do nothing but doze, half-hearing the sighs / Of this or that breeze drift aimlessly over the failed farms / And wasted gardens" (13–16). These lines present us with a sad, eerie juxtaposition of death upon the life-giving forces of earth.

Clearly, in this world without a poetic counterlife, all is wasted. Those who call themselves poets do not utilize imagination, he complains. They "do nothing but count the trees, the clouds, / The few birds left" (19–20), instead of re-creating them, troping them anew, within a poem. Then they rationalize their inaction by saying, "[Besides], wasn't the church of the world already in ruins?" The would-be poets of today are stagnant; they ignore the angels who would inspire them, writing only of the doleful realities of the external world and charting its squalor; or not writing at all, and making excuses for avoiding their artistic responsibilities as they go. It is a scathing critique of contemporary confessionalist poetry and vapid tabloid-angst trends. Other poems in this collection seem to reveal a Strand who has spent considerable time considering this issue, and who expresses concern over the state of poetry and comment in similar ways. This is but one reason for this collection's extensive references to some of Strand's "masters." It also seems to call forth Strand's own great work, *Dark Harbor*, only a few years down the road. If one may be so bold as to attribute such hubris to Strand, this poem, and much of *The Continuous Life*, appears to be his re-creation of Emerson's calling for the next great poet. However, unlike then, Whitman does not answer the call; Strand will answer his own with *Dark Harbor*. His presentation in *The Continuous Life* of the ruinous state of poetry helps foreshadow his great work to come. When he makes utterances such as "Where was it written," in "Se la vita e sventura . . . ?" he prepares himself to answer, *It hasn't been, so I will write it.* When he later invokes, "Imagine a poem," he begins to prefigure the long poem that will follow ("Reading in Place" 1).

Ultimately, Strand returns to directive poems and reasserts in "Reading in Place" and "The End" the capacities of the imagination that only need to be tapped to be fruitful. "Reading in Place" begins by asking us to "Imagine a poem that starts with a couple." Throughout the poem, Strand befittingly demands that readers be attentive to the subtle shifts in perspective to understand their place in the creative mode. For, indeed, when the poem is completed, it is via our "imagining the poem" that *we* readers have created it: a talented metanarrative trick. But this is not the mere act of imagining ourselves the prince of Paraguay as in the simpler "What to Think Of." Indeed, here we not only imagine the poem and the couple within the poem, but also a reader of the poem who slips the poem into a book. We are then to imagine the couple's continued existence in stasis, for while they are stuck within the unread book, they are "feeling nothing is lost" (9). We then follow their imaginations as they engage in a pastoral escape.

The reader, we then are told, "out for a stroll in the autumn night, with all / The imprisoned sounds of nature dying around him, forgets / Not only the poem, but where he is" (13–15). Where Strand indicts the contemporary poet in "The History of Poetry," here he indicts the reader. Ignoring his own powers of imagination, not tapping a la Poulet into the imagination of another's poem, not going to the source of the waters of his childhood, the reader thinks of the real world and when he recalls a house, "He cannot remember whose house it was, or when he was there" (20).

But all does not end in despair. Strand has other requirements for his readers. In a similar admonition to those of "The Continuous Life," he tells us to reimagine—reinvent?—the man six years later, rediscovering the poem anew. The couple is blissfully ignorant of their own condition as fictional creations, and are safe in their belief "That they will continue to live harm-free, sealed / In the twilight's amber weather" (25–26). Finally, the speaker poses the question: "[H]ow will the reader know, / Especially now that he puts the poem, without looking, / Back in the book, the book where the poet [yet another character for us to consider!] stares at the sky / And says to a blank page, 'Where, where in Heaven am I?'" (26–29).

Strand makes a commentary on the sad life of this almost entirely imagination-deprived reader, and poems such as this one cause Kirby to masterfully assert that "art . . . fails Mark Strand. But artistry is another matter altogether. Art is static; a book on the shelf may as well be a doorstop. But artistry is dynamic, including the artistry of the passionate reader or viewer (or translator, in the case of *The Monument)*" (82–83). Without engaging in the creative act of imagining the poem (which is what engaged readers do when they read a poem, Strand asserts), the reader is living without any kind of redemption. He will not know the gifts the imagination can bring (i.e., the ability to reorder the universe). Instead, he will be trapped in a perpetual autumn. The poet, meanwhile, is faced with that ever-ominous, ever-promising "blank page," where tomorrow he may once again reinvent himself. It is an intriguing journey on which

Strand has taken his readers in this poem, one in which he gives them greater imaginative responsibilities. In doing so, the poet presents an imaginative creation stronger than at any time previous. "The world is ugly, and the people are sad," Strand may have repeated for this volume, adding, "But the imagination is 'the necessary angel of earth, Since, in my sight, you see the earth again' " (Stevens, *The Necessary Angel*, epigraph). At no point in Strand's career before does he seem more committed to that principle.

CHAPTER 3

EARNING ONE'S WINGS:
DARK HARBOR

In *Dark Harbor* (1993), Strand's career evolves to a new level poetically, if not philosophically. Possessing the strength of conviction and finding a need to create a more sustained enterprise in light of such recent masters as Ashbery, Strand felt ready to undertake a more substantial project:

> I tried to enlarge my vision and write something new, and I think *Dark Harbor* is an attempt to make an enlargement. I had just come back from Washington being Poet Laureate and had no place to work. It was a very social year, and I wrote "Suite of Appearances" (in consideration of the social obligations I had had to make). John Ashbery's *Flow Chart* had just appeared and I had always thought he was a great poet of the generation just ahead of me. [Inspired by *Flow Chart*] I felt I needed to write a long poem. . . . So, with "Auroras of Autumn" [in mind], I wanted to engage in an exercise in good spirits.   (Interview, Jan. 26, 2002)

This single poem in 46 parts continues the ascent of the imagination to its most expansive form. Strand readdresses the poet's place in today's world, and makes some of the most bold, confident statements about poetry's value in his entire body of work. At the apex of Strand's career of subtle changes, this volume represents one of the broader leaps in his poetic evolution, and his most integral success. Now the "perfect moment" of engaged imagination is 47 pages long— or perhaps it is more precise to say there are 46 small moments of engagement that link together in one radiant sustained effort.

Although the poem contains more flourishes of brilliance than many of Strand's less-comprehensive efforts, it is probably due to the overriding attempt to create a unified poetic whole that makes the work less accessible at the outset. Strand has, after all, built a poetic voice based upon evanescent visions and temporary moments of sufficiency. To maintain a vision as long as Strand does here would appear to alter the ground rules for his readership, but, as we will see, only in superficial ways. The work as a whole is rewarding to the careful reader well versed in Strand's poetry. Immersing oneself in it can shed light on Strand's career, yet can also break new ground for Strand's most mature stage yet. "The overarching plot of *Dark Harbor* is the poet's counterlife in art," says Christopher Benfey, in an assessment with some merit, "from his initial departure from the enclosure of family and home, to his journey through a place of . . . uncertainty, to his final sense of safe harbor within the community of other poets" ("Books Considered" 37).

This poem has few entirely new concerns. Structurally, the individual parts are tighter in their strictures than any previous Strand work; the 46 sections are almost exclusively tercets, between 18 and 24 lines long, linguistically less playful, and in general tonally consistent. Strand's sentences are longer; he uses even more enjambment than usual, and his syntax also is a good deal more challenging than before. Most noticeable, however, little action occurs narratively; the poem is more concerned with a reflection upon things that *have* happened or *may* happen. Ultimately, the effort reveals a distinct determination on the poet's part, and also shows the poet up to the task of sustaining such an effort. It is one thing to be ready to undertake such a poem, quite another to succeed at such a mission.

As a single entity comprising loosely connected threads, *Dark Harbor* owes more to the sonnet sequence, as Benfey deftly identifies, than to the epic poetry tradition. It is an almost exclusively serious work that contains engaging philosophical discourse focused on the fictional harbor that protects the poet from the storms with which the world has threatened him since 1964. The poem represents the longest engagement of Strand's career and the fullest treatment of his poetic ideology. "The tone is graver than what one has come to expect from Mark Strand," identifies Richard Tillinghast (292). Benfey is even more discerning in his assessment of the poem as "a kind of summing up: of the poet's task in dark times; of a poet's engagement with predecessors and contemporaries; of what poetry can make, and make happen. *Dark Harbor* is a fine occasion for making sense of Strand" ("Enigma" 34).

Though its form is distinguishable from Strand's previous work, *Dark Harbor* represents more of a reassertion, with updates, of his poetic philosophy than a presentation of newfound beliefs. Most of Strand's hopes and fears, as well as his concerns about and attitudes toward the power of the poem to present a source of wonderment between two great darknesses, are recast here. Nonetheless, it is the enlargement of Strand's vision—and the concomitant compression of his philosophy—that makes *Dark Harbor* Strand's magnum opus. Instead of succeeding in fits and starts, providing frequent glimpses of greatness, Strand provides here an enduring counterlife in art, and a lasting monument.

"Proem" ignites *Dark Harbor*'s imaginative creation and is a springboard from the philosophically attuned poetry of *The Continuous Life* to this extended vision of a town built around a dark—with all its attendant Strandian associations—harbor. One might say this poem puts into practice the previous volume's theory. It almost uninterruptedly expresses the creation of an imaginative world replacing the natural world, a concept Strand has espoused throughout his career. "This is my Main Street," it begins as the speaker relates the words of an anonymous man who leaves the town for the rest of the world and enters "the high-woods tipped in pink" (3). "My main street," of course speaks of a private reality, and Strand has frequently used purples (and in this case, its sister color, pink) to represent artifice. "It's a color of exoticism; it's the color of shade," Strand admits (Interview, Nov. 2, 2002). Thus, right from the start, the poem establishes an erasure of the world in favor of the imaginative creation. The man then blazes a path for the speaker, containing the requisite elements of absence, "a stark sea over which / The turbulent sky would drop the shadowy shapes / Of its song" (7–9). This man, like Strand's speaker, is confident in his ability to conjure up the imagination at will, for he is "sure" of "the great space that . . . / Would open before him" (6–7).

Like any good poet-creator, this anonymous man does not merely count the few remaining birds. Instead, he valuates the world, reordering it, reimagining as he goes, marking "The passages of greater and lesser worth, / the silken / Tropes and calls to this or that" (11–12). "He would whip them / Into shape" the speaker says (13–14). The speaker follows this man-magician-conjurer to the edges of the familiar sea, that birthplace of the planet and of the imagination. When Strand ends his "Proem" by stating that the man "began to breathe" (18), we easily recognize that the rest of the poem is his—that the poem is what he has breathed into existence. Although

Henri Cole says of *The Continuous Life*, "The poems are difficult to excerpt, except for their ethereal, cumulative effect" (54), the truth of the statement is borne out more certainly in *Dark Harbor* than at any time previously in Strand's career. The "cumulative effect" of these poems, which do on the whole require reading their counterparts, is Strand's construction of a poetic community within which he can find his station. When we return to Dark Harbor's "Proem" after reading the whole volume, we understand this man to be representative of the "masters" of poetry that Strand searched for most recently in *The Continuous Life's* "The History of Poetry." We also understand that the poem breathed out by him is Strand's subjective world, and "Proem" to be his own Genesis.

The first few segments of *Dark Harbor* serve as introductory forays into this world—cognitive road maps, if you will. They convey, in subtle ways, the sense of loss the Strand speaker has experienced throughout his career, and they address many of the concerns the reader has confronted before—death, the fear of the loss of poetic voice, and the place of poetry in the world. What seems increasingly certain throughout the poem is that the effort sustained by the speaker within this harbor does somewhat successfully "perpetuate the balance between the past / And the future. They are the future as it / Extends itself, just as we are the past / Coming to terms with itself" (IV 16–19).

Returning to Dark Harbor's "Proem," it is apparent that when the walker "leav[es] the town to the others," it is his precursor poets to whom he refers (2). Because *Dark Harbor* seems to owe more to the sonnet sequence than to the tradition of epic poetry, its "Proem" must be considered in light of the other parts of the poem, and for our purposes, the concluding segment. In that segment, Strand addresses those poets as "angels," and, as *Dark Harbor* is more circular than linear, they conclude by promising to sing, just as the walker in "Proem" begins to breathe. At the outset, however, the walker needs to leave them behind, seek out new ground for himself before finding his own niche within the poetic community at the poem's end.

The concept of darkness as both the starting place and ending place of the poetic activity has long been established as a quintessential Strandian notion. Within these periods of darkness, however, exists a finite, fleeting moment of poetic apotheosis: when the poet writes, he banishes the darkness. The light that shines in the absence of darkness is his poetic world. As this walker moves through the darkness

> he watched
> For the great space that he felt sure
>
> Would open before him, a stark sea over which

The turbulent sky would drop the shadowy shapes
Of its song.

(5–9)

Indeed, Strand's speaker is confident at this stage of his career that an opening will present itself to him within which his poetic world can be erected. This is characteristic of Strand's poetic style; the blank page upon which he will create his own work is that "stark sea." His tone, here as in most of his work, is linguistically unadorned. From his earliest incarnations, Strand has projected the world as a violent, indeterminate place within which shadowy shapes ambulate. It is unsurprising to find that, as the song begins to take shape, the language does come to life. Polysyllabic words such as "turbulent" and "shadowy" give the line a quicker pace than the monosyllables of line six, in which the walker is still waiting. As Willard Spiegelman says of a later segment, "Like Frost and Hopkins, in addition to Stevens, Strand knows the pathos a line of monosyllables can bring" (140). Likewise, Strand knows how the alliterative effect of "shadowy shapes" will then animate "Proem." He goes on to say:

he would move his arms

And begin to mark, almost as a painter would,
The passages of greater and lesser worth, the silken
Tropes and calls to this or that, coarsely conceived,

Echoing and blasting all around.

(9–13)

In writing these lines, Strand replaces the passivity of the opening stanzas with the actual "shapes" of the song he himself describes. Strand excels at producing this marriage of form and function. Here, we encounter the shadowy shapes of the man moving his arms in ways that are indistinct to us as readers. The "silken / Tropes" are also nonspecific, aimed at "this or that, coarsely conceived." Similarly, they "echo" and "blast" in every direction. The great space, indeed, *has* opened up for the poet, almost recklessly so, in the second half of this poem. But shadowy shapes do not a poem make. The poet, for writers such as Strand or Stevens, must establish some order among and between the shadowy shapes. When he is done, "Everything would have an edge" (14).

The sense of vagueness harnessed into a tight poetic creation continues here, as often elsewhere in Strand's poetry, until the very last word. When the walker says, "This is the life," it is a literal as well as a figurative statement. After all, the "life" has been created within the poem out of the ash of a privative darkness. As the *Virginia Quarterly Review* states, "Meditative in tone, and one step removed from direct experience, these poems create their own reality" ("Dark Harbor" 136). Of course, at the poem's end, we can expect the poem—and Strand's reality—to retreat to another darkness. After all, it is only when the poem is speaking that "the life" exists; when the poem stops speaking, there is silence. At some points in his career, Strand fears this silence will be the final silence from which no more poems will rise. Here, as has been the case in the latter part of his career, he is secure in the belief that the silence at the end of the poem is equivalent to the silence out of which the next poem *will* surface. Here he calls the end of the poem "the first / Of many outer edges to the sea he sought," referring to the end of this one part of a many-edged poem, this one page in a many-paged book (16–17). After all, as he has said, "Everything would have an edge." When he begins to breathe at the end, Strand leaves us with the sound of his expiration. The experienced Strand reader recognizes, of course, the certainty of this silence, sometimes referred to as darkness, sometimes as whiteness—in each case an absence of some sort. When this person begins to breathe, we rightly expect a poem to follow, and it does—the most sustained imaginative creation of Strand's career.

Segment I opens "In the night without end," a surprising choice of choruses for Mark Strand, whose nights end when his poems *begin*. Yet there is a bit of irony in the statement, for while the night may not end, the speaker is "wearing a white suit that shines / Among the black leaves falling" (203). It is a sad irony, however, for this attempt at poetry—this white-suit-wearing—is apparently unsuccessful. The Strand poem we have come to know through 30 years of poetry *affects*—i.e., tropes—the world. When he speaks, images move, drop from the skies as he says in the proem. Here, he attempts to shine light, but though his white suit does shine as he walks through the world, it lights only him. The concern that his poetry serves only to illuminate him and not any great purpose in the world has troubled Strand at various stages in his career. In *Dark Harbor*, it presents itself as a central dilemma. *This* night without end is the final night, death, which looms as a larger presence than at any time previous.

The first poem of the sequence, along with poems II–XII, presents a world in stasis, the only movement being the speaker. Of course, this speaker is not Strand himself, or the speaker of the poem as we know the term: that is, the one presenting the poem. The "speaker" we will speak of throughout the sequence is the *walker* that the original speaker presents in "Proem." *Dark Harbor* is that walker's "breathing."

By absenting himself and, in fact, the speaker-as-we-know-him from the poem, Strand amplifies the speaker's—and his own—presence. The absence of a first-hand speaker calls greater attention to the actual second-hand speaker of the poem. In several segments of *Dark Harbor*, Strand engages in similar speaker-switching and speaker-hiding, and in places such as part V, allows wisdom to be passed on by secondary or tertiary characters.

The first 12 parts to the poem establish the sense of quietude and absence. In them, we are in a static world, sometime before dawn. We are *preparing* to leave, but the preparation seemingly involves little more than wandering and ruminating on things past. Little actually occurs in the narrative of these poems. "Though there are flashes of action and illumination in *Dark Harbor*, the majority of these poems work toward a stylized, static quality found in the paintings of Edward Hopper or William Bailey" ("Dark Harbor" 136). The narrative depends on the speaker's imagination to focus upon some object within the poem in much the same way Bailey's globe focuses the viewer's imagination in the equally stark still life that adorns the book's cover.

Midway through part I of Strand's masterpiece, the poetic vision takes center stage and alights itself in the reader's mind, thus taking on the light that banishes the darkness of the non-poem that existed before (and will exist after) this poem. When the speaker says, "Soon we shall travel through the soundless dark, / With fires guiding us over the bitter terrain," he is again predicting the very vision that he will be presenting (10–11). Yes, the fires that will guide him are the fires of the poem, the poem that banishes "the bitter terrain" of the world that his poem replaces. When he invokes his "suit that outdoes the moon" (13), indeed that suit becomes the locus of the poem, the radiating light of imaginative creation. The confidence contained within the Strandian imagination is evidenced by this statement. When the imagination is engaged, the world poses no threat. Even the moon is not a threat—for it does not give light of its own, but merely reflects it.

Still, the ambivalence toward the value of poetic achievement is a concern in *Dark Harbor*, and the negativity is present in the first poem of this sequence. The "wings [that] can be had / For a song" (17–18) refer to the wings owned by the good poet-angels of the concluding poem, the precursor poets both admired and, to a degree, feared by the Strandian speaker. Indeed, the wings *are* earned by writing songs—poems. Yet, the value of those wings is in doubt; after all, they could be had "for a song or by trading arms." Therefore, the value of poetry may be inconsequential, after all. And in light of the ominous darkness awaiting the poet at the end of this poem—death, the loss of poetic voice—one's dedication to poetry can be a fearful thing.

Indeed, one poem into the sequence, and there is a troublesomeness to this departure. The desire to "leave" may be explained as Strand's *clinamen*, to use Bloom's term for "a poet['s] swerve away from his precursor. . . . This appears as a corrective movement in his own poem, which implies that the precursor poem went accurately up to a certain point, but then should have swerved, precisely in the direction that the new poem moves" (*Anxiety* 14). In the early part of *Dark Harbor*, there is a distinct focus on leaving as a necessity to find one's poetic niche. For the speaker, there seems to be, in the first 12 parts of the poem, a lack of a place both within the poetic community and the world. At this stage, he is in "the place that is not a place" (IX, 4). The world, as the Strand reader is well aware, provides no joy; it is in the silencing of the world where the poet can achieve temporary gain, through the creation of a subjective reality that supplants the world. As he says in part V, "I would have to invent my pleasure, carve it out of the air" (11). As a pleasant consequence, his invention gains him a voice; earns him a place in the poets' pantheon.

Segment III returns us to the sense of circularity that Strand describes as a defining quality of life—and the act of writing poetry. "Go in any direction and you will return to the main drag," it begins. Likewise, if we were to read this poem front to back, or back to front, we would return to the main concern of *Dark Harbor*. At the end of both the proem and the concluding segment in the series, a poet prepares to speak. Within these two bookends exists the poem itself, breathed by the walker if read front to back, sung by the good angel, if read from back to front. In both cases, the poems are necessary attempts to reorder the world, to create the "new" world that exists within these bookend poems; in both cases, and throughout Strand's corpus, "the useless items / . . . turn into necessities, a sense of direction" (2–3). Regardless of which direction one chooses to read, as reader (and, as poet) fully engaged in the imagination, one "loses oneself."

This is a contention Strand has endorsed right from his early work, since he became the "new man" who "romp[s] with joy in the bookish dark" in "Eating Poetry" (16–18). Yet Strand also knows that poetry's redemptive powers can be sustained only for the moment that the poem is being written, or read. In part III of *Dark Harbor*, he speaks of "becoming yourself on your return" (4), and this "becoming yourself" is a more inclusive return to the world than the customary

Strand tradition. This is not just a poem of return to the extratextual world. This is a poem of the inescapability of one's past, and is a consequence of his intense inward-lookingness of *The Story of Our Lives* and outward-lookingness of *The Continuous Life*. Strand is, as it were, primed for this magnificent work.

In part III, the speaker's departure represents the recognition that any attempt to escape one's heritage is futile. The going and coming back along the unerringly circuitous route may very well be a blessing, a chance "To escape your origins as you would yourself" (15). When the speaker issues this quasi-religious dictum, it invariably must come true. Indeed, Strand the speaker-creator never fails to put forth that which he says he will put forth. It is thus unsurprising to find the speaker at the end of part III invoking, "look, there in the kitchen are Mom and Dad, / He's reading the paper, she's killing a fly" (23–24). The escaping of one's origins has lasted but 22 lines, for here they are. The "useless items" that gained a sense of direction, return to preeminence in the form of the mundane suburban kitchen. These useless items indeed are from the origins that the speaker attempts to escape, yet those items turn into poetic necessities. This is one of Strand's successful presentations of executing in the poem that which he articulates in the poem.

In part V, Strand confronts the same privative absences that have left him so frequently displaced from the world. "The soldiers are gone, and now the women are leaving," it begins. "I wonder if I shall ever catch up" (3). The melancholy evoked in many stages of this poem recall "Leopardi," when Strand again took time to be retrospective. Here, there is reconsideration of his poetic life taking place, and the poem attempts to find a new sanctuary. Strand has presented the challenges involved in pursuing the artistic life before. Reinvention, the re-creation of self and the world within the poem, this time requires a more sustained effort.

Halfway through part V, Strand relates what we have known already of his philosophy: "I would have to invent my pleasure, carve it out of the air, / Subtract it from my future. And I could have no illusions" (11–12). But the officer who instructs him to invent his pleasure also advises the speaker of the benefits of his toil:

> "And listen," the officer said, "on any morning look down
>
> Into the valley. Watch the shadows, the clouds dispersing
> Then look through the ice into nature's frozen museum,
> See how perfectly everything fits in its space."
>
> (15–18)

This is the nature of the great poets. Strand echoes a theme he has had since "Keeping Things Whole." Nature is a whole; it is perfect in every way, even when it threatens man, who decidedly is external to nature. In fact, here the speaker is external to the scene; looking down into the valley, he is not interfering with the landscape as he would have been in "Keeping Things Whole." Presumably, then, he does not have to move out of the scene. While there is the danger of believing that Strand has suddenly found harmony in nature, it is important to remember that this is *re-created* nature. All that occurs in this poem is *of* the poetic community created *by* the great masters and *passed on* to Strand should he choose to take up the gauntlet. Bloom would concur. He likens Strand to Emerson, Whitman, Bishop, and Stevens, saying, "Like his precursors, [Strand] stations himself just before sunrise, in order to hear 'again the luminous wind of morning that comes before the sun.' Stevens said of this moment that it brought a 'difficult rightness' and Strand . . . is adept at just such a rightness" ("Books Considered" 30).

Strand relates his setbacks and accomplishments along his path in the poems that follow, part VI standing out for its narration of the goals of this poet. Here desire has

> reached not for the whole earth which everyone
> Thinks is its likely object, but instead grew
>
> Into an enlarged desire, a desire that wished for even more,
> For an unthinkable conclusion, an impossible satisfaction,
> Itself increasing, enclosing within its appetite
>
> The elaboration and extension of its despair.
>
> (5–10)

In fact, Strand's imaginative capacities *have* grown. Yet, as this passage ably conveys, the imagination cannibalizes itself and desires more than even *it* can attain. The search for something beyond this world brings only temporary satisfaction when it is fulfilled; then, there arises a need to discover something beyond the range of comprehension; then, something beyond even the scope of the imagination, ad infinitum. The more he desires, or achieves, "There is only / Larger and larger dissatisfaction" (16–17).

The Strand speaker ultimately tries to sustain the moment of inspiration with the threat of being poetically silenced looming. This gives the moment so much additional weight that the speaker can become too inhibited to write. Still, despite "the weight of the future saying / That I am only what you are, but more so" (19–20)—in a revision of

"Leopardi's" "I do not give you hope"—the words Strand also hears from this place give him a reason to pursue the imagination: "because / It is yours, the loss that is continuous / Will be all yours and will only increase" (22–24). At the height of despair, knowledge that one has something of one's own brings some minimally redemptive value.

Both the reason for engaging in the poetic struggle, and the primary obstacle to finding satisfaction in writing, are summarized in part VIII of *Dark Harbor*. Here Strand spells it out rather lucidly. "If dawn breaks the heart, and the moon is a horror, / And the sun is nothing but the source of torpor, / Then of course I would have been silent all these years," the speaker begins (1–3). It is important to note that Strand has never asserted—and still does not assert here—the inherent value of anything in nature:

> People think of me as an extremely dark person, but I don't think of myself [that way]. I mean, don't get me wrong, I don't believe in any kind of afterlife or anything like that, and I don't have too many great things to say about my fellow man, but that doesn't make me gloomy. I don't believe it adds up to gloomy.   (Interview Jan. 26, 2002)

The possibility of *knowing* what levels of benevolence and malevolence exist in the world has plagued him as a poet, as does the endurance of his poetic creation. But while engaged in the moment of the poem, while indulging in the *placement* of value upon the objects he *selects* from nature, Strand can momentarily believe "how good life / Has been and how it has culminated in this instant. / The harmonies of wholesomeness have reached their apogee" (7–9).

Still, death looms over him, and he is now so familiar with death that he considers its perpetually looming threat as a "my partner, my beautiful death, / My black paradise . . . / My symbolist muse" (14–16). In this poem, which Tillinghast says, "is a dramatic moment that places Strand firmly in the line of serious European poetry with roots in the French nineteenth century" (293–94), he invokes death, imploring it to give him the answers to questions that beleaguer him. Of course, death has not been the sole villain in Strand's poetry. *Life*, after all, is equally unknowable. He wants his muse to assure him that his poem will have enduring value, that something of the world will persist. He asks death the most fundamental questions in this apostrophe:

> Tell me I have not lived in vain, that the stars
>
> Will not die, that things will stay as they are,

That what I have seen will last, that I was not born
Into change, that what I have said has not been said for me.

(21–24)

Couched in these words, the request seems both sincere and reasonable, and indeed the speaker wishes for some sense of permanence, if not in the world, then at least to his endeavors. He wants to touch a reader, to bridge the gaps between people that arose first with the man in "The Tunnel." Throughout his corpus, Strand wants to reach his ancestors (in the past), his daughter (in the present), and his unborn son (in the future). Until this moment, the answer that has come back from the universe—or rather the lack thereof—reveals that what he has said, *has* been said only for him.

Still, in *Dark Harbor* he continues to struggle, and ironically he finds some lasting value in the final line, the very line where he names his worries about his faith in poetry. After all, it is Ashbery whom he paraphrases here. His delight and his anxiety are united in such a line, for in having this doubt yet in invoking a fellow strong poet's doubt, he unifies his voice with another. This voice-strengthening exercise finds him his place within the poetic pantheon. As Coleman says,

> The poet's duty, then, is to write the world, to define it, inventing language as he goes, making something "out of the unsayable," whether or not it is forgotten. A hopeless proposition? Perhaps. Perhaps not. Poets since Cassandra have stood outside the pale, listening, singing, reaching out to an uncaring, unheeding audience. (179)

Part IX opens, however, with a discouraged voice, the voice of a poet who ostensibly has been silent until this moment. The fear Strand expresses about the silence and darkness that replace the poem at its conclusion ironically calls greater attention to those silences. The space between poems VIII and IX is just that kind of space. The voice that opens part IX begins in a dismal state, completely bereft of hope. The experience from the previous page is gone and forgotten. Yet he tries again, with a blank page. "Where is the experience that meant so much, / That carried such weight?" he asks in a familiar Strand commencement. At these moments, the questions seem as though they are rhetorical. Yet, we readers must keep the question in mind as we read the rest of the poem, and we must not discount the imagination. Here Strand answers that question very early in the poem: the experience is "lodged in memory, in the air of memory, / In the place that is not a place, but where / The mortal beauty of the world is stored" (3–5). This "air of memory," of course, is an absence; the "place that is not a place" is the blank page of imagination.

The rest of this episode vacillates, as does the rest of the poem, between confidence and skepticism. The good moments in one's life are, as always for Strand, difficult to sustain and communicate: the moon is found "giving back a silent O of surprise / Each time we try to explain how it was, / How fleeting, breakable, expensive it was" (7–9). Certainly, Strand knows that language necessarily tropes any experience, thus creating something "new" despite every best intention to perfectly re-create that "old" experience. Still, the "new" is not bad, just different. The past, present, and future are untenable in their "natural" states, but unified in the imagination, they become one. Despite the inability to convey understanding, or to have the past, present, and future communicate with one another, the promise of possibilities spurs the poet onward: "We are always about to take off into a future / Unencumbered," he says, before oscillating back to cynicism: "as if we could leave ourselves behind, / But of course we never do" (10–12).

Ultimately, in this segment, Strand decides that he must return to those waters of childhood, re-create himself in a quasi-Freudian therapy session, and "work on the past to make the future / More bearable" (18–19). As we remember from part III, the speaker has attempted to jettison the past, and realizes that the attempt was a foolhardy one. There he resolved to embrace his origins. Part IX finds him still very much in the same condition—the narrative, as has been said, proceeds at a snail's pace if one chooses to find linearity at all. Uncertain of his vision because of his disconnectedness from the past, he frets:

> Who can face the future,
>
> Especially now, as a nobody with no past
> To fall back on, nothing to prove one is
> Like everyone else, with baby pictures
>
> And pictures of Mom and Dad in their old-fashioned
> Swimsuits on a beach somewhere in the Maritimes.
>
> (12–17)

In the Strand tradition, this speaker has again created a presence more palpable as an absence than it could be as a presence in itself. When he conjures up the family album that he does not have, he creates the past that was not and makes it the past that was. The Mom and Dad who were not there in the world *are* there—in the poem. We can attempt to leave the past behind, but in bringing that desire to consciousness, of course, we re-create it. We can attempt to re-create the past, but in *that* act, we trope it with imprecise language and, as such, create something new instead.

Despite the wavering confidence of the poet, his effort ends with promise, for he is certain that the imagination, as strong as it has become, will perform its magic: "Ah, the potential past, how it swells, / How it crowds the days before us with feelings / And postures we had dismissed until now" (19–21). The "potential past" is one of Strand's facile strokes of oxymoron. Here again is the speaker becoming the creator of self by creating the not-self. That is, he has created a fictional "who he was," and he already has acknowledged that who we *were* is more important than who we *are*. In this deft application of his philosophy of poetic creation, he has thus fathered someone who is more him than he himself is—the "he" who he was when he was younger. It is malleable clay, this "potential past."

Segment X returns to the past to provide us with increased under-standing of *Dark Harbor's* impetus. It opens with a Stevensian pathetic fallacy of a "dreadful cry" that is "Hoping to be heard" (1–2). Immediately, we are reminded of the theme of a return to the past. With segment IX still fresh in our minds, we can marry this cry to a psychological need to restore one's present health by a reconsideration of one's childhood. The poem begins in its natural Strandian state: at the moment of waking. Soon it confirms our suspicions about the redoubled attempt to voyage to the past, as the speaker informs us, "your day will be spent / In the futile correction of a distant longing" (3–4). Then when he speaks of "All those voices calling from the depths of elsewhere," he presents a multiplicity of potential voices (5). Are those voices simply the family of the past from poem IX? Or are they the voices of the poets, his precursors who at the same time inspire and awe him? Is the "futile correction" then an attempted rewriting of these earlier poets, the Wordsworths and Stevenses and Bishops? Or perhaps the voices are alternate selves of the person he did not become because of the acts that he now feels need "correction?"

Whatever choice the reader makes, the first half of this segment necessarily begins with a statement of fear and worry. It is the central part of the Strand poem that tries to organize these "useless items," to give them direction, to create a meaningful experience from them. "You have no choice but to follow their prompting," he says in a vague echo of Bishop, "Saving something of that sound, urging the harsh syllables / Of disaster into music" (9–11). And as the reader proceeds with the poem, he finds the image of a cloud making itself known. It is the third such reference in the first ten parts of the poem, and one that Strand will continue to use rather consistently as the figure of the imagination—the capable imagination, if you will.

As "You stare out the window, / Watching the build-up of clouds," Strand's whipping the world into shape becomes recognizable (11–12). As the imagination is engaged, the clouds draw and focus the reader's attention on them and provide the organizing force for the images from within the poem as the poet provides the organizing force for the images from without. It is the clouds and the wind that are "sending a rain of leaves / To the ground," the phrasing suggesting a consciousness owned by the wind and cloud (13–14). Surely, the motions of wind and cloud are the motions of the imagination. When the speaker follows this line by asking, "How do you turn pain / Into its own memorial, how do you write it down" he provides the question that he has already answered in the poem (14–15). The imagination must send its own rain of leaves to the ground.

At this point, it is important to recognize the Whitmanian use of leaves in the poem. Indeed, while *Dark Harbor* is in many ways Strand's most Stevensian poem (at times Stevens appearing to be a rewriting of Strand), it also owes more to Whitman than the typical Strand poem. The leaves here, as in part I and in several segments to follow, are the poetic leaves of *Leaves of Grass*. Here, when the wind excites the clouds to rain down upon the willow, the act of imagination is defined in a rather lucid metaphor. From here, wind and clouds as the imaginative force that rains poem-leaves become familiar motifs.

The speaker's question in segment X does not end here, however. Indeed, the final tercet reminds that the poet's task is to take pain and "Turn . . . it into itself as witnessed / Through pleasure, so it can be known, even loved, / As it lives in what it could not be" (16–18). The speaker suggests that he tries to deal with his pain in the poetic endeavor ("witnessed / Through pleasure"), troping it in order to know it more fully. And how does one know it more fully? By absenting it from the poem. Yes, by turning the pain into a creative force behind the poem, or the *materia poetica*, in fact, it is no longer the former pain, but the troped hurt. It now is transformed into "what it could not be," and by being what it was not, the speaker is more prepared to confront it.

The speaker can confidently confront his fears in segments such as XI, where he in fact sustains his imaginative vision. The poem opens with the disappearance of sorrow, ostensibly overshadowed by the imaginative creation of part X. The "rough stone walls" of experience are not erased, however, in so much as outshouted by the poet (4). It is an important distinction that the speaker says he "saw *beyond* the rough stone walls" (italics mine). "The flesh of clouds" that compel the speaker's and reader's attention are necessarily a choice—a purposeful engagement of the imagination that minimizes the obstacles the walls present (5). When the speaker continues his indulgence in the powers of the imagination, we recognize the motif:

>   It seems like yesterday
> When . . .
>   the pollen-filled breath
>
> Of the wind drew the shadow of the clouds
> Around us so that we could feel the force
> Of our freedom while still the captives of dark.
>   (7–12)

Once again, it is the imagination—the breath of the walker in "Proem," whom we now recognize as our speaker—that is the cloud drawn by the walker's breath. Or, in more succinct terms, the walker's speaking (breath) gains strength as he speaks, grows into a wind, which then acts upon the imagination (the clouds) so as to present a redeeming virtue within a world of darkness: a poem.

Before part XI concludes, however, the speaker must ask again: "how to explain / Our happiness then, the particular way our voices / Erased all signs of the sorrow that had been, / Its violence, its terrible omens of the end?" (15–17). Yet, again, in one of Strand's magnificently facile strokes of irony, the act of asking the question answers the question. The poem that asks such questions provides answers merely by being a poem. One confronts and defeats one's pains by seeing through them, seeing into the "flesh of clouds." However, the poem does not *explicitly* provide answers. In the double-irony then, one answers the question by creating a poem within which one can *ask* the question, and by not providing answers, one provides answers.

If there were any doubt about the cloud's importance as a vital motif in the poem, part XII silences it. Of the opening segments, part XII is the keystone. The cloud is grand in its presentation here, and from the tone of the poem, all previous segments sound as though they were leading up to this point. The movement of the speaker in the previous sections was practically nonexistent. As the *Virginia Quarterly Review* has said, "Each moment seems freighted with significance, as if time had slowed nearly to a stop" ("Dark Harbor" 136). Part XII then begins in a biblical tone: "So it came of its own like the sun that covers / The damp grass with its luster and drives the cold / Into the dark corners of the house; out of silence / It came . . . "(1–4). In another incarnation of a loud absence, Strand does not mention the cloud by name until line 15. In doing so, the "it" mentioned in line one grows in stature as "its" qualities are enumerated in the first five stanzas of the segment. "It" takes on oversized proportions in these lines, keeping the reader focused on its qualities until the reader learns, indeed, "it" is the cloud, the imagination yet again narrated as being mobilized by wind.

This imaginative power then alters the scene of the natural world: "The panorama of the lake was charged / With the arrival of a cloud," the poem says (14–15). In case his reader has forgotten how to perform acts of imagination, Strand reminds that the cloud's purpose "We would have to decipher and apply / To our own ends" (16–17). The subjectivity of the imagination is underscored here, yet lest one should foolhardily trust in the persistence of the subjective world provided by the imagination, the speaker reminds that it ends "in either dismissal or doubt" (21). The poetic mind must deal in a fixed realm of reality. It cannot endure forever, and therefore must end. The world that had been silenced by the poem returns in full force. At best, it leaves the poet in doubt about the enduring value of his creation. At its worst, it results in a complete dismissal of the poem's consequence.

The establishment of the imagination as focal point and organizing medium, and the subsequent presentation of the impossible task in store for the imagination, provides the quintessential thesis of *Dark Harbor*. It also provides the primary role and challenge of the poet. As Ehrenpreis says, "Strand does not open the lyric to the world but makes it a self-sustaining enterprise" (47). Indeed, the solution to the poetic dilemma of death, of the silence of the voice, involves no interaction between worldly and poetic images. The goal, Strand clearly provides, is to blot out the world, silence it in any imaginative endeavor, so that the lyric can speak in the absence of the world. When the poem is over, however, the world must necessarily return, for the poem was that which silenced the world, and the poem cannot work its magic when it is gone. For Strand, one is either in the world or in the poem, and never will the twain meet harmoniously.

The commencement of part XIII reinforces the fact that part XII is the culmination of poetic thought in *Dark Harbor*, while also heralding the dawn, and thus, a second phase of the poem. "The mist clears," it begins, in a matter of fact manner, inaugurating a new concern of the poet. As this monograph has discussed, one of the poet's primary challenges is to silence the world long enough to present the poetic world in its place. In part XIII, the reader finds daybreak challenging the poetic vision. As the speaker says, this "is the moment to resist the onset / Of another average day, to beat the daylight / For exotic instances of this or that" (5–7). The "this or that" echoes the "useless items" of part III or the "harsh syllables" of part X, both of which require the poet's artistic engagement to transform them into something "exotic," something no longer belonging to just another "average day." When one recalls "Proem," the walker's "silken / Tropes" were also aimed at "this or that."

Confronted with a new task—the challenge of "Mak[ing] imprecision the core of the school / Curriculum" (11–12)—the speaker admits, "There's lots to be done" (12). In this poem, perhaps for the first time in *Dark Harbor*, there is a sense of urgency in the speaker's tone. "There is little time left," he says, intimating a poetic death (17). "We must get down to work," he says, sounding liked the determined forgetters of "Always" in his attempt to summon the imagination (20). Perhaps the desperation is evidenced by the fact that it is only in the final few lines where the speaker does succeed in invoking the power of poetic language. In another example of Strand's answering the question by asking the question, he creates an image of a spruce by wondering, "If only it were possible to spruce up the air / Without buying a spruce, the day might begin / To take on a light of its own, green and piercing" (23–25). Indeed, by mentioning the desire to spruce up the air, he has done that very thing. And, once again, we must note that it clearly is *not* a spruce that he conjures here, but an air "sprucer," if you will. It is, after all, the artificial that this poet calls for, not the natural.

These middle episodes of *Dark Harbor* bring the speaker to the point where his ability to create moments is strengthened at the same time as he is attempting in vain to sustain these moments and transform them into lasting subjective realities. The results are wavering levels of security and satisfaction, because there seems to be no outlet—no audience for the poet, whose voice grows increasingly disgusted with the world around him. In XIV, the speaker's ability to transcend reality temporarily is obstructed: "The ship has been held in the harbor. / The promise of departure has begun to dim" (1–2). And of course, the world does not care: "The radiance of the sea, the shining abundance / Of its blue are nevertheless undiminished" (3–4). He finds another moment of fulfillment: "the writing surfaces, / Shines a moment in the light," but does not sustain itself, for it "sinks unread" (16–17). Such a line reasserts one of the primary fears that have bedeviled Strand throughout his career. That is, that his work is only "for him." This segment ends, in fact, without an exultation, or even a fleeting recognition, of the imagination, for "It has been / Years . . . / Since the cloud behind the nearby mountain moved" (21–24).

*   *   *

The sense of stasis that Strand conveys to describe the world in which we live is troubling. In this postmodern era, the poet's role is not clearly established. Indeed, often it is not recognized at all. Strand's poem challenges the stagnancy that permeates the world. Yet, for now, he speaks of those who seem to have lost their imagination, and thus, for them, time stands still.

The anxiety in this poem intensifies, particularly as dawn breaks and casts light upon the real world to challenge the fictive world of the poet, and the authority of the poem. In the moments before dawn— segments I through XII—the poet can reign, for the imagination is the only light-casting medium available. In poems such as this one, it is hard to disagree with Spiegelman when he says, "An eye for clear detail . . . turns some of the poems into exquisite literary landscapes" (134). When the sun shines here, however, it shines as a competitor to the poet. In poem XV, a moment of apotheosis *is* generated when Strand settles for an instant of authority: "even the green trees can be saved / For a moment and look bejeweled" (2–3).

Yet, Strand does not assert the trees' salvation, but rather questions whether they truly can be saved: "What light is this that says the air is golden, / That even the green trees can be saved, . . . / That my hand . . . / becomes a flame pointing the way" is how he couches the phrase (1–5). In this echo of "Se la vita e sventura . . . ?" Strand questions the power of his poem, that fruit of the hand. Here he seems to acquiesce to a smaller place within the world's indeterminate fate: "The sheen of the possible / Is adjusting itself to a change of venue: the look / Of farewell" (7–9). And here, too, as the poem ends, the vision ends, and with both goes the poet's sovereignty. This "new place" last is seen "going under, becoming what no one remembers" (11–13). Words like "promise," "potential" and "possibility" dominate the middle stage of this poem, for the imagination is valued for all three. Still, in each case, promises do not equal fulfillment: "the wind / That pursues is the perfumed wind of spring / That promises much, but settles for summer" (XXV 22–24).

This middle section of *Dark Harbor* is fraught with settling, in fact. In poem XVI, the poetic imagination proves a feeble beast, indeed, in the face of death, and the speaker in a defeated manner acquiesces:

> It is true, as someone has said, that in
> A world without heaven all is farewell.
> Whether you wave your hand or not,
>
> It is farewell, and if no tears come to your eyes
> It is still farewell, and if you pretend not to notice,
> Hating what passes, it is still farewell.
>
> Farewell no matter what.
>
> (1–7)

As Benfey says, "The someone here is Stevens, who didn't quite say this in 'Waving Adieu, Adieu, Adieu.' But Strand's poem is itself a tribute to Stevens' mythmaking, in a world unsponsored by paradise" ("Enigma" 36). Whether or not this speaker acknowledges ("It is true") the primacy of the natural world, whether or not he creates ("waves" his hand), the world will go on as unconcerned with the poet as with anyone else, and death will come.

How to confront such a rigid fate, is the poet's next task, and he begins to take it on in part XVII. In a Nietzschean acknowledgment of the futility of any endeavor, the speaker says farewell to a friend, watches cornstalks being burned and the smoke covering up the sun, and characteristically owns a Strandian "blank face" of indifference (4). Though there is some hope of imagination, found in the "Someone . . . playing a tape of birds singing" (8), ultimately nothing is created in this poem. It is a poem of possibilities, but unrealized possibilities, the first of Nietzsche's progression toward nihilistic freedom. Here Strand recognizes "the seasonal possibilities" inherent in autumn (10). After all, he does require burning off of the world, darkening its presence in order to erect his poetic world in its stead. And while he tried to invoke the "pretty densities of white on white!" ultimately, he concludes this poem entrenched in a state of looking at the blank page—the white on white possibilities (11). At this poem's conclusion, nature reigns in the form "Of ice and snow, the straight pines, the frigid moon" (16). They are white items of possibility, but for this poem, they remain only possibilities. He has not transformed them into anything yet, and thus, for the first time in *Dark Harbor*, his effort comes to nothing. The items of the natural world remain items of the natural world, frigid and empty.

The natural world that the speaker has confronted in the last two poems overwhelms him to a degree in segment XVIII. Here he makes an effort to stop fighting nature and instead attempts to unite with it. In an echo of his "Keeping Things Whole," 30 years earlier, Strand expresses a wish to absent himself and instead

> be on the other side, and be part of all

> That surrounds me. I would like to be
> In that solitude of soundless things, in the random
> Company of the wind, to be weightless, nameless.
>   (3–6)

Yet, even if he could achieve a truce with the world, he recognizes that—like Frost's birch-tree swinger—it would be momentary, as all imaginative endeavors are: "in no time / I would be back" (9–10). But in that moment where he is absent from the world and resurrected, as it were, in the poem, he could find himself. In that "sleep," as he here calls it, the poet finds "My grief is ponderous," as in worth pondering (11). And in that moment, "the streets are long" and "the sky is great" (12–13). Yet, in a reverse irony of the presences created by absence, here, though he speaks of these presences, it is all wishful thinking. Speaking of presences only accentuates their absence. These images are not conjured for indulgence; they merely are mentioned as desires. And again this crisis-poem segment ends with only a wistful hope "of the inmost dancing (15), which ultimately "cannot go on" (14).

Strand opens part XX with the familiar but relatively absent "you" to whom he has addressed a number of poems in the past. This "you," who is concurrently himself, the reader and the imagination, is a prime imaginative creation, sired simply by its verbal invocation in the poem's lines. When Strand asks, "Is it you," he creates the "you" in the poem, thus assuring the question's affirmative answer. The doubt so prevalent in the previous seven segments now yields to a willful reassertion of poetic imagination. Here, "you" is also equated with a phantom wind, recognizable as the force that reorganizes the world's slovenly elements in the opening parts of the segment.

This wind, this creative force, is "Rising from the script of waves," as clouds do, and, also as clouds do, is "casting a sudden shadow over my hand" (10–11). Says Spiegelman of this phenomenon, "Between the event and the imagination falls the shadow" (139). As the speaker writes the wind and the clouds, they come to life. The *you* that is not in the poem—after all, he is still asking "*Is it* you?"—becomes a formal part of the poem. When he says the wind "moves / Over the page," it necessarily must (12–13). In fact, it is the *you*, the imagination, that moves over the page. While, in previous verses, the speaker was paralyzed in possibility, here he can create. Imagination is, of course, the genesis of the poem, and indulgence in the imagination does create.

Before this indulgence, however, in the previous segments he could not generate, but only ruminate on the possibilities. Here he can consummate the kiss that he could only hope for previously, and yet even the kiss "is only the beginning / Of what until now we could only imagine" (15–16). Still, the unstable footing of this poet quivers again. As the imagination is about to depart with the end of the segment, the speaker again questions the powers of the imagination.

Is this wind the creative force, summonable at one's will, or is it just a phantom wind that comes and goes on its own fickle volition? Does it engender creativity for a purpose, or does it leave the creator empty, repeating a forlorn "alas, alas" at the poem's conclusion? (18). Even when he can re-create the world in his chosen image, the poet is left with doubt as to its consequence, and as to its likelihood of returning.

The natural world continues to get reinvented throughout *Dark Harbor*, only to find the creative vision sinking back into nothingness at the end of each part. Such repeated attempts convey the sense of a poet frustrated by the ephemeral nature of his creations. Yes, there are redemptive *moments*, but only while the writer is engaged with his craft, rarely afterward. Note the blissful communion achieved in this passage as it transiently slips away:

> There is a luminousness, a convergence of enchantments,
> And the world is altered for the better as trees,
> Rivers, mountains, animals, all find their true place,
>
> But only while Orpheus sings. When the song is over
> The world resumes its old flaws, and things are again
> Mismatched and misplaced and the cruelty of men
>
> Is tempered only by laws . . .
>
> (XXVIII 1–7)

In the latter half of this poem, Strand begins to associate himself with the community of poets, commencing, of course, with the most famous poet of all. This is not coincidentally where he begins to find condolence. For in his recognition that "Orpheus can change the world / For a while, but he cannot save it, which is his despair," he discovers another being who understands his plight (7–8). The possibility for communion is thus fulfilled in the land of the poets. For even if the world is made sadder by the attempted creation of a song, and even if, as both Strand and Ashbery worry, "my voice is just for me" (16), in the poetic undertaking, "Still, we feel better for trying" (18). Although here too he remains unfulfilled at the conclusion, the *promise* is now more *promising*. Yet this is the last in a triad of segments that gestures the ultimate concern of Strand in *Dark Harbor*. Although in general the poem's quandary is finding the place of the poet in the community, more markedly is Strand concerned with this *particular* poet's place within the community of other poets.

In segment XXVI, the poet recalls his poetic origins and calls forth an unnamed precursor poet. In doing so, he confronts what Bloom calls "poetic history. . . . [S]trong poets make that history by misreading one another, so as to clear imaginative space for themselves" (*Anxiety* 5). The stage of his career that Strand reviews, however, is the stage of the weaker poet. As Bloom says, "Weaker talents idealize; figures of capable imagination appropriate for themselves" (*Anxiety* 5). It would be intriguing to chart *Dark Harbor* as a progression of the poet—not Strand the poet, but *Dark Harbor's* own speaker-poet—through the stages of development from *clinamen* to *apophrades*. The poem does not move in linear fashion, however; thus it would not be accurate to assert that all the later segments illuminate a stronger poem than the earlier ones.[1] In this segment, in the face of his "master," Strand presents himself "unshaven, limping, / My clothes ragged, I came in my vileness, believing / That you, understanding my passion, would forgive me" (12–14). In his wretched quest for acceptance by the precursor poet that the poem presents, this neophyte poet desires but a kind word in a book from the precursor: "So that on the worst days it will be possible / For me to open it and feel wanted" (21–22). This poet is subservient and deferential to his master. His belief that a mere signature could serve as "wisdom as you have passed it on to me" is a startlingly naive one (24). Indeed, here is exhibited Bloom's contention that "Influence is *Influenza*—an astral disease. If influence were health, who could write a poem?" (*Anxiety* 95).

Although the desire for an unchanging place in the society of poets is a sincere one, the speaker's tonal presentation of himself as little more than a fan club member surely cannot win him that place. This desire to find a place from without—the approval of a master—is the very goal that will assure failure. After all, when successfully engaging the imagination, the most a poet can hope for is a momentary redemption for himself from *within*. The autographed book, then, is nothing other than the poem's words on a page. They hold no meaning unless one is fully engaging the imagination in writing or reading the words. It is only in doing so that they become more than words; they "live in what they could not be." As words, they are only words. So, again, the book is useless. Yes, but were not those useless items named the stuff of poetry by Strand? Though it does not happen in this poem, ostensibly a representation of the Strand as younger poet, when the poet matures, as he does, he becomes capable of transforming those items into "necessity, a sense of direction"—into poetry.

Part XXVII represents a stride toward that poetic maturation. In this delightful segment, Strand is no longer a fan club member, but a capable reader of his precursors. Poet #1 appears to be Whitman, #2 Stevens, #3 echoes Hart Crane, #4 Bishop, #5 perhaps Marianne Moore, #6 Pound or Eliot. But, as Benfey correctly notes, "More important than any particular identification are the terms of appreciation here. Three poets who verge on absurdity and chaos, three poets who verge on revelation. What Strand admires is the pushing to extremes, the flirtation with the pointless" ("Enigma" 36). Indeed, the essential element is that the indulgence in these predecessors' works, "that leaves this one of the side of his mountain, / Hunched over the page, thanking his loves for coming / And keeping him company all this time" (19–21). As reader of poetry, this time, Strand is sufficed.

There is a distinct ambiguity present in this concluding tercet. Yes, the speaker is glad to be joined by his idol-poets. And yes, there was a union established while he was engaged with them in reading their works. And there is a third "yes" in that he has achieved a unity with his reader as well. Yet, there is a wistful note present: he is, after all, alone. At quick glance, one might say he was on the other side of *one* mountain from his precursors. In fact, upon closer review of this twisted cliché, it proves to be an entirely different mountain, leaving the reader to conclude that at this stage of development, the poet is still two steps removed from those with whom he wishes to commune.

The presentation of this triad of segments (XXVI–XXVIII) reveals a remarkable temporal regression. Part XXVI began with the poet's own roots, his master presumably still alive and writing. Part XXVII goes back further, to the poets of the Romantic tradition. Then part XXVIII returns to the father of all poets, Orpheus. In each case, ironically, the further he retreats, the more successful he becomes in finding his place within their ranks. As we have discussed of segment XXVIII, Strand finds a unity with Orpheus, perhaps because Orpheus, too, was an unsatisfied singer. Also ironically, when he goes so far back, Strand also returns to the present, in the form of Ashbery, with whom he commiserates. Thus he completes the union on two fronts: the origins of poetry and the present of poetry.

Yet, though the poem presents to the Strandian speaker "the well of our wishes / In which we are mirrored" (20–21), it is "darkly as though / A shadowed glass held within its frozen calm image / Of abundance, a bloom of humanness, a hymn in which / The shapes and sounds of Paradise are buried" (21–24). Clearly, this poet's work is not done, nor is his place within the community of poets secure. And so, he writes on.

From segment XXIX on, other poets and new challenges await this increasingly capable poet. Part XXIX bemoans the current state of poetry, and takes stabs at confessionalists and critics. Their poetry and criticism is that of "formless affirmation, / Saying selfhood is hating Dad or wanting Mom" (9). He then mocks the confessionalists' purported invocation of Whitman, saying that their poems sounded, "like flies—/ Me at my foulest, the song of me, me in the haunted / Woods of my own condition" (12–13). He comes to the gloomy conclusion: "These are bad times. Idiots have stolen the moonlight. / They cast their shadowy pomp wherever they wish (14). It is one of the most pointed criticisms Strand has made in his career, and because Strand typically refrains from such frankness, the statement is both refreshing and biting. As Strand has said in a personal interview, "I'm not a poet who testifies to the ills of the world; I don't want to draw attention to the poor, the meek, what have you. That would be too self-congratulatory. I propose a metaphorical world, and not a metonymic world. They propose a slice of life and if you read it so much you're doing nothing about it. It's a hideous act of self-love" (Jan 26, 2002).

Part XXXII opens with the speaker on the coast of Labrador, in a state much like that of Stevens in "The Auroras of Autumn." The poem originally appeared in *The New Republic*, August 3, 1992, as the first of a three-part poem with the distinctly Stevensian title, "From the Academy of Revelations." It is a mountainous region that intimidates this poet. What he learns in this "academy" is that "The idea of our being large is inconceivable, / Even after lunch with Harry at Lutece, even after / Finishing *The Death of Virgil*" (7–9). This segment becomes, then, a counterpoint to the Strandian theme of artistic redemption. Here, no work of art can compare with the natural landscape; no indulgence of the imagination can dwarf these mountains. Even the poet is impotent, and leaves the speaker overwhelmed to the point of submission: "The image of a god, / A Platonic person, who . . . / brings whole rooms, whole continents to light, / Like the sun, is not for us" (9–12).

It is a complete reversal of fortunes for the Strandian speaker, this relinquishing of the poetic creation. The question then, is: *What to do when faced with such an immutable world?* Strand turns the trick by acquiescing to the mountainous supremacy of the natural world—evocative of the years he lived in Utah—and instead seeks a small niche within, say, a fissure in the rock. He says: "We have a growing appetite / For littleness, a piece of ourselves, a bit of the world, / An understanding that remains unfinished, unentire, / Largely imperfect so long as it lasts" (12–15).

With this utterance, the speaker also demands of the reader a reconsideration of the previous stanza. The image of a god being "not for us" now probably suggests not defeat, but a conscious choice—a *rejection* of the image of a god. It is not a large world the speaker requires, but a small one, a subjective one within the confines of the natural world, one within which his own imaginative gestures predominate. It is one of Strand's most assertive attempts to unite the dualities of the private and public worlds within which he lives. The theme here is, if you cannot beat the mountain, hide within a cave, light a match, and make shadow puppets on the wall. Yet, if, as the saying goes, defining the problem is half the battle, the union is not completed here. The speaker has established the quandary and defined the possible solution. It has not been achieved by the poem's end, however, for just as the poet issues the final words, "so long as it lasts," the poem ends—stops "lasting"—thus canceling the successful "littleness" that he achieved within the poem.

These interior sections of *Dark Harbor* identify the quintessential concerns of the poem. Strand asserts many of the themes he has offered in earlier volumes, but here he provides a keener vision of those themes. It is the moment of salvation in the imaginative endeavor he still seeks, but presently it is a small, sad salvation, a short-term goal. The task of blanking out the world now too daunting, he seeks a quiet haven, a dark harbor that he can call his own. Yet, at these late middle stages, potential remains larger than the reality. The lovers in segment XXXIII thus reach the pinnacle of their relationship by looking at each other's naked body in a mirror. The speaker and his paramour can esteem the beauty of their bodies, but know that the moment cannot be equaled by anything more than this mutually voyeuristic act. The speaker "admitted somewhat sadly, 'in the mirror the body / Becomes simultaneously visible and untouchable' " (17–18). Their joy is that they can stare at each other's bodies, but consummation is not achieved, and so the joy is tempered. The imagination can be awakened as their bodies become visible. But if touch were to enter the equation, imagination would have to submit to reality, and here they are mutually exclusive concepts.

This issue persists through parts XXXIV to XXXVIII. In XXXIV, the connection to nature seems completely severed, and the only poetic satisfaction comes in the form of mutual commiseration among those who recognize the loss. In XXXV, those people are recognized as the poets, and we again see Strand returning to the poets to find security, enlightenment, and that previously mentioned commiseration. "The sickness of angels is nothing new," he opens, sounding very much like a poet who has lost his voice and is desperately trying to convince himself that the loss is temporary, that it has been experienced by others and thus there is nothing to fear. "I have seen them . . . / chewing their tongues, not singing," he says (1–3).

The sense of loss in this segment culminates in a reassertion of the *power* of potential to both raise one's spirits and a reminder of the *limits* of potential. The poets, who retreat amongst themselves to some postlapserian commune when they lose their voices, seem to find redemption in the process, yet the "pure erotic glory of death without echoes" they experience is fleeting (12). Yes, they enjoy "The feel of kisses blown out of heaven" (13), but the poem is careful to mention their "Melting the moment they land" (14). Once again, that fleeting sense of contentment and joy is gone in the instant the segment is completed.

Parts XXXVI and XXXVII contemplate the purposelessness of any act in the face of such melting kisses, and seem to become bogged down in inaction. It is as though the speaker considers quitting as a means of escape from his plight. But segment XXVIII finds him unsaved, and so he must try again. Here he meets a mysterious stranger, ostensibly another of the angels. In a move in line with Bloom's description of *apophrades*, the speaker-as-poet discusses the reconsideration of his precursor. After all, in the first line, the stranger "appears." In the succeeding lines, Strand says, "The rest is up to me. To say, for example, / Why he has come and where he has come from" (2–3). The speaker's task, it appears, is to write, as Bloom would say, "as though the later poet himself had written the precursor's characteristic work" (*Anxiety* 16). In the 20-line sentence that ends the segment, Strand presents a blurring of the line between precursor as inspiration to ephebe and precursor as rewriter of ephebe.[2] He is described as "a stand-in / For somebody or something, an idea / Of withdrawal or silence" (10–12). He, too, appears to have lost his voice, for he is described as entrapped by "an invisible net / . . . paralyzing him, / Turning him into a watcher as well" (14–16). However, as Strand rewrites this precursor poet, he has the latter teach him to speak again, for he is "A watcher who sees and must say what he sees, / Must carve a figure out of blankness, / Invent it in other words so that it has meaning" (17–19). Of course, this is the poet's task, to reconstruct a world out of the ashes of silence. This carving from blankness is a magnificent turn on Strand's part, containing a synesthetic double irony. After all, carving is a cutting away of what is already present; Michelangelo had often said that his sculptures were a setting free of form already existent in the stone. Here, Strand's carving is away from a nothingness. The synesthetic element that doubles the irony is that blankness refers to sight, yet carving requires a sense of touch.

In an atypical Strandian twist that can be viewed in a Freudian light, the precursor is transformed, one might say, into the poet's father in order that this poet can kill his father. Yet, the perspective becomes skewed here as well, for poet and precursor begin to become one and the same. When the speaker is shown painting a gun into the precursor's hand and pointing it at "the one who assumed / The responsibility of watching" (24–25), it becomes difficult to decipher who that "one who assumed" is. Indeed, it seems to be both men, and attempting to distinguish the shooter from the victim seems immaterial; when the trigger is pulled, neither dies. Instead, "something falls, / A fragment, a piece of a larger intention, that is all" (26–27). The poetic noise uttered at the conclusion of part XXXVIII then leaves us with another Strandian silence that must be, and is, confronted in the following segment.

In part XXXIX, the speaker seems to make a new attempt, and takes a deep breath in preparation for the final stages of this monumental poem. He begins in a state of uncertainty, issuing a sentence fragment that hesitantly declares his intention to write without actually beginning the poem (of course, he *has* begun, for the two stanzas *are* present; yet, in their assertion that they *will* begin a poem, they declare the *absence* of poem).

With the struggle to recapture the poet's voice thus brought to the fore again, Strand coolly declares, "Today I shall consider Marsyas," the mythological figure flayed after battling Apollo in a musical contest (2–3). The pieces that remain at the end of part XXXVIII are picked up here as the remains of Marsyas, useless items again needed by the poet to reconstruct something of the world of the past—even if that world is the previous poem. Again, the poem finds the speaker wondering whether or not he should bother to try, whether the effort is worth expending. After all, Marsyas' fate may be what awaits him.

Benfey is correct to note that "The company of poets [to which Strand seeks to belong] can be intimidating, . . . and in *Dark Harbor* this fear is embodied in the figure of Marsyas" ("Enigma" 36). His further assumption, however, that "the link" in this poem "is clearly that of fear of not being good enough, the writer's 'block' that is both obstacle and punishment" overlooks the redemption that ends the poem (36). In elegiac style, the poem spirals upward. Strand "considers" Marsyas in the first, third, and fourth stanzas, seemingly lamenting that poet's—and, by extension, *this* poet's—fate. Yet, in each *re-consideration*, Strand brings something new to the mix, and thus rebuilds the poet in the making. By the time the poem ends, it exhibits a certain revitalization.

The grieving that dominates the early moments of this segment gives way to a reuse of this *materia poetica* called Marsyas. Strand transforms his flayed flesh into "the flesh of light, / Which is fed to onlookers centuries later" (12–13). The poetic influence of Marsyas is felt by, of course, Strand the "onlooker," who then repays Marsyas with the poem at the same time as he rewrites Marsyas. "Can this be the cost of encompassing pain?" the speaker now asks (14), as much of himself as of his predecessor. He, too, has felt the pain of "a long silence" (15), and attempts to use the experience as a unifying feature for him and his predecessor. Yet, the "correct" reply requires some reassessment, and a useful Strandian conjunction: "Or is a body scraped from the bone of experience, the chart of suffering / To be read in such ways that all flesh might be redeemed, / At least for the moment, the moment it passes into song?" (19–21). Yes, for a moment, there is redemption; there is hope, in the singing—that minute instant of engagement. As Spiegelman says, "Hopefulness, even muted, is hopefulness still" (135).

Yet, if part XXXIX ends with an acknowledgment that the poet can be redeemed in the moment he translates his experience into song, that song, of course, ends at the poem's conclusion, and the new poem, XL, begins after the latest silence. It necessarily must address loss, for the "moment" of segment XXXIX has passed. And now, he asks,

> How can I sing when I haven't the heart, or the hope
> That something of paradise persists in my song,
> That a touch of those long afternoons of summer . . .
>
> Will find a home in yet another imagined place?
>
> (1–5)

The other imagined place is the mind of the reader, or the poem of another. His incessant goal as poet: lasting value for his creation. "[W]ill I have proved / That I live against time," he asks (8–9). Or is the final answer: "whatever I sing is a blank?" (12). Though the indecision is maddening, it is the indecision that is the subject of his writing, and *as* the subject of his writing, it is the indecision that *keeps* him writing. It is a painful temporary redemption for this poet, indeed, and the concluding quintet of poems does its utmost to speak up against the perpetual fear of the speaking being ineffectual.

Segment XLI's solution to the meaninglessness of "the night sky" (2), to the realization that "I have no idea / Of what I see" (2–3), and to the number of the stars being "far beyond / What I can reckon" (4–5), is a "who knows," that seems to speak more as a "who cares?" (13). This poet speaks, he now says, because he must speak—of his joys, of his fears, of his inability to speak, and of his need to speak. Where the poem goes from there is now immaterial in the face of the poet's requirement to write. Of tomorrow, he says, "We are already travelling faster than our / Apparent stillness can stand, and if it keeps up / You will be light-years away by the time I speak" (13–15). Indeed, this segment's point of utterance is already far removed from the reader's point of reading. The poet's ability to affect the reader has long ended, and, in the scheme of real time, several poems already have been penned between this one and the reader's reception of it.

Time continues to race past unconcerned with the world's human inhabitants in segment XLII, and now none of it matters to the poet, or so he says. Marsyas, the hero of segment XXXIX, has been "asleep for centuries" (9), and "Arion, whose gaudy music drove the Phrygians wild, / Hasn't spoken in a hundred years" (10–11). Both are dead, and the poet is sure of this one "truth": "Soon the song deserts its maker" (12). Yet, Strand seems to be establishing a potential for union by linking these early poets in their silence. Hints are present when he says, "The airy demon dies, and others come along" (13). The others include himself, and though no union is established just yet, the experienced Strand reader can see it just around the corner, in the next poem. Surely, while there is no celebration here, when Strand says, "A different kind of dark invades the autumn woods, / A different sound sends lovers packing into sleep" (14–15), it is still a sound, whether it is a sound of poetry or of erasure to make room for poetry. Likewise, while "The air is full of anguish," the poet can potentially transform that anguish (16). As for tomorrow, this poet seems to leave it where it is—in that unreachable realm expressed in the previous segment of *Dark Harbor*. He now says, "The Beyond is *merely* beyond, / A melancholy place of failed and fallen stars" (17–18, italics mine).

Consequently, with the old poets discussed and put to rest, part XLIII begins to establish some continuity among and between poets. Though the piano music is no longer played, and the players are also gone, Strand links Jules Laforgue and Wallace Stevens in an extension of the torch-passing theme of the previous poem. He resurrects these poets and their poems in his reconsideration of them, but, as in the previous segments, he ends without resurrecting poetry to a place of honor. The connective bridge sustained here again is poetry's mutability: "The snows have come, and the black shapes of the pianos / Are sleeping and cannot be roused, like the girls themselves / Who have gone, and the leaves, and all that was just here" (13–15). Strand's own poem ("all that was just here") is unified with the poets who created the precursor poems, and their poems (the leaves) themselves. Though they "cannot be roused," there are commonalities being established in these final segments, which will ultimately be tied together in the celebration of the final segment's song. But for now, "all that was just here," the momentary salvation experienced in the writing of *this* poem, as well as all the delight achieved from the previous poems and their poets, are gone. They are united, yet only in their absence. Or, one might say, they are unified *in* their absence.

Part XLIV begins in a reminiscence of earlier days and ends in a recognition of the sea as an enduring, generative force that awed the speaker as a child and has intimidated the poet as an adult, for it was the enduring force he wished his poetry could be. Indeed, *Dark Harbor* ends at the sea, considering the past, the same place from where the proem was issued. For the speaker as a child, there was also something frightening about the power of the sea's loud voice. But "now years later / It is the sound as well as its size that I love" (8–9). Indeed, the sea has both the voice and the endurance that *every* poet seeks so fervently. And from the dawn of history, the sea has been speaking *to* these poets. Here, this poet has lost his voice "in my inland exile among the mountains" (10).

Ah, those mountains from part XXXII, those mountains that have intimidated him into submission, are the same mountains that separate him from his angel-poets in part XXVII. They, too, are enduring, but they do not speak. Ironically, the speaker now admires the ocean's changeability. Like the poet—or, perhaps more accurately, like the poet wishes to be—the ocean creates and destroys and is varied in its appearance from day to day, wave to wave, and moment to moment. This poet's mountains "do not change except for the light / That colors them or the snows that make them remote / Or the clouds that lift them, so they appear much higher / Than they are" (11–14). The ocean is the imagination at its strongest, capable of effecting change. This poet's mountains "are acted upon and have none / Of the mystery of the sea that generates its own changes" (14–15). And this eternal sea cries, too. These are the cries the poet now recognizes as a poetic need for him, as well. Gone are the days of childhood. Now, despite the futility of his situation—or *because* of the futility of his situation—as mere mortal, he must face the silence, face death, and face the insecurity of the future:

> [I]n those days what did I know of the pleasures of loss,
> Of the edge of the abyss coming close with its hisses
> And storms, a great watery animal breaking itself on the rocks,
>
> Sending up stars of salt, loud clouds of spume.
>
> (19–22)

This poet once again recognizes that poetry is not merely a bulwark against pain and suffering, but that loss is also a *source* of poetry. Instead of railing against the darknesses that exist before and after the poetic invention, the poet now focuses on that invention that *does*, regardless of its origins and its fate, exist.

This brings us to segment XLV, which ends *Dark Harbor* by radiating from itself, calling out to the future and to the past "masters" of poetry. Finally, it presents that bonding for Strand within the community of poets. This concluding poem-within-a-poem originates in a primal scene that the speaker is sure his audience would find "misty," one that seems to be left over just as the great forgetters of "Always," from Strand's *The Continuous Life*, are completing their erasure of the world. The speaker discovers "Groups of souls, wrapped in cloaks" (3) in the fields. This place reminds the speaker of another location, where a stranger who mysteriously recognizes him:

> Approached, saying there were many poets
> Wandering around who wished to be alive again.
> They were ready to say the words they had been unable to say—
>
> Words whose absence had been the silence of love,
> Of pain, and even of pleasure.
>
> (10–14)

Surely, these are not those inspirational poets wishing to return to earth, the place of love. More likely they are the "lazy poets" of Strand's "The History of Poetry," who, no longer having the power to create that they had on earth, have gathered together to mourn missed opportunity and to unlearn their bad habits. For they have a new teacher now, and they are learning to speak of the imagination. They have found communion, discovered that "the golden lights of sunset / And sunrise are one and the same" (18–19). Their teacher is "an angel, one of the good ones, about to sing" (21).

Yet, upon closer scrutiny, perhaps, Strand is saying that this is the fate of all poets once they have been defeated by death. In the face of such eternal silence, Strand's hedging throughout the poem appears to be a waste of effort. Here, he seems to recognize that there will be plenty of time for silence. Any words unsaid now will be regretted in the long silence after the imagination has been abandoned, after *life* has ceased. The "Someone, / who claimed to have known me years before" (8–9)—this mysterious speaker within the speaker's poem—has a lesson to teach. He is a liaison between the world of the now-silenced precursor poets and the living poet. It is he who summons the good angel to speak to his now-rapt audience, and the silence that ends the poem is the most promising silence of all silences, for it awaits the angel's impending poem. Strand has not ended a collection with as forward-looking and promising a hope as he does within the figure of an angel—the imagination that Stevens calls "the necessary angel"—hovering over this dark scene, right at the moment when the song is about to be sung. Few things are more promising than the promise of song. And if we indeed see the poem as circular—or at least spoken in both directions—the promise bears itself out in this most successful work of art, this angel-song.

LIVED EXPERIENCE BETWEEN THE BOOKENDS OF DARKNESS

Critics disagree on the tone of *Dark Harbor*. Tillinghast remarks that Strand presents a sincerity of emotion in *Dark Harbor*, noting an "elevated, classical tone that unifies its disparate parts" (292–93). Spiegelman disunites the poem by identifying the "faux-naif tone" of certain poems (136). Benfey reminds that Strand also exhibits startlingly playful brashness in segments such as XIX, XXII, and XXIII.

In general, Strand also appears in different forms to different people. Those with a penchant for European literature reasonably recognize Frenchmen Baudelaire and Rimbaud and German Rilke in Strand. Those who specialize in British Romanticism, see in him Keats and Wordsworth, again with well-founded opinions. It would be remiss to ignore the Dantesque quality of the three-line stanzas of *Dark Harbor*. And yet, there are a few critics who correctly note his affinity with certain Latin American poets, a few of whom he has studied and translated. On one thing, critics (other than Gregerson) seem to agree: his work is oddly familiar despite the apparent originality of its bluntness in the face of the perpetual annihilation. Pinsky may not have been entirely complimentary when saying, "Strand is an original writer, but not of the kind who challenges our idea of poetry. He confirms that idea, rather than enlarging it" (300–301), but few poets can hope to reach the level of imaginative achievement necessary to "confirm" our idea of poetry as compellingly—and, I might add, definitively—as he does. Indeed, Strand is a well-read writer who seems unafraid to reconsider any of his precursors, and that brings *Dark Harbor* to its heights. It is this universality of influence that probably identifies the accuracy of Spiegelman's contention, "Many of Strand's elegiac notes sound reassuring rather than threatening, precisely because of the familiarity of their tone" (135). Remarkably, they seem familiar to everyone, though for different reasons.

While given labels such as confessionalist, surrealist, fantasist, and postmodernist, Strand is a serious poet in the Romantic tradition contemplating and contending with the possibilities of poetry in a world where faith in religion and most other institutions has been lost. Throughout Strand's career, the poet exhibits an increasing imaginative strength. That strength has its peaks and valleys, but on the whole, Strand's voice grows louder in its capacity to call forth an imaginative vision. In *Dark Harbor*, he charts the whole territory anew, summarizing the growth of a poet from *ephebe* to strong poet. In paying close attention to what the poems do and how they do it, we have assayed to achieve what Henri Cole rightly calls "the cumulative effect" of Strand's vision. Indeed, it is our contention that *Dark Harbor* intends to produce such a cumulative effect. Despite its variations, it is a single-minded poem aimed at expressing the obstacles presented to the contemporary poet, and in particular, this mature contemporary poet. As Spiegelman says, "Wedding his cool Stevensian side to a more strapping Whitmanian feeling for the sea and its combination of terror and maternal comfort, Strand acknowledges certain adult emotions of which the young are deprived" (135). Ultimately, *Dark Harbor* asserts the vitality of "poetry itself, the naked poem, the imagination manifesting itself in its domination of words" (Stevens *Imaginary* viii).

In Strand's assertion of the primacy of the imagination, he has utilized many repeating images—primitive and privative absences and darknesses, the desire for safe haven amid the world's tempests, and the assertion of the imaginative gesture as temporarily redeeming. Ultimately, *Dark Harbor* comes down to the celebration of the subjectively meaningful action in the face of an apathetic world. In imagining the poem, Strand continually reinvents himself in a place of poets that we too are given when we accompany him. And in imagining the poem, he provides for himself and his reader temporary joy. Although Strand's imaginative powers have grown steadily from the weak attempts to stave off the storms of *Sleeping with One Eye Open*, to the multiple-layered creative powers of *Dark Harbor*, for now, Strand is still asking his blank page, "Where, where in Heaven am I?" And now, even if the imagination does not sustain, "Still, we feel better for trying."

CHAPTER 4

REINVENTING THE SELF:
BLIZZARD OF ONE

E is for endings, endings to poems, last words designed to release us
back into our world with the momentary illusion that no harm has
been done. They are various, and inscribe themselves in the ghostly
aftermath of any work of art. Much of what we love about poems,
regardless of their subject, is that they leave us with a sense of
renewal, of more life. Life, on the other hand, prepares us for nothing,
and leaves us nowhere to go. It stops.

—Strand, *The Weather of Words* 5

OVERCOMING THE ANXIETY OF ONE'S
OWN INFLUENCE

The neophyte poet's work combines a prepossessing manner, a singularity of vision, and some sense of resonance with a past master. Though current trends may privilege such essentials—and often they do not require them in great supply—these qualities alone do not automatically qualify a poet for greatness. A good poet has the capacity to compellingly depict his impressions of the world. The stronger poet is able to plot fresh space, perform some generative act in the face of the life's maelstroms, creatively confront the page that will consume his words once they are said, and bestow upon his reader a perception of having engaged something sufficiently potent as to be productive and primary.

We have discussed the incumbencies of using such concepts as precursors and poetic strength. Although applying Harold Bloom's model to Strand's entire career is not the ultimate intention of this project, we do recognize Bloom's terms as vital in this chapter, while we chart the intriguing if subtle departure of Mark Strand from his precursor, Mark Strand.

As we previously considered, Strand mournfully relates in "The History of Poetry" the tale of those weak poets who "do nothing but count the trees, the clouds, / The few birds left." This defines one of Strand's important qualifications for poetry. The strong poet must attempt to exceed mere accounting of the items and events of his day-to-day existence. The strong poet needs to effect his world, trope what *is* into what *may be*.

In *Dark Harbor*, Strand's speaker achieves communion within the fellowship of the great angel-poets, and seems pleased with his status. If that were completely true, and I suggest that to a great degree it is, Strand's pen might have had nothing left to do "but count the trees, the clouds, / The few birds left." He could not, after all, write another long poem along the lines of *Dark Harbor*. Nor could he go backward, as it were, and write another fear-inspired *Sleeping with One Eye Open*. Certainly, he could write prose (as he does with *The Weather of Words*) and translations, and continue to create playful experiments (as he does with *Chicken, Shadow, Moon and More*). But a creator of worlds, as I contend a strong poet needs to be, cannot create a world that is already in existence. He must map out new territories, continually.

The blank page that Strand faces after *Dark Harbor*, then, presents him with a singular dilemma. He has attained, after all, what only a rare number of poets could hope to accomplish in a career. He—or at least his speaker—is in the fraternity of the masters. In recommencing with a corpus such as his behind him, he must ask himself, *What is left to write?* "I just let things happen in *Dark Harbor*, and got carried away," explains Strand of his confidence at writing that work. "There's a certain amount of trust you [develop] in yourself. . . . I wish it continued. Those feelings come and go" (Interview, Nov. 2, 2002). To resume right from the conclusion of *Dark Harbor* would be to risk becoming merely an imitation of himself. Certainly there is an anxiety of influence Strand feels: however, as he himself admits, "The anxiety of self-imitation is the great anxiety of the poet" (Interview, Jan. 26, 2002). Strand's own success in the course of overcoming the world's whirlwinds has led him to become his own precursor. Indeed, any poet who creates work that satisfies his need for expression, will reach a point in his career where he must repeatedly outdo what he has done previously.

Blizzard of One thus finds Strand considering what to do now that he has become "the great dog . . . myself" ("Five Dogs" #2, 1–2). Why transform his angel from *Dark Harbor* into a dog? As the self-effacing Strand has said in a November 2002 interview, "It was a little too grand to have an angel up there; I needed to take it down a peg before [proceeding]." *Blizzard of One* then becomes both a capstone to Strand's career and a new movement forward. It is a necessary attempt—or rather, several different attempts—at a reinvention of the poetic self. Strand does revisit previous motifs, yet also paves the way for something further, perhaps bolder, along the line. Clearly, Strand has shown himself adept at humor—and at humoring himself. Here, he is equally at home with wittily deconstructing his work, while at the same time charting new space in his latest resurrection of the self. Only through the examination of this work as Mark Strand's attempt to swerve from his precursor, Mark Strand, can we recognize the subtleties of success that *Blizzard of One* attains. He takes the motifs, sounds, and sentiments generated by the Mark Strand who precedes him and, in his own new ordeals, discovers the puissance to create askew from his progenitor.

CHARTING THE COURSE AHEAD

Upon first reading, the experienced Strand reader might find few surprises in the tone and structure of the poems of *Blizzard of One*. Although the poems seem to contain more humor and playfulness, Strand has not suddenly become a nonsense poet. In fact, the primary modes of many poems here are sadness and loss, noticeably traceable, if one would so desire, to the dissolution of his second marriage. Yet, poetically, the lyrics gradually strike the reader as a reformulation of that which already was. Strand has continued to revert to the shorter, starker formal presentation of his early work, yet the themes are more approachable than the self-conscious poems of his early years. It would seem that in his desire to reach the perfect imaginative moment, Strand, with some exceptions, seeks the least conspicuous form. In doing so, he even seems to approach no form whatsoever. Strand has often presented poems that have eschewed conspicuous structures in order to allow the visions contained *within* the forms to come to the fore. Of course, achieving apparent formlessness is a sophisticated task.

In order to recognize Strand's attempt in *Blizzard of One* to clear new ground—to make his *clinamen*, a subtle Bloomian revisionary swerve away from himself—it will be beneficial to recall the concluding canto of *Dark Harbor*. Part XLV radiated from itself, calling out to the future and to the past "masters" of poetry, offering a unity for Strand within the community of poets. The "lazy poets" of Strand's

"The History of Poetry," no longer having the creative power that they had on earth, gathered to mourn missed opportunity and to unlearn their habits. There they found communion, discovered that "the golden lights of sunset / And sunrise are one and the same" (18–19). Their teacher: "an angel, one of the good ones, about to sing" (21). The silence that ends *Dark Harbor* is the most promising of all silences, for it awaits the angel's impending song. Few times has a pause been so pregnant with hope—with an angel hovering over this dark scene, right at the moment when the song is about to be sung.

The first small surprise *Blizzard of One* provides is in the opening lines, for the untitled poem begins *in medias res*. It does not begin with a silence, or with a silence-breaking proclamation reminiscent of "What to Think Of." More precisely, the poem seems to begin in the middle of an argument. The speaker seems to be recounting his opponent's previous contention about a supposed poem titled "The Adorable One." "As for the poem," he begins contentiously, and finishes the characteristically long sentence with "It has been years since you bothered to read it" (1–4). It is noteworthy that the poet has not chosen to say, "It has been years since you read it," which would have been connotatively neutral; or "since you *managed* to read it," which would have expressed desire but inability; or "since you *cared* to read it," which would have asserted indifference; or even "since you *hazarded* to read it," which may have suggested fear. Indeed, there is some sarcastic acid presented in his tone. But continuing to analyze the poem as merely one half of a dialogue would diminish the several resonances created in these four lines alone.

In the opening line, we have to account for the juxtaposition of the apparently angry tone with the chirpy title of the intertextual poem. It is hard to read "The Adorable One" without smiling. A likely first instinct on hearing the word "adorable" is to think of infants. It is rare to see the word "adorable" in common usage applied to an adult, and when it is, it carries a nonthreatening connotation. So, the collection, and the poem, open by reminding readers that, when reading Mark Strand, they must recognize several layers of troping happening at one time.

Further rumination reminds us, of course, that adoration—a connotative brother to adorable—is also something heaped upon a god. As the next pair of lines unfolds, and we marry them to Part XLV of *Dark Harbor*, we may distinguish several things. First, we recognize the intertextual poem's *own* playful beginning. More importantly, we also identify that poem's speaker with the superhuman flying angel-poet from the concluding section of *Dark Harbor*. Furthermore, if we properly identify the speaker of "The Adorable One" as the speaker of the untitled poem—i.e., Mark Strand—then the speaker is also recognizing himself as the formerly strong poet. This leads us into our discussion of Strand's own anxiety of influence.

First, Strand acknowledges the precursor poem as a superior achievement. Second, as creator of that precursor poem, Strand recognizes that his intended audience, the "you" of the untitled poem, has not even bothered to read it. Furthermore, "The Adorable One" was, in the context of this new poem, written a long time ago, for "It has been years" since it has been read. The narrative time that Strand has placed here between Part XLV and "Untitled," puts *Dark Harbor* in the distant past so as to make new space for his new poem. In this way, we understand it is not so much a silence that begins this poem, but it is the diminishing of the voice's effect: the tree that has fallen in the forest but has not been heard. Thus, the Strand dilemma is not the presence of absence, but the presence of a presence: himself. His *Dark Harbor* poem reminds him of his status within the poetic pantheon, and he distances himself from it, paves ground for the new poem, the new attempt, by first giving it a different title and belittling the earnestness of it, then having his reader indifferent about reading it, then pushing the creation into the past—all this before even four lines are completed.

"But now," Strand hides in an enjambment at the end of line four, " . . . the time [itself enjambed at the end of line five] / Seems right" (4–6). Remarkably, within the text of "Untitled," Strand rewrites the poem in the characteristically artificial lavender light. "Untitled," then, in resurrecting "The Adorable One," is a translation of that former poem. As such, it then becomes its own entity, makes its own *clinamen*.[1] But I digress. "The Adorable One," as we stated, will be reread or translated, "[i]n this lavender light under the shade of the pines" (5). Lavenders and purples while evoking dusk also have come to represent the artificial for Strand, that strange darkness necessary to create an alternative universe to the natural world. Strand's readers recognize and appreciate that when colors turn to lavender—just as when an old man waves his hand, or a person begins to speak, or leaves or snow fall, or when steam rises—this is a trope. More precisely, it is a trope for the making of a path for the artificial universe to replace the natural world.

There is something else noteworthy about the second sentence of this poem, and it revolves around that word "Seems" that projects defiantly at the commencement of line six. The independent clause of this sentence syntactically reads, "But now the time seems right." Such a sentence is so familiar to the American reader as to appear a cliché.

However, first there is the addition of the aforementioned "In this lavender light under the shade of the pines" that injects a certain mystical magic. Second, it is no accident that the three pairs of words ("But now," "the time" and "Seems right") are placed, respectively, at the end, end, and beginning of three successive lines. One might expect that the "But now" would find a prominent place; after all, it should be a bold (if hackneyed) proclamation, "But now, the time is right. . . . Change is going to occur; *this* is the moment!" Instead, the only words that find positional distinction are "Seems right." Only an inattentive reader would discount the pair of words enjambed at almost the center of the poem. The speaker does not feel the time "is" right, but merely "Seems right." From what we already have ascertained in the first six lines of the poem, the speaker's tone is anything but confident. Thus, this "Seems right" seems to be a stab in the dark, if you will. He may just as well have chosen to say, "But now, since I can't think of anything else . . . well, I guess I might as well try *something.*"

So, the speaker seems to open the book and attempt to read the poem. But, like Stevens' scholar of one candle, he is immediately shot down. What does the poem contain? Some lofty pursuit? Some bold statement? Some proclamation of beauty and wonder? No, instead, "The dust of a passion, the dark crumble of images / Down the page are all that remain" (6–7). It is a deflating moment. The opening three-and-five-sixths lines began with a consideration of the past. As the speaker turns to say "But now," he tries to resurrect something lost within himself, his listener, his poem, and directly is struck by the ineffectuality of the attempt. Thus, he quickly turns to his attempt to translate that poem, that "something lost," even before the seventh line ends: "And she was beautiful, / And the poem, you thought at the time, was equally so." But this attempt, too, fails. As much a master of poetic form as ever, Strand voices his speaker's dejection with the three shortest sentences in the poem in little more than one line. It is a voice that has grown weary within ten lines. Even "[t]he lavender turns to ash. The clouds disappear. Where / Is she now?" (9–10). That "she" is ostensibly the listener of this poem, to whom he alternately refers as "you."

Ultimately, this poem needs to map out its space by returning to the past. This time the speaker travels further, to the boy he was. Or rather, he *attempts* to find the boy he was, for he asks, "And where is that boy who stood for hours / Outside her house, learning too late that something is always / About to happen just at the moment it serves no purpose at all" (9–12). The poem ends with a familiar sense that whatever is about to happen is about to happen momentarily, *right here*, at the conclusion of the poem. And in that, it reminds us of so many earlier poems that conclude with someone *about* to speak, yet recognize that, since that someone in fact does *not* get to speak before the poem ends, the words *will* "serve no purpose." Still, one realizes that, as the first poem in the collection, there will be words to follow. However, at this point, the speaker's contention is that what will "happen" in this collection will occur when "it serves no purpose at all."

In other words, the woman-listener has already left the room and closed the door. So, remarkably, the poem returns to its previous trope. The woman has not bothered to read the first poem, and here she will not read the next one. We therefore can recognize this poem as an addendum to "The Adorable One." Unlike that poem, however, this one concludes with an unremitting sense of futility. In the former poem, the good angel would not get to sing until it concluded. In this one, singing will get done, but will be heard by no one. Strand is left to consider *What can I do, and what can become of it,* "Now that the great dog I worshipped for years / Has become none other than myself" ("Five Dogs," #2, 1–2)? He discusses this in Part III of *Blizzard*. It is *apropos* to look to the dog poems of Part III presently not only to facilitate my contention that Strand acknowledges himself as a difficult precursor to follow, but also because two of the poems were written and published shortly after *Dark Harbor's* publication. As such, they immediately addressed the theme of anxiety, if you will, and most of *Blizzard of One*, having been written later, is an attempt at a solution to the problem that at least two of the dog poems discuss.

Were one to doubt the contention that Strand harbors any anxiety toward creating a new self at the outset of *Blizzard*, one need only consult the poem Strand wrote in 1995, called "Great Dog Poem #2." This poem, reprinted as "Five Dogs" poem #2,[2] begins by claiming in no uncertain terms that he is the eponymous canine:

> Now that the great dog I worshipped for years
> Has become none other than myself, I can look within
> And bark, and I can look at the mountains down the street
> And bark at them as well. I am an eye that sees itself
> Look back, a nose that tracks the scent of shadows
> As they fall, an ear that picks up sounds
> Before they're born. I am the last of the platinum
> Retrievers, the end of a gorgeous line.
> But there's no comfort being who I am.
> I roam around and ponder fate's abolishments
> Until my eyes are filled with tears and I say to myself, "Oh, Rex,
> Forget. Forget. The stars are out. The marble moon slides by."

It requires a confident—perhaps a hubristic—poet to declare himself the great dog, and this is one eye-opening start to any poem. Nonetheless, this is no vainglorious speaker. He desires not to tout his accomplishments, nor to rest on his laurels. Instead, he uses this opportunity as consummate poet to "look within / And bark" (2–3), and to "look at the mountains down the street / And bark at them as well" (3–4). Whether it is a bark of joy or of despair, it is a bark of power. I *can* speak, this dog utters, and the utterance—so long as it is heard, Strand will sometimes append—is all that matters. With a confident voice, this dog-poet focuses his attention upon the utterance. It matters not *what* he barks, but rather *that* he barks—and perhaps *when*. There is nothing more gratifying, Strand explains, than for a poet to be able to write, than for a dog to be able to bark. Indeed, it *is* a dog's life that the confident poet leads.

In the face of the mountains that imposed themselves upon many scenes in previous Strand poems, this dog does not have to cower. Yes, the mountains are massive, an ever-present reminder of the natural world's ability to infringe upon even the most grandiose of human efforts to construct a viable alternate reality. Still, the dog's poetic utterance is valuable as a creation of its own, despite the fact that the mountain will always be there. Yes, the Strand speaker has matured. Now poetry is a reliable ally against the natural world. Now, as successor to his precursor-self, he has "an eye that sees itself / Look back, a nose that tracks the scent of shadows / As they fall, an ear that picks up sounds / Before they are born" (4–7).

This declaration thematically echoes Emerson while also being unmistakably Strand. Is Strand truly Rex, the King, metaphysically aware of all his surroundings? How far does this poet's pride go? Or are these lines merely a reflection of the poet's quiet confidence in himself? When he becomes the "eye that sees itself / Look back," is it more accurate to say that this poet no longer speaks his poetry out of desperation? Is he now saying, "I can write poetry, and create myself within the poem looking at myself outside the poem?" Is it a poet now confident that his poetic vision can be sustained, at least for a while, in the face of an oppressive reality?

If his nose, synesthetically, can track "the scent of shadows / As they fall," and his ear "picks up sounds / Before they are born," is he not the preternaturally sensitive poet? Is what he saying decipherable as "I am in tune with the world, and can translate any occurrence in the world into a language suitable for poetry?" In the literal world, shadows have no scent, and nor do they fall. The human ear can pick up no sounds before they are uttered. For the speaker then, he is more interested in the items of the world as the building blocks of poetry. The world's objects as they stand are all-too-menacing, or at least apathetic, to human lives. Before they become "real" shadows, "real" sounds, the confident poet must take from them what he needs, turn them back upon themselves—as the eye that sees itself look back—and use them to create shadows and sounds of his own. His concern is to seize the world's shadows and sounds, and before they can be interpreted as what they *are*, turn them into what they are *not*. Then he will be using them for his own ends, and not to the erratic and unpredictable ends nature has in store for them. In short, the world's items are more valuable as tropes than as what they might be in and of themselves.

Before we delve too deeply into the poem's philosophical underpinnings, however, this is, of course, not meant to be a wholly solemn poem. One must not undervalue the playfulness inherent in a poem about "great dogs." Indeed, one of the remarkable transformations in Strand's career, as he has progressed from an insulated, nightmare-haunted speaker to a confident architect of imaginative alternatives to the dismal world—is his ability to laugh at that world. Does not self-directed humor reflect positively upon a person's security? In calling himself "the last of the platinum / Retrievers, the end of a gorgeous line," Strand makes an overt reference to his now-gray hair. And indeed, he is a striking man. But perhaps more important is to recognize that the platinum retriever is a fabricated species. It is a hybrid of two natural entities—the element platinum and, of course, the canine breed. Juxtapose the two naturally occurring items and what one has is a non-natural Strandian metaphor—nature cultivated, nature transmuted. Strand has previously described this process in *Dark Harbor*:

> There is a luminousness, a convergence of enchantments,
> And the world is altered for the better as trees,
> Rivers, mountains, animals, all find their true place,
>
> But only while Orpheus sings. When the song is over
> The world resumes its old flaws, and things are again
> Mismatched and misplaced . . .
>
> (XXVIII 1–6)

In a stunning proclamation of confidence, Strand asserts the "true place" of things as that designated by the imagination expressed in "the song." In their native habitats, things are but "mismatched and misplaced."

But let us return to those quietly omnipresent "mountains down the street" in "Five Dogs" #2. The mountains are the same ones from *Dark Harbor*'s canto XXXII, the same mountains that have intimidated him into submission, that separate him from his angel-poets in segment XXVII. Like everything in nature, they are enduring, speechless, and, as such, inaccessible in themselves. This poet's mountains "are acted upon and have none / Of the mystery of the sea that generates its own changes" (14–15). In "Five Dogs" #2, filled with the conviction that he can speak but insecure about the value of speaking, this speaker knows he is able to bark at the mountains. He knows his barking will not make them go away, but the exercising of voice is the life-affirming act.

Still, despite the speaker's confidence, in no way is his creation permanently entrenched. The poem must end, and when it does, the speaker no longer exists. The poet is only a poet when writing poetry. Thus, as the poem approaches its conclusion, the speaker realizes, "there's no comfort being who I am" (9). For a poem that begins with such gleeful power, it ends with apparent mournful helplessness. If one were to desire to do such a horrible thing as to summarize a poem, one might do it to this poem as follows, "Well, I may be the great poet I always wished I could be, but so what?"

As the great dog ponders "fate's abolishments"—which bemoan the state of poetry as underappreciated and speak of postpoetic silences—he grows melancholic. After all, whatever fate has abolished leaves a gap in the world of what once was. Hence the need for poetic vision—to replace the beauty that has been torn from the world. "Forget. Forget," the speaker advises himself. In a beautifully subtle redundancy of negatives, this command requires him to "forget" what the world has "abolished." Hence, he is telling himself to erase not only what the world has erased, but also the memory of it having been erased. Forget not only the other platinum retrievers who have now gone, but also the very fact that he is the last in the "gorgeous line."

What, then, remains to build the poem with? Start from darkness. After all, "The stars are out" (12), and the nighttime obscures the world's terrifying features. In the night, all is black—the primitive darkness out of which this powerful artist can create. His marble moon—a white canvas upon which he can paint—represents, importantly, not the authentic moon, but an impressionistic one. Strand does not seek out the artificial, as Yeats would. However, as we saw him juxtapose platinum with retriever, he selects common, accessible objects from *within* the natural, and applies them in new combinations. On first glance, both a platinum retriever and a marble moon are easily digestible metaphors. However, each calls for more than a quick glance. Hence the natural marble juxtaposed with the natural moon resulting in an unnatural trope. Whatever the world had for us, if anything, is no longer available for us. We must "forget" about that possibility. Nature, however, can be practicable, Strand asserts, just not as itself. And so, our great dog-poet leaves us saddened, yet not without the hope of transforming the natural scene into something useful—an alternative world constructed by the imagination. In the natural world, nothing has inherent meaning. As the speaker of part XXVIII of *Dark Harbor* says, one must be "[a] watcher who sees and must say what he sees, / Must carve a figure out of blankness, / Invent it in other words so that it has meaning" (17–19).

Thus, Strand recognizes himself as an imposing precursor, and tries to clear ground in this poem by forgetting. In part three, Strand endures a crisis of desire, before being able to proceed to the more vital part four. Dog Poem #3 begins, again, with a smile-inducing attempt at dog-think: "Most of my kind believe the Earth / Is the only planet not covered with hair" (1–2). In an apparent non sequitur, Strand follows with "So be it, / I say, let tragedy strike, let the story of everything / End today, then let it begin again tomorrow" (2–4). A striking statement to the uninitiated, perhaps, but the Strand reader has long since been inundated with such demands for erasures to clear space for future creations. What *is* striking, however, is this apparent throwing up of hands:

> I no longer care.
> I no longer wait in front of the blistered, antique mirror,
> Hoping a shape or a self will rise, and step
> From that misted surface and say: You there,
> Come with me into the world of light and be whole,
> For the love you thought had been dead a thousand years
> Is back in town and asking for you . . .
>
> (4–10)

The passivity expressed in these lines is uncharacteristic of the later Strand. For that matter, the early Strand occasionally may have cowered in fear from some imposing force, but rarely waited for some good to occur. This waiting he claims to endure is, in fact, a double waiting. He is waiting, foremost, for the love he thought had been dead a thousand years. But it is important not to overlook the fact that *first* he is waiting for a "shape or a self" to rise out of a Strandian mirror to *tell him* that the love he professes to have been waiting for is alive.

So, this love is therefore doubly unattainable, and this is before we consider the hyperbole of her being "dead a thousand years." To consider the theme of doubles on a different plane, it is reasonable to recall Strand's divorce with these lines. Is he feeling sorry for himself? Is he trying to get back on the romantic horse after being thrown? In times of loneliness, does not one index one's past loves and wonder *what if*? On the other hand, perhaps the love he speaks of is not of the romantic kind, but of the poetic kind. After all, all Strand's dog poems equate dogs with poets or poetry readers. Perhaps he has been waiting for inspiration from some past poet—and perhaps in that way, the thousand-year-old death is not, in fact, hyperbole.

Two words later, we find what starts to become a recurring methodology for Strand in *Blizzard*. The speaker unequivocally, bluntly answers himself with an enjambed "Oh no," before the end of line ten. "I'm done with my kind," he continues (11). This is a human making a typical "I'm through with love" statement, but also a dog-poet surprisingly eschewing poetry. When he concludes the poem with a quiet "I live alone / On Walnut Lane, and will until the day I die," he provides an unredeeming solitude (11–12). This may be viewed as Strand's *kenosis* against Strand the precursor. "For, in *kenosis*, the artist's battle against art has been lost, and the poet falls or ebbs into a space and time that confine him, even as he undoes the precursor's pattern by a deliberate, willed loss in continuity" (Bloom *Anxiety* 90). Had this poem been written in 1980, one might have recognized it as the work of the blocked writer that Strand then was. Nonetheless, here in the middle of *Blizzard of One*, it echoes the sentiment of failure. Maybe this dog will bark again, but, as the great dog in a place where great dogs are aberrations (they are, after all, living on the universe's only hairless planet), he is confident his barking from #2 will not be heeded. The desire to speak to others in this poem is muted. How to follow up one's magnum opus? How to deal with one's own achievement? "Five Dogs" #3 seems almost a throwing up of hands and a declaration of: "I will speak only to myself." In this way, Strand rewrites—and thus clears new ground for himself as he simultaneously professes to surrender to silence—*Dark Harbor*, part VIII. That poem concluded with the plea:

> Tell me I have not lived in vain, that the stars
> Will not die, that things will stay as they are,
> That what I have seen will last, that I was not born
> Into change, that what I have said has not been said for me.
> (21–24)

This dog poem's speaker seems confident that what has been said *has* been said only for himself, and so ends in an unfulfilling retreat. Any barking he has done is useless, he now believes, if done only for himself. And so the poem ends with the unusual, for Strand, use of the word "die" in the moment of poetic silence at the conclusion. Furthermore, this speaker seeks the change that *Dark Harbor* canto VIII's speaker feared, until the conclusion when he *resigns himself* to the fact that "things will stay as they are." The remarkable duality is, of course, that in throwing up his hands in defeat, Strand *has* done what "Five Dogs" says it cannot do. That is, it says it cannot find a new way to speak. Its new way to speak, however, *is* to speak in such defeatist absolutes. As such, it is a negative progression. At this point, one might say Strand's answer to following up his most powerful work, *Dark Harbor*, is to become powerless. As Bloom says of *kenosis*, "The later poet, apparently emptying himself of his own afflatus, his imaginative godhood, seems to humble himself as though he were ceasing to be a poet" (*Anxiety* 14–15). In this way, the poem of apparent weakness is the natural successor to the strong poem. This is then a ritual cleansing, a necessary feeling sorry for oneself, a cathartic "I am no good and nothing good can come of this," before finding a ray of light to begin a new day. Hence, it is a more painful path to privation than Strand's poetry has ever encountered. To return to Bloom, "[T]his ebbing is so performed in relation to the precursor's poem-of-ebbing that the precursor is emptied out also, and so the later poem of deflation is not as absolute as it seems" (*Anxiety* 15). Indeed, this poem— and the Five Dog poems in general—may go as far as becoming an *apophrades* for Strand. They are such strong poems, revealing Strand

> already burdened by an imaginative solitude that is almost a solipsism, hold[ing] his own poem so open again to the precursor's work [Strand's earlier seminal dog poems]. . . . [T]he poem is now *held* open to the precursor, where it once *was* open, and the uncanny effect is that the new poem's achievement makes it seem to us, not as though the precursor were writing it, but as though the later poet himself had written the precursor's characteristic work. (*Anxiety* 15–16).

Few things are more promising than the promise of song, and in "Five Dogs" #4, "the howls of the great dogs practicing fills the air" (5).[3]

> Before the tremendous dogs are unleashed,
> Let's get the little ones inside, let's drag

The big bones onto the lawn and clean the Royal Dog Hotel.
Gypsy, my love, the end of an age has come. Already,
The howls of the great dogs practicing fills the air,
And look at that man on all fours dancing under
The moon's dumbfounded gaze, and look at that woman
Doing the same. The wave of the future has gotten
To them, and they have responded with all they have:
A little step forward, a little step back. And they sway,
And their eyes are closed. O heavenly bodies.
O bodies of time. O golden bodies of lasting fire.

The world is the same one that said to him in "Leopardi," "I do not give you any hope. Not even hope." Here, the moon gives a "dumbfounded gaze." Yet the poets seem to have taken over this world. The dogs that we saw "on the basement stairs and coming up" in "Eating Poetry" have completed their ascent now. And though "the end of an age has come," this poem begins, in a sense, a resurgence on the dogs' part. These poets are not "romping with joy," as they were in 1968, but they *are* "practicing" to regain their voices. If #3 was the low point in *Blizzard*, #4 is the attempt to get back on his feet. After all, the modus operandi for the great dog to make some worthwhile creation is defined here as: "A little step forward, a little step back." Thus, #4 is that step forward, that new attempt to recreate Mark Strand, the poet.

The poem begins, as do each of the first four dog poems, with a witty reference to the canine world. But this poem maps itself out not as a monologue of existential angst. Instead, it presents a visual renaissance. One need only recall the good angels in the concluding part of *Dark Harbor*. They are the ones the poet-ghosts gathered to hear. Similarly, the tremendous dogs are here to shepherd the little ones. The great dogs' howling and the man and woman's dancing under the moon, strike one as an Orphic ritual. Certainly, there is the disconcerting acknowledgment that "the end of an age has come." In Strand's personal and professional life, those words hold true. Yet, instead of holing themselves up after consideration of thousand-year-lost loves, these figures look to the future. And, in a remarkably direct line praising the power of indulgence, "they have responded with all they have."

"Five Dogs" #4 readdresses Strand's earlier signature piece, "Eating Poetry," at the same time continuing his later quest—the consideration of the poet's place within the world. Ergo, it brings much of Strand's career into play as it attempts to stake new territory for the future. Though the poem is "After a line of John Ashbery's," it speaks strongly of Strand's own poetic vision. Ever the master of revising other poets in ways that truly transform their words irrevocably into his, Strand opens with a projection of a primal world, albeit one in which there, as here, it is "the end of an age." These creatures are celebrating a return to the earth as source of power; they give of themselves wholly in the glorification of song, and they dance in a unified acknowledgment of the eternal gift of art.

Strand and his companion dogs ostensibly have escaped from their library prison in "Eating Poetry," and are simply biding their time, waiting to be "unleashed" (1). This is no insecure poet now, hesitant of the world's, i.e., the librarian's, reaction to him, but one reminding him of his capacity to summon forth the poetic creation with a word. Strand uses familiar motifs to invoke the imaginative act. Strand's rather frequent—until this collection—use of the imperative is present here. When the speaker commands us to "look at that man" and "look at that woman," he is invoking the reader's imagination to bring the reader into the participation of the poetic tropes. For, to "look at that man" requires the conjuring of just such a figure. In doing so, the reader is a creator, as well. Reader and poet thus share the experience of poetic redemption. In using the imperative, Strand seems to be reaching back again, not to recall long-lost loves as in #3, but long-lost tropes from poems gone by. He seems himself to be, like the dogs, practicing. He is preparing to write valuable poetry, if only indulging in trope making at this point. His final invocations, using the infrequently used "O," may be shooting in the dark at effective metaphors, or may be a sincere invocation, but as an utterance, they *do* call forth their images; they do "speak." If the reader recalls the concluding words of the first of these five dog poems— "That's when I, the dog they call Spot, began to sing"—the speaking is an act both celebratory, and worthy of celebrating.

In "Five Dogs" #4 the indulgence of the imagination in the moment is evidenced by the men and women responding "with all they have." These lyric eaters find redemption by accessing their primal selves through their immersion into the poetic endeavor. They metamorphose from dogs to "heavenly bodies . . . bodies of time . . . golden bodies of lasting fire." Indeed, the lasting fire here evokes those guiding fires from *Dark Harbor*; they are the inspiration a poem brings to its reader. Strand's earlier works ordinarily portrayed no less than a somber vision of dying fires, silenced voices coincidental with the poem's end. The end of the imaginative vision represented the speaker's silence, for voice is all the poet has. When he creates his private life in the poem, he has a world in which to live. Concurrent with the conclusion of that poem, there must, by definition, be an ending of that world. Hence, the poem's conclusion often begets an ominous silence.

Here, the fires that the speaker lights are, at best, just ignited at the poem's conclusion. This trope is designed, at least, not to exist only within the physical strictures of the poem, but within the minds of the readers who are reading and *have read* the poem. Thus, what has occurred in this poem is not a self-contained motif designed to live its life within the mere lines scribbled by a desperate poet, but one that attempts to outlive the poem. As the reader finishes the poem, he is asked to contemplate the final trope. In doing so, the act of the imagination does, in fact, outlast the physical limitations of a 12-line poem.

Before proceeding to the final poem in the "Five Dogs" sequence, we shall return to the first. This will allow us to add another element to the mix. That is, we can also examine the poem *as* a sequence of poems, and understand the unfolding of the themes as they present themselves before turning an eye to the poem that has the last word.

The first of the dog poems begins with a simple declaration that, when revisited at the poem's conclusion, gains force and meaning. "I, the dog they call Spot, was about to sing," it starts, and at this point the utterance seems matter-of-fact. The speaker's reference to himself as "the dog they call Spot" is made not merely as an acknowledgment that a dog is given a name by its human "owner." It also bears testimony to some sort of celebrity status. He is, one would say, *known* as Spot. The speaker continues with a visual description of autumn, with a "tarnished / Moonlit emptiness" that serves as a subtle harbinger of the winter to come (2–3). When he says, "I wanted to climb the poets' hill before the winter settled in; / I wanted to praise the soul," it is one of the more straightforward utterances in Strand's career (4–5). This poet is looking for perspective, climbing the top of the hill to see his world below. His goal is to sing in praise of his own creation. Instantly, however, he is disparaged: "My neighbor told me / Not to waste my time" (5–6). Why? First, the neighbor says, *it is too late; your career has already crested, and the silence of death is closer than you think*: "Already the frost has deepened" (6). Spot, a dog with desire but waning confidence, seems to look around him and concur: "[T]he north wind, trailing the whip of its own scream, / Pressed against the house" (7–8). The wind's balefulness is revealed in having not just a whip, or a scream, but in a verbalization that multiplies the effect; it "trails" the whip of its *own* scream.

To reassert one of the major themes Strand needs to deal with at this stage in his career, we point to the neighbor. In a kind of antithesis to

Frost's neighbor in "Mending Wall," this voice reveals the pragmatism of the day: "'A dog's sublimity is never news,' / He said, 'what's another poet in the end?'" (8–9). Strand's own sublimity is thus called into question; he is, after all, the dog they call Spot. And his existential crisis centers around that aforementioned question, *Now that I have achieved something poetically, what is the purpose of speaking anymore?* As Spot (a reasonable synonym for "Mark"), he seeks to make a new and lasting "mark."

Spot seems to take a moment or two of silence after the neighbor's counsel. Unlike "Mending Wall," however, the neighbor does not get the last word. Instead, in a beautiful string of words, Strand has Spot stare out into the nighttime sky, "watching the great starfields / Flash and flower in the wished-for reaches of heaven" (10–11). The flashing and flowering, presumably a meteor shower display, does not serve to intimidate the dog-poet. This scholar of one candle seems to accept the starfields' transcendence and uses them as fodder instead (after all, they have already provided the stuff of two magnificent lines of poetry). Inspired to reach for greatness by the examples the sky provides, Spot reiterates the opening line: "That's when I, the dog they call Spot, began to sing" (12). The first time he professes to sing, the reader notices, he is deterred, first by his own accounting for why he wanted to sing, then by his neighbor's censure. This time, bolstered by the force of nature—and his narration of his first attempt, which, of course, *was* his first song—this speaker *will* sing, and the four poems of "Five Dogs" follow. Poem #2, of course, attempts to find something lasting to say, while #3 indulges in impotence and isolation. And #4 finds him inspired yet again to take "a little step forward" after more than "a little step back."

Noticeably, the final poem of the pentalogy does not begin with any reference to dogs. Consequently, the humor that seemed to mask more serious poems in the first four cases, is eschewed in favor of a seriousness that nearly undercuts itself by being a poem about a dog. The poem begins with a personification of nature that occurs only occasionally in Strand's later work. By saying, "the weather came up with amazing results," Strand presents, of course, that nature had been *trying* to create the effects that follow (1). What is not immediately clear, however, is whether nature is, at this point, attempting to create hazards or beauty. One's inclination at the outset is to believe it is the latter. After all, Strand describes the results as "amazing": "The streets and walks had turned to glass. The sky / Was a sheet of white" (2–3). Mirrors and blank pages are, after all, prime Strandian tropes.

Our dog then arrives in line three, and this dog, unlike those in the previous four poems, seems misplaced. The reader easily could substitute the word "man" for dog here, and not skip a beat. What follows is another indulgence akin to "Five Dogs" #3. There the dog-speaker indulges in self-pity, one might say, and retreats to a life of loneliness. In this poem, the third-person dog seems thoroughly overwhelmed. If this is a different dog from the one in poem #3 or #4—and one could assume that by reading the subtitle "Five Dogs" literally—then this dog does not go forward as does dog #4. Thus, one might read "Five Dogs" as five potential futures for the Strandian speaker. More likely, however, one would read "Five Dogs" as a passage through the emptiness and absence prevailing throughout *Blizzard of One*. If so, then poem #5 ends a downward spiral. Poem #1 begins with a desire—in the face of objection—to sing, and to celebrate singing. However, poem #5 ends with the desperately sad truth that he will *not*, in fact, get to sing, because literally nobody is there to listen. If the Strandian dog-speaker is buoyed by the self in #1, or the promise of other poets in #4, now he seems earnestly discouraged and disheartened, and "nothing would ease his tiny heart" (4).

This dog is found "Calling home," a phrase noticeable first in its placement at the beginning of its line (4). Strand links this dog, then, with such forebears as Whitman and Shelley—not as living poets, but as silenced ones: "For years the song of his body was all of his calling. Now / It was nothing. Those hymns to desire, songs of bliss / Would never return" (5–7). The attitude of this dog resembles that of poem #3. There, the dog is sure he will live alone for the rest of his life; here, he will be silent forever. Strand brings the absence closer to home by then using his own lexicon: "The sky's copious indigo, / The yellow dust of sunlight after rain, were gone" (7–8).

Strand again uses his remarkable facility for enjambment to underscore the sadness of the silence that follows: "No one was home. The phone kept ringing" (9). These two brusque sentences reveal the lack of poetry that prevails as the poem's theme. These lines imbue in the reader a palpable parallel between the dog's calling home and that of a broken marriage. When Strand reveals the darkness that will ensue, it is a more powerful darkness—a denser blackness—than perhaps we have ever seen in his work, for it is unrelenting and permanent: "The curtains / Of sleep were about to be drawn, and darkness would pass / Into the world" (9–11).

This curtain of darkness brings us to the concluding lines, which seem as much an unsuccessful stab at black humor intended to distance himself from pain as a whistling in the dark. The pain identified with the dog seems almost too much to bear, for instead of continuing in line 11, the speaker trails off: "And so, and so . . ." When he concludes with "goodbye all, goodbye dog," the joke necessarily falls flat (11). Accordingly, the despair and silence reverberate uncomfortably, as when someone tries to tell a joke to alleviate one's own pain but no one in the room believes the speaker's humor is sincere.

This sequence of poems proceeds naturally, as it were, from the great harvest of autumn in the first poem, to the eternal death of winter in the final one. Strand's speaker opened the series with the acknowledgment of self as reputable and accomplished. He is "the great dog," but finds "no comfort" in being so. After all, the poet's indulgences here do not "praise the soul," as he has desired. He can summon forth no "hymns of desire, songs of bliss." Once again, he needs to confront the question, *Even if I can speak, what should I say, and what power will it have?* This is no poet content to "do nothing but count the trees, the clouds, / The few birds left" ("The History of Poetry" 19–20). He needs to be a creator here, and in ways that have either delighted or disconcerted his critics, he intersperses the humorous with the gloomy. Before doing so, however, he must engender an absence, a killing off of they great dog himself. As such, *Blizzard of One* charts the many stops and starts Strand makes in his journey, and does so with remarkable expression of his ambivalence.

Dark Harbor: Revisited/Revised

If the untitled poem that opens *Blizzard of One* reminds readers of *Dark Harbor*, and reveals a stage-setting attempt to revise the poet Mark Strand, the second poem, "The Beach Hotel" offers an intriguing antithesis to *Dark Harbor*. Where the eponymous harbor seemed to be a place worth remaining in, this poem commences with a hurried, "Oh, look, the ship is sailing without us! And the wind / Is from the east, and the next ship leaves in a year." Still, the tone is humorous, at least at first glance. It is here that the reader may first consider whether the speaker is laughing in the face of nature, or, again, whistling in the dark. Indeed, the speaker seems unconcerned by his fate of being stranded: "Let's go back to the beach hotel where the rain never stops" (3). From here the poem almost becomes macabre. The hotel's garden is "green and shadow-filled," and whispers, "Beware of encroachment" (4–5), probably not motifs of hospitality.

What can one *do* at such a hotel? "We can . . . visit / The dead decked out in their ashen pajamas" (5–6). The reader naturally finds him/herself asking, "Are these dead people the corpses of the angel-poets, now silenced?" After all, on concluding our visit with them, "we" are not inspired to poetic heights, but instead "lie on the rumpled bed, watching / The ancient moonlight creep across the floor" (7–8). Now, instead of flight, there is stagnation. The darkness that arrives in line nine is "uncalled-for," and instead of erasing the world to make way for a new creation, this darkness "[w]ill cover us" (10). Claustrophobia may be the end result of this darkness; the sleep that results from its blanket is "close and mirrored" (10). In the end, the speaker becomes the dead decked out in his own ashen pajamas. If the etymological origins of inspiration are "a breathing into," this is a poem of "expiration," where dead poets suck the breath *out* of this poet. Instead of becoming the fodder for his future poem, or at worst the precursor around which he must work, these figures are the dead that enshroud and suffocate him. Indeed, Strand presents formidable barriers to success here, and by establishing such obstacles, perhaps ultimately paves the way for greater heights to be achieved. The higher the stakes, the greater the reward.

"Old Man Leaves Party" is Strand's first effort in this collection to reverse the declension of the opening poems. This verse begins with the speaker making a conscious effort to exit the public eye—forget that he is The Great Dog. Perhaps, one might deduce, the party was in his honor. After all, he is decked out, and concerned that others might see him as he disrobes. Strand chooses, in this poem, to strip off the accouterments, leave the social sphere, and return to the private sphere, alone in the woods. When the speaker reminds us of one of the Strandian rules of poetry, "The moon shone down as it will / On moments of deep introspection" (3–4), he invokes the lunar muse of sorts, almost as if reminding himself of its power. The light of the moon, after all, is reflected light, not originating from its source, which is why it makes such a potent trope for Strand. Luna the thief steals her light from the sun in the way Strand needs to steal natural-world objects to trope them for his artificial constructs. Nature then becomes personified by holding its breath, and we recognize we are not in the natural world but rather the poetic one, and Strand brings us along to witness the transformation.

What follows is the Strandian moment of creation wherein nature conforms to the poet's needs. It is the ceremonial stripping away that Strand sees as necessary for the private creation. He takes off his shirt, and "[t]he flowers of bear grass nodded their moonwashed heads" (7). He takes off his pants "and the magpies circles the redwoods" (8). The stagnation of "The Beach Hotel" is replaced by life: "Down in the valley the creaking river was flowing once more" (9). From a phenomenological viewpoint, when one is socializing, a theme reiterated in the succeeding poem, there is no bear grass, nor magpies, nor flowing river for he who merely experiences a party. The speaker needed to repair to the woods and disrobe to get the river flowing again. In a way, the poem could be considered complete at this point. Though fairly simplistic, it would still state a major tenet of "living in the poetic moment." The concepts of artificial and natural worlds, and poetic and public spheres, are contained in these opening nine lines.

But Strand performs his *volta* outside the movement of the poem in the concluding five lines. This time he does not alter tenses, but steps outside the poem to directly address the reader. "I know what you are thinking. I was like you once," he says in another example of staccato sentences squeezed into a single line. What he does not say is what is presented as rhetorical: "What *are* we thinking?" He does not elaborate, but instead leaves us behind as he looks forward: "With so much before me, so many emerald trees, and / Weed-whitened fields, mountains and lakes, how could I not / Be only myself, this dream of flesh, from moment to moment?" (12–14). The veteran Strand reader will remark at the first use of the characteristic mellifluous alliteration of "weed-whitened" in this collection. The short celebration of being "only myself" is also the first we see in three poems. It is also the first time in *Blizzard* we see the esteeming of moments—ever so fleeting but ever so present—in the last words of the poem. Juxtapose these moments with the "moment it serves no purpose at all" in the opening poem, and the contrast is striking. *Something* creative occurs in "Old Man Leaves Party," where it was only *about to* in the previous poem, and even then was going to be impotent in any case.

Some of the lightheartedness that presented itself in "Old Man Leaves Party" continues even in the whimsical tone of the title of the next poem, "I Will Love the Twenty-first Century." Initially it sounds like an affirmation the speaker is using to convince himself. "Dinner was getting cold," it begins, and we wonder if the party from the previous poem is waiting for the speaker to return from his trek to the woods. Jovial yet striking, the poem's timbre is amusing at the outset, but this hides the emptiness and meaninglessness that is at the heart of matters. After all

> The guests, hoping for quick,
> Impersonal, random encounters of the usual sort, were sprawled
> In the bedrooms. The potatoes were hard, the beans soft, the meat—
> There was no meat.

> (1–4)

On two planes there is a kind of ironic failure: one a failure of passion, the other of sustenance. Were there no dinner, one would have viewed this house as a whorehouse. But even at that, one might expect that the *guests* would be looking for something a little more passionate than "the usual sort." The meal that is getting cold, meanwhile, is no prize, either. Thus, one would say the guests are missing an inadequate meal by *waiting for*, not even having, inadequate sexual experiences. It is reminiscent of the old joke of the couple at dinner, one complaining, "This meal is terrible," the other adding, "Yes, and such small portions."

In a way, the opening of the poem *is* but a joke. When Strand continues with his visual description of winter, he seems to go into a more characteristic mode of versification. One might say—despite the thoughtfulness of a line like "Deer were moving down the road like refugees" (5)—that this second part of the poem is Strand's own "random encounter of the usual sort." They seem to be easy lines for Strand to write, and in fact, seem as if they have been written by him before. That said, the poem turns to a second speaker, who provides the "meat" of the poem:

> Then a man turned
> And said to me: "Although I love the past, the dark of it,
> The weight of it teaching us nothing, the loss of it, the all
> Of it asking for nothing, I will love the twenty-first century more,
> For in it I see someone in bathrobe and slippers, brown-eyed and poor,
> Walking through snow without leaving so much as a footprint behind."
> (6–11)

With these lines in hand, the reader can, first of all, attribute sincerity to the title, even if it is not the credo of the original speaker. That being done, we can address the philosophy contained in the man's monologue. Essentially, he decides to love the new century because he anticipates that the future that will leave nothing is more desirable than the nothing that already is past. For him, the promise of something that will *turn to* nothing is better than the nothing that is currently here as a negation of something that *was* but is gone. In other terms, he prefers the primitive darkness that will become a privative darkness to the privative darkness that was once a primitive darkness.

Before we delve further into this discussion, we should note, however, the speaker's final utterance: "'Oh,' I said, putting my hat on, 'Oh'" (13). The repeated response is doubly negative. First, it is said twice, and it is a nonresponse at that. Second, the utterance itself is a nothingness—i.e., "Oh" = zero. Before we indulge further into the deliberation of privative and primitive darknesses, we need to recognize that the speaker *negates* the man's discussion of negations—as if the issue were not already complicated by double negatives compounding double negatives. We can then attribute the speaker's state of mind to one of two things. Either he is unimpressed by, or not in love with, absences of any kind, or he is one of the aforementioned guests who does not *want* this discussion, only the "quick / Impersonal, random encounters of the usual sort." In either case, this speaker is unlike the conventional Strandian speaker who thrives on such considerations. This is a tired man who stands here listening; one who perhaps wants encounters to be easier, unencumbered by complexity and nuance. Hence, the poem is a failure in its success, or a success in its failure—and once again we return to the poem's conflation of apparent dualities. That is, the poem is very much an antipoem, *if* one of our requirements of poetry is that it contain complexity and nuance. Its speaker narratively cancels any discussion of complexity and nuance that the man attempts to provide. As such, the poem itself becomes a champion of ease and depthlessness. A man speaks, presents an idea, and the speaker, literally—and poem, figuratively—puts on his hat to leave. The idea then does not echo, as it does in so many Strand poems. What echoes is the speaker's "Oh . . . oh." The blankness of that negative utterance is as somber as Strand has ever presented.

Our poet changes gears—tonally, at least—as he looks for some personal redemption in "The Next Time." Part I begins with an assertion that "the architecture of our time / Is becoming the architecture of the next time" (1–2). On one hand, one might interpret this statement as *What we have created today is lasting until tomorrow and making a new name for itself.* However, the syntax of the phrasing suggests that the architecture of today is being *taken away* from us. After all, it is *becoming* something else, not *growing into.* One has the sense that Strand feels no capacity to affect architecture's change into what it will be. Further, the phrase "the next time" pushes the architecture to a place that is *not* of our time, and so distances the architecture from us. Any reader who believes that the phrasing suggests some positive, lasting outgrowth of art into another age should be persuaded otherwise by the succeeding lines:

And the dazzle

Of light upon the waters is as nothing beside the changes
Wrought therein, just as our waywardness means

Nothing against the steady pull of things over the edge.
Nobody can stop the flow, but nobody can start it either.

Time slips by; our sorrows do not turn into poems,
And what is invisible stays that way. Desire has fled,

Leaving only a trace of perfume in its wake,
And so many people we loved have gone,

(2–10)

Part I of "The Next Time" seems to encounter the problem of
absences as described so many times in Strand's poetry, but most
recently in "I Will Love the Twenty-first Century." One cannot dis-
pute that these lines describe an unalterable current toward death that
everything falls into. As the poem unfolds, we recognize this opening
as a presentation of dilemma that then gets addressed in the succeeding parts. One may decide, perhaps, to pursue the poem as a syllo-
gism. In any case, the progression of the natural world—with all its
constraints and finalities—is presented in no uncertain terms in the
opening part of the poem.

Of note is the despondent statement "our sorrows do not turn into
poems." Certainly Strand *has* used his sorrows to create many poems.
However, any belief in such alchemy is gone here. When the speaker
notes that "Desire has fled," he reiterates the stagnancy presented in
"Untitled" that comes to the fore in "Five Dogs." After all, it is one
thing to say "so many people we have loved have gone," which he does,
and it is quite another to assert that *desire* itself has gone, as well.

Strand's most resonant lines come at the conclusion of part I:

And no voice comes from outer space, from the folds
Of dust and carpets of wind to tell us that this

Is the way it was meant to happen, that if only we knew
How long the ruins would last we would never complain.

(11–14)

The double sense of negativity so powerfully redundant in "I Will Love
the Twenty-first Century" turns instead against itself here. That is, the
"no voice" that is acutely sought by the "we" of the poem to say something *does* in fact get to say something. The speaker gets to say what the
absent voice should be saying. Of course, "we" will continue to complain because it is the speaker who says it and not the voice from outer
space. But first of all, the reader needs to recognize that if nature must
be belligerent, "we" desire it also to be beneficent. "Say something to us

we can learn / By heart and when alone repeat / Say something!" Frost demands in "Choose Something Like a Star" (9–11). Here, Strand asks "outer space" to tell us with finality that this is all there is to existence. It is the indeterminacy that causes Strand's speaker so much woe.

The last line-and-a-half, then, turns the nonspeech required of outer space into a speech. By making the words into a behest, the fact that the words are not said becomes a potent warning, nonetheless. They *would* be said, Strand's speaker asserts, should the voice from outer space speak. What is in question is the speaking of the words, *not* the truth of the words, should they be said: "[I]f only we knew / How long the ruins would last we would never complain." This nihilistic admonition leaves the speaker staring into a darkness that he has now convinced himself is of unbearable duration.

Part II of "The Next Time" proceeds from the premise, then, that what the voice from outer space did not say was true and that immutability is the only certainty. Once that has been accepted, one can heed the advice: "never complain." As such, part II seems to possess some of the Strandian trademark tongue-in-cheek playfulness that has been chiefly absent from this collection until now:

> Perfection is out of the question for people like us,
> So why plug away at the same old self when the landscape
>
> Has opened its arms and given us marvelous shrines
> To flock towards? The great motels to the west are waiting,
>
> In somebody's yard a pristine dog is hoping that we'll drive by,
> And on the rubber surface of a lake people bobbing up and down
>
> Will wave. The highway comes right to the door, so let's
> Take off before the world out there burns up. Life should be more
>
> Than the body's weight working itself from room to room.
> A turn through the forest will do us good, so will a spin
>
> Among the farms. Just think of the chickens strutting,
> The cows swinging their udders, and flicking their tails at flies.
>
> And one can imagine prisms of summer light breaking against
> The silent, haze-filled sleep of the farmer and his wife.

As we discussed earlier, in the poem "Se la vita e sventura . . . ?" Strand writes:

> Was it written that I would be born into myself again and again,
> As I am even now, as everything is at this moment,

And feel the fall of flesh into time, and feel it turn,
Soundlessly, slowly, as if righting itself, into line?
                              (29–32)

Here, too, Strand seems at peace with—or at least acquiescent to—
having to be born into himself again: "Why plug away at the same old
self?" Instead of seeking larger and deeper tropes, he uses simpler
ones: the "marvelous shrines / To flock towards" are nothing more
than "[t]he great motels to the west." His third stanza continues the
humor with a dose of playful irony. As he and his companion ostensibly "drive" westward, they encounter first a "pristine dog" who for
some reason hopes they will drive by. The description of the dog as
"pristine" surprises because the word does not have a natural-world
connotation; one might accept an infinite number of pristine artificial
objects, but very few animal ones. One might coin a phrase and define
the unnatural adjective to describe a natural object as an artificial/nat-
ural synesthesia. In doing this, Strand seems to make the dog a "new"
one; that is, a dog that has never had an owner, not had experiences,
and never run through the woods. Strand thus appropriates the dog
for himself, erasing the dog's life to this point so that it, too, can be
born again into itself. This might be one way of understanding the
role of a trope itself, for in troping, the poet gives the object new
meaning; hence it must be understood/experienced as a new entity.

In the very next line, Strand seems to reverse the artificial/natural
synesthesia. When he says, "And on the rubber surface of a lake people
bobbing up and down," he creates an image along the lines of
Marianne Moore's "imaginary gardens with real toads in them"
("Poetry" 41). In the previous line, the natural dog was modified by
the artificial adjective "pristine." Here, the artificial rubber lake is
impacted by the natural "people." When he does this, Strand forces the
reader to consider his universe in two different ways, yet each demands
that the world considered is the imaginative one. The juxtaposition of
artificial with natural teaches the reader how to read the poem: not as
some model of the natural world, but as a transfiguration of it. Strand
not only presents the object, but illustrates how to transform it into
something functional.

Strand's speaker then encourages his reader to hurry up and participate in the imaginative creation before there are no objects left to
trope: "The highway comes right to the door, so let's / Take off
before the world out there burns up." Speaking as much to himself as
to his readers, Strand attempts to whip up some enthusiasm for his
venture westward: "Life should be more / Than the body's weight

working itself from room to room. / A turn through the forest will do us good, so will a spin / Among the farms." The solitude that Strand evokes ("the body's weight working itself from room to room") stands in direct contrast to the imaginative constructions that Strand's poetry has provided for almost 40 years. Strand seems to be remembering that fact as he talks us, and himself, into getting off of our imagination-poor couches and into the creative world. "Why plug away at the same old self?" indeed. This earth-bound poet is seeking to recreate himself in a place where poetry again matters—or at least where one might find the fodder for poetry, if one views the journey westward as a return to Strand's previous poetic locale, Utah.

Accordingly, when Strand concludes, he is not using imagery to convince the reader to take the trip *eventually*, he is advising the reader on precisely how to take the trip *now*. That is, we have been going all along, and when we "think of the chickens strutting, / The cows swinging their udders, and flicking their tails at flies," we *are* taking the imaginative voyage Strand describes. After all, when "one can imagine prisms of summer light breaking against / The silent, haze-filled sleep of the farmer and his wife," one *is* imagining prisms of summer light. Furthermore, "one" is also using the artificial/natural synesthesia technique that Strand has advised us to use earlier. After all, *sleep* is not a tangible object that can have *light* shed upon it. Therefore, we readers are engaging our own imaginations in imagining the "sleep of the farmer and his wife."

For a moment, then, Strand has some success in rousing the muse, at the same time as reminding that the effect is short-lived. As part II of "The Next Time" ends, the sleep, after all, is about to be interrupted by the prisms of summer light that we, the poet-readers, have created. This creative capacity is a tenuous gift, for as soon as we turn our imaginative beams on an object, we transform that object. In so much of *Blizzard of One*, Strand advises (himself) against engaging the imagination for so many reasons, not the least of which is to preserve things as they are, to keep things whole. Here he remembers that, even if for but a moment, *something* can come out of the act of imagination. But, keeping in mind that the poem is "The Next Time," and also that this is part II of three parts, the diaphanous nature of the creation is made that much clearer.

Part I has served as a prologue to the central utterance that is part II of "The Next Time." Since the ruins do last such a long time, part II is the attempt to momentarily *stave off* those ruins. In the act of imaginative participation, at least one is engaged and not merely bemoaning the losses of the past or the absences to come. Part III, then, is the afterword, a reflection that ties back to part I, back in the ruins, one might think. The crucial utterance in the former part involved that voice from outer space that the Strand speaker sought to hear utter, "[T]his / is the way it was meant to happen." When part III commences, it resumes where part I left off: "It could have been another story, the one that was meant / Instead of the one that happened" (1–2). In this Prufrockian articulation, Strand reverses the thought. Maybe, he seems to say, something else *could* have happened, and things would have turned out better. In this configuration, the word "meant" has been reconfigured from the previous usage. That is, the way it was *meant* to be in part I referred to the immutability of fate; here, *meant* refers to the desire of the speaker to affect his reality *despite* fate.

When the speaker laments that "hoping to revise what has been false or rendered unreadable / Is not what we wanted," he bemoans that all he has is the hope of troping a painful reality into something bearable. In other words, he is reconsidering the value of what he has done in part II: "Believing that the intended story / Would have been like a day in the west when everything / Is tirelessly present . . . was overly / Simple no doubt, and short-sighted" (4–9). *What a waste of time to think a poem could make it all better*, is one possible translation of these lines. A stronger one is, *What a waste of time to think that the intended story would have been devoid of painful absence, more enduring, or more enjoyable*. The speaker may be laughing at—or chiding—himself for previously believing in some enduring adventure where the mountains, wind, and trees all beneficently participate in the creation and maintenance of some grand romance. At this point, one might contend that Strand seems to be admittedly reporting the process of *kenosis* in this self-emptying poem. As Bloom relates,

> Where the precursor was, there the ephebe shall be, but by the discontinuous mode of emptying the precursor of *his* divinity, while appearing to empty himself of his own. However plangent or even despairing the poem of *kenosis*, the ephebe takes care to fall soft, while the precursor falls hard. (*Anxiety 91*)

Strand's speaker tries to cushion his fall; he seems to be regaining composure after allowing his emotions to get away from him. He reminds himself that all things end in death, and therefore his intended reality, even if it *could* have been summoned in the face of fate, would have been short-lived: "For soon the leaves, / Having gone black, would fall" (9–10); he empties canto I of *Dark Harbor*.

When he says, "the annulling snow / Would pillow the walk" (10–11), it is a smothering that this pillow performs, not a softening, not the "pretty densities of white on white" of canto XVII. Ultimately, what would occur would be what *has* occurred. That is, the same erasing, restarting, revising: "we, with shovels in hand, would meet, / Bow, and scrape the sidewalk clean" (11–12). *Whatever* the story, whether it was meant by the participant, or by fate, it has the same ending. Hence, all Strand presents are the myriad starts and stops, doings and undoings, erasures and recreations.

Because the poem follows "I Will Love the Twenty-first Century," and concerns the passage of things into nothingness from today into tomorrow, one might reassess the accusation against the speaker of "The Next Time" that he is negating the man's speech. One might consider that he has put his hat on to leave in order to ruminate on the man's words, or to find some personal redemption in the face of the universal darkness that awaits all. In any case, this speaker certainly does not "love" either the past or the future. He is struggling to make peace with the negations of *both* past and future, and in doing so, he creates a poem to replace the previous antipoem.

"What else would there be . . ." Strand's speaker now understands, "but desire to make amends / And start again, the sun's compassion as it disappears?" (12–14). He recognizes what he has forgotten, yet what has happened repeatedly in his career—that understanding, compassion, redemption all are infinitesimally narrow moments. When he connects "What else would there be" with "the sun's compassion as it disappears," he summons the pattern of discovery at the pinnacle of imaginative creation. That is, he recognizes "that something is always / About to happen just at the moment it serves no purpose at all"; and "We'll . . . discover . . . the bitter remains of someone who might have been / Had we not taken his place"; and "how could I not / Be only myself . . . from moment to moment?" Those Wordsworthian moments, that something that is about to happen and that compassion, however ephemeral, are all one can aspire to attain. There is very little left to rally so late in poetry's day.

That in hand, Strand ruminates on the dark fate in "The Night, The Porch." He is keenly aware of death, but no longer nonplused by that awareness. Evidence how in a matter-of-fact manner he says, "To stare at nothing is to learn by heart / What all of us will be swept into" (1–2). Furthermore, he recommends acquiescing to death's ultimate authority, for "baring oneself / To the wind is feeling the ungraspable somewhere close by" (2–3).

When line four arrives, it presents its compelling case in poignant monosyllables: "Trees can sway or be still. Day or night can be what they wish." On one level, the line attributes the power of free will to nature, thus implying that we humans do *not* have the power to be what we desire. After all, we desire at best the oxymoronic *something* that is always just *outside* our grasp: "the comfort / Of being strangers, at least to ourselves" (5–6). On another level, one can read line four as a throwing up of one's hands, as Strand advises earlier, and giving in to fate. Where he once wanted to hear the voice of outer space provide answers, or trope elements of nature, singing or whipping winds, clapping leaves, and annulling snow—here he has turned away from all motifs. He is no longer looking for them to provide rational answers, or even merely atmosphere, because they will not give us any. It does not matter if trees sway or are still, and nor should we try to discern any lesson from the day or night. Let it go, the speaker says, and in this poem, he is in a more tranquil, Zenlike state of mind. He is now thinking clearly about fate's abolishments, resigning himself to his fate instead of fighting emotionally to circumvent it. What we need, he says, is not the pursuit of any intrinsic meaning gleaned from a nature external to us. We are waiting for the imaginable. Once that imaginable becomes available to us, becomes tangible, it is no longer imaginable and merely "real." It has to be the sound of less than one leaf—perceivable but never experienced. It must be something we can never achieve—that cabin in the woods "that should remain empty"—because once we do achieve it, it *has been achieved*, and is thus a *past* achievement.

Strand concludes his exhortation with another compelling duality: "There is no end to what we can learn. The book out there / Tells us as much, and was never written with us in mind" (10–11). First of all, *if* our experiences are short-lived and transient, then at least they will be manifold, and as such, come with their many concomitant lessons. The last sentence then is both a referral to and admonition against "the book." It does, after all, support Strand's thesis, "There is no end to what we can learn." On the other hand, like the trees, the day, and the night in line four, they were "never written with us in mind." That is, just as we should not look to the trees, the day, or the night for answers because they do not care to give them to us, neither should we look to the book. In this Emersonian locution, Strand advises against the outward-lookingness that he, himself, has been sporadically guilty of in this collection of poems. Stop looking to the book out there, he says, even if it has lessons, for its lessons are not meant for you and can provide you with very little solace.

"Precious Little" contains the lessons learned in the previous two poems, and seems to turn them outward to teach them to his readers more than to himself. As such, the poem contains some didactic elements that serve to make it a somewhat lesser poem than, say, "The Next Time." It begins by expressing the lesson that Strand's speaker seems to have learned in the early stages of *Blizzard of One*—i.e., how to regain one's vision: "If blindness is blind to itself / Then vision will come" (1–2). The wind as synecdoche for the natural world again plays a role in the poem, as the listener—or very easily, the self—finds himself taking a risk by "opening the door that was your shield" (3). When the listener twice declares to nature, "Out of my way," for a moment, the natural world is erased: "In a trice the purple thunder draws back, the tulip drops / Its petals, the path is clear" (7–9).

With these words declared, we quickly recognize the poem has room to breathe, and create. What follows is what the experienced Strand reader expects. Once again, the West plays the role of ideal world: "You head west over the Great / Divide and down through canyons into an endless valley. / The air is pure, the houses are vacant" (10–12). The wind returns again, and in a reversal of "The Night, The Porch," *is* imbued with a capacity to imagine in such a way that causes our speaker to become emotionally committed. In fact, the wind is "*all* ice and feeling" as it "Invents a tree and a harp, and begins to play" (13–14, italics mine). The speaker ceases to be a listener to the performance—and, in fact, stops the reverie of creation himself—to ask the rhetorical question, "What could be better—long phrases of air stirring the leaves, / The leaves turning?" (15–16). The lines, Stevensian certainly, are nonetheless marvelous expressions. The wind becomes properly personified by speaking in "long phrases of air." However, the long phrases of air that stir the leaves are also the long phrases of *poetry*, and the turning of leaves nothing less than the troping of leaves into the aforementioned harp players. One might have expected the poem to have reached its apogee here, but Strand turns back on himself and attempts to nullify his own creation: "But listen again. Is it really the wind, / Or is it the sound of somebody running / One step ahead of the dark?" (16–18). The speaker is talking about himself, of course: so many earlier poems seem to sound like "somebody running one step ahead of the dark," instead of someone attempting to create from his own darkness. This latest self-conscious intrusion in the creation of poetry again interferes with the reverie; in doing so, it reinforces a theme now recognizable in *Blizzard*. Strand begins with an attempt to do what he has done so many times before. When he clears away space for the poem, the veteran Strand reader recognizes that the poem's visualization is about to dominate. But unlike as in *Dark Harbor*, here that does not suffice. The speaker cannot become unselfconsciously absorbed in the imaginative world. The destructive losses of the world external to the poem are too omnipresent, and they bring him back.

Ultimately, Strand is left to consider yet again the purpose of the poetic ambition, the value of recreating himself anew: "And if it is, and nothing turns out / As you thought, then what is the difference / Between blindness lost and blindness regained?" The compounded difficulties of blindness that is blind to itself being lost and then regained can be maddening. If we recall "The Next Time," Strand presents the reconsideration of the theme of one's life turning out differently than intended. But he also now considers that once one has accepted that things do not turn out as planned, is that any better than having *rejected* that things do not turn out as planned?

For now, the question is left unanswered, though the tone suggests resignation. This ultimate acquiescence to privative darkness temporarily defeats this speaker. The poem thus adds its voice to the many ups and downs that become *Blizzard of One*. One might in fact say that such attitude and tone shifts are as much responsible for the titling of the collection as the line from "A Piece of the Storm." This constant re-creation of self that Strand hopes will happen, among other places, in the mirror, in the West, in the wind, is sought so vigorously, so self-consciously, that the struggle to do so becomes the primary engagement more than the actual re-creation. As such, the utterances that are these poems often plunge the speakers into enervation. The speakers rarely seem sure that the already difficult task of deleting the natural world and creating something that will suffice is worth the effort, but they often cling to the small hope that the *next* creation *will* satisfy. For now, all they have is the tiny moment where "[t]he air is pure, the houses are vacant," and the promise of creation remains pure. This topic leads, then, to the title of this poem. At first glance, we are inclined to read "Precious Little" as *very* little. Coming full circle with the poem as we do, we are more inclined to read it as: *Our solace may be little, but it is precious.*

If so much of Part I of *Blizzard* is plagued with the unsilenceable echoes of things lost and fears that "I have not lived in vain," at least the concluding poem ends with a tone of rejuvenation after some spring rain. It is only a short metaphoric jump from considering Strand as the Great Dog to the Great Poet of his "The Great Poet Returns." Initially, this poem differs from "Five Dogs" in that it does not begin in the Strandian moment. That is, the poem does not begin simultaneously with the utterance of some such statement as, "*This is my poem.*" Here, the poem begins with a consideration of an event *past:* "When the light poured down through a hole in the clouds, / We knew the great poet was going to show. And he did" (1–2).

Certainly, Strand is equivocal about the poet's role in the present world, but he has endured such vacillations in the first section of *Blizzard* that we must tread gingerly when making such statements. "Five Dogs" #4 claims at least a handful of tremendous dog-poets ready to take the world into the new era. In "Five Dogs" #2 he is the only one left. In "The Great Poet Returns," the poet once again holds a revered place in society.[4]

At the inception of this poem, the speaker recalls the anticipation of the great poet in the world, yet one must submit to Strand's vision to accept this as an everyday occurrence. Indeed, when was the last time a poet was introduced by "light pour[ing] down through a hole in the clouds"? No, indeed, this light occurs only within the mind of the sensitive reader, whose own imagination is set alight by the anticipation of receiving the poet's vision. Nonetheless, this light does foreshadow the great poet's coming, for his role, as we have seen, is to cast light upon the darkness. "And he did."

Lines three and four present him arriving in a merging of popular culture and religious icons. Indeed, he drives up in the limousine of the rock star, but it contains the hallowed "stained-glass windows" of a cathedral (3). Neither rock star nor priest, this poet possesses the power and respect of both. In a remarkable oxymoron bordering on pathetic fallacy, the speaker recalls how "with a clear and soundless fluency, / He strode into the hall," and we know instantly that this star-priest-poet is also a man of no small magic (4–5). As he *prepares* to speak, all listen with baited breath. Before he *does*, however, the speaker feels the need to interject something odd about the poet. Besides noting that "His wings were big" (5), evoking the angel image that has worked for Strand before, he notes that "The cut of his suit, the width of his tie were out of date" (6). Despite the respect and attention he receives, the poet remains liminal and atemporal. Or perhaps this line reasserts the contention that *this* poet has remained in a time past, and needs to reconstruct himself. Perhaps he desires to reorder the world to match the cut of his suit and the width of his tie, or perhaps it is not until he speaks that he *does* in fact update himself. In any case, the poem definitively declares; he does speak.

"When he spoke, the air seemed whitened by imagined cries" (7), is a lovely paraphrase of a central Strandian poetic principle, evocative of *Dark Harbor's* "Proem." In the generative principle of the poet-creator, the poet needs merely to write to evoke his world. When he speaks of light pouring down through a hole in the clouds, the reader has no choice but to envision that very image. In an instantaneous sense, then, when the poet speaks, the air *is* "whitened by imagined cries." It was imagined by the poet, and is now reimagined by the reader. And no listener is untouched: "The worm of desire bore into the heart of everyone there" (8).

When the poet finishes, it is coincidental with "the end / of the world" (10–11), for it is the end of this "imagined" world created by the poet, re-created by the sensitive listeners, filled with "imagined" cries. Indeed, it *is* "only the end of the world as you know it" (11). The poet's role, Strand seems to remember here, is to pose new possibilities. The end of the world is, in fact, a dual one. It is the end of the imagined cries issued by the poet. Yet, Strand suggests that something of the listener's life must change as a result of the encounter with the poem. Thus, the ending of the world *as you know it* frees those engaged in the imagination to reorder their existence, to participate in the *new* world that awaits those who have indulged in the poem.

La volta in this poem occurs in lines 12 and 13: "Then he was gone, and the world was a blank. It was cold and the air was still." Indeed, when the reader is engaged in the poetic creation, the world enacted in the poem is vibrant, alive. And when the poem ends, that world *is* a blank; in the form of a characteristic Strandian darkness, whiteness, or, simply, blank page. What comes before and after the poem—words on a page—but a blank page? What comes before and after the song but silence? What comes before and after the light of day but darkness? What, finally, comes before and after the imaginative creation but oblivion?

At this point, the speaker steps out and addresses the reader directly—unexpected at this point in the poem, but a common motif for this poet. When he asks, "Tell me, you people out there, what is poetry anyway? / Can anyone die without even a little," he focuses the readers back on his own poem and continues to create in their imagination (13–14). The Strand speaker knows he must die at the end of each poem, and knows that the poem's final utterance brings about his death. Yet, the Strand creation known as "The Great Poet Returns" asks the reader to continue pondering the ideas the speaker has evoked. For one of only a handful of times in his career, Strand issues forth an imaginative vision that does not end simultaneously with the end of the utterance. When the utterance ends in the interrogative form, the poem continues to resonate in the reader's mind in ways reminiscent of Dickinson. After all, the reader must consider the questions. In doing so, the reader is "keeping alive" the poem, even if only for a moment. In changing the reader's life in this way, Strand again attempts to recast himself in the role of the great poet. Has he not poured his light through a hole in the clouds? In some way did he not arrive in his presentation of the stained-glass limousine? When he leaves, is the reader's imagination not left as a temporary blank, capable of being filled by his or her own consideration of the question, "Can anyone die without even a little?" While Strand may not yet be convinced of his ability to re-summon poetry's power to suffice, part I of *Blizzard of One* ends with the strongest push to revive poetry's potency.

Major questions of Strand's assertion of poetry's capacity to create an alternate life can be summed up in Strand's previously uncollected poem from 1992, "Our Masterpiece is the Private Life." That poem begins part II of *Blizzard*, and indeed, it would seem the title, repeated in the lines of the poem, presents a quite lucid theme.[5] The private life—that one constructed in the imagination—is the superior life worth living. If we use the poem as one example of the imaginative act, then indeed, it is the masterful poem that creates a private life for the poet and reader. This second attempt at re-creating the self appears to be a retreat into the solipsistic self, one that has served Strand well in the past. Time—i.e., the poems that are spoken within part II of *Blizzard*—will tell if this second attempt will succeed.

The poem opens with a natural object that refuses to become "useful" to us because it remains inaccessible— "something down by the water, keeping itself from us" (1). More particularly, this image appears to be something of ourselves—a painful loss, perhaps, subsumed in the mind— "Some source of sorrow that does not wish to be discovered yet" (3). Whether or not the individual wishes to revivify the "source of sorrow," here, Strand says, "desire cast[s] its rainbows over the coarse porcelain / Of the world's skin, and with its measures fill the air" (4–5). Considering the two primary forces at work in this part of the poem—the "source of sorrow" and "desire"— the former is clearly an item out of the past, while the latter is a future-looking emotion. That is, sorrow is an emotion reserved for some event that already has occurred. Desire is, by definition, an emotion one feels for something that has yet to occur. Keeping in mind the losses that inform this collection, the speaker seems to be turning his back on those and looking hopefully to the future and new desires that will "fill the air." When he says, however, "Why look for more?" we are not sure if he is asking the question rhetorically, or if he is sincerely questioning himself (5). In fact, the entire second stanza potentially may be read as ironic. Has this speaker truly put the past behind him and become forward-looking, or is he merely trying very hard to convince himself that he is doing just that?

In part II, Strand confronts poets of cynicism, or confessionalists, at whom Strand has taken stabs in the past—those "advocates of awfulness and sorrow / Pushing their dripping barge up and down the beach" (6–7). His admonishes his purported lover here: "let's eat / Our brill, and sip this beautiful white Beaune" (7–8). The speaker tries to talk himself into taking the fodder of his life's ruins—perhaps the "source of sorrow" from part I—and turn it into something productive. While others open up their private lives for public display, he attempts to turn his sorrow into sustenance—food and wine. As the cliché goes, if life gives you lemons, make lemonade. The speaker acknowledges that the real world consists of "dripping barges," and "the light" of *his* imaginative creation—the world he asks his love to live in—"is artificial" (9). And yes, like the Great Poet, he and is companion "are not well dressed" (9).

Still, Strand is unruffled, asserting, "So what. We like it here" (10). Yes, it is artificial, and the sound of wind over the grass is not the sound of nature, but the sound of poetry—the wind becomes the voice of the poet and grass becomes the Whitmanian leaves of verse. In fact, the enjoyment of the occasion is entirely "[t]he way you speak" (11). Noticeably, Strand has not emphasized *what* is spoken, but the *manner* in which one speaks, "disclosures" connoting something vital being shared (12). Here, Strand does not concern himself with what happens when the utterance is finished, or where the words go, whom they are for, or what value they have. Simply speaking is a creation, equally vital, and equally worthless, and so in asking, "why live / For anything else?" he echoes part I's "Why look for more?" (12–13). The speaker's confidence in this second part, a reconsideration of the first, seems to have grown. Our masterpiece is not the public poem that earns one the title Poet Laureate of the United States. It is the private disclosure shared with a single other late one night.

Indeed, the imagination is the point. The dripping barges will always be there, along with the whipping winds and every other natural element that either plans man's undoing or cares not about man in the least. When one can share the personal moment retained by the two lovers reminiscent of Arnold's lovers in "Dover Beach," indeed, "Why live / For anything else?" There is nothing else for us. Indeed, the world is for itself, or for nothing at all. The individual imagination projects an existence specifically and ideally suited for the individual.

And so, Strand creates the logical Mobius strip, "Our masterpiece is the private life" (13). To create a "masterpiece"—a Strandian poem—requires creating a "private life"; yet, to create a "private life" requires creating a "masterpiece."

Part III of "Our Masterpiece" readdresses the task of private creation in the face of growing cynicism, describing it in terms of "the moment of pleasure taken / In pleasure vanishing." While the world is a place where such "pleasure" is "vanishing," for this speaker, "the moment of pleasure" taken in his and his lover's intentional ignorance of the vanishing pleasure of the natural world "seems to grow" (15–16). However, Strand never escapes completely into a Romantic vision that supplants reality. He knows that the imaginative indulgence must end, and when it does, reality will come flooding back. Thus, at his poem's conclusion, the speaker prepares for that eventuality.

Strand begins with the speaker in a liminal zone, somewhere between sea ("Roving Swan") and sky ("Star Immaculate")[6] (14), simply taking in the moment and enjoying it not *despite*, but *for* what it is—a fleeting respite from "awfulness and sorrow." When the speaker describes the moment as having "self-soiling / Beauty" (16–17), he wistfully acknowledges that the moment grows old, and as it is contemplated, it loses the purity that is concomitant with being a thought, and instead becomes *thought about*. Once that momentary spot of time passes, it "can only be what it was, sustaining itself / A little longer in its *going*" (17–18, italics mine). From here, Strand straightforwardly reveals his metaphor-making in the comparison of this fleeing moment to his and his lover's "passage . . . / Into the ordinary" (18–20), becoming what they are instead of what the imagination desired to make of them. With the effort to sustain unsuccessful, the Strand speaker finds that such effort "leav[es] us a little more tired each time, / A little more distant from the experiences which in the old days / Held us captive for hours" (20–22).

As expected, Strand leaves the reader with considerable ambivalence. If there were lasting joy in the indulging of a poem, the need to write or read a second poem would not exist. If the poem ended in a declaration of its ultimate worthlessness, this too would preclude the necessity of writing—or reading—a poem. To continue, there must be the *need* for a further attempt to create a poem that *will* work, an imaginative vision that *will* last. Thus, while Strand ends with a description of the things that used to but no longer hold them captive for hours, the writing of them here does, in effect, re-create their power. While he mourns the passing of "All the day's rewards waiting at the doors of sleep . . . ," at the poem's conclusion, promise remains (25). After all, the imagination at the end of the poem can be said to "go to sleep," and this brings "rewards": the hope of another imaginative act to recreate those imaginative acts that have gone before. One also cannot underestimate the use of the ellipsis to end the poem, suggesting in a somewhat Dickinsonian manner that there is, in fact, more to come after this lyric. This poem is certainly more than an epitaph for "The drive along the winding road / Back to the house, the sea pounding against the cliffs, / The glass of whiskey on the table, the open book, the questions" (22–24). It is a reminder of the things that *used to* bring joy, at the same time as a reminder that other things, too, may some day bring satisfaction. This is a poem as much about beginnings as endings. Those "old days" that they have grown "a little more distant" from, have been recreated in some small way here (21). Likewise, by concluding with the "open book, the questions," Strand projects the beginning—or at worst, the middle—of the relationship, where there is more to be read from the book, where there is more to learn about each other through questioning. The second part of *Blizzard of One*, then, represents a second beginning, perhaps a second route through the trials that have afflicted this poet so conspicuously thus far.

The tripartite structure that has become a favorite for Strand in this collection returns in "Morning, Noon, and Night." The poem reverberates the themes of loss and wonder, struggle and acquiescence. It also continues to illustrate the mood swings that *Blizzard* demonstrates. It begins with the poet awake and in the middle of a self-deprecating rant: "And the morning green, and the buildup of weather, and my brows / Have never been brushed, and never will be, by the breezes of divinity. / That much is clear, at least to me" (1–3). This may be viewed as Strand's *kenosis* against Strand the precursor. As Bloom reminds us, this is "a breaking device similar to the defense mechanisms our psyches employ against repetition compulsions; *kenosis* then is a movement towards discontinuity with the precursor" (*Anxiety* 14–15). Important, of course, is to note that this humbling of the self is a *seeming* "as though he were ceasing to be a poet" (*Anxiety* 15). Bloom lends further insight into Strand at this point when he says, "[I]n kenosis, the artist's battle against art has been lost, and the poet falls or ebbs into a space and time that confine him" (*Anxiety* 90). Here, Strand certainly seems confined—this time, to perpetual mediocrity—even as he seems to then take the same stance as that of the *Dark Harbor* speaker.

The speaker opens with that tone of complete surrender this "morning," then promptly relates the story of a dreamlike *yesterday* where he "noticed / Something floating in and out of clouds, something like a bird, / But also like a man, black-suited, with his arms outspread" (3–5). These lines immediately bring to mind the poet-angels from the conclusion of *Dark Harbor*. We do not need Strand to tell us that this is a good omen for the poet-speaker, but he does, anyway: "I thought this could be a sign that I've been wrong" (6). When the speaker shifts back again to negativity by saying, "Then I woke," it is easy for us to forget that he never does, in fact, even intimate that what he experienced was a dream in the first place. What he does say, when we look again, is "yesterday I noticed." Thus, we are three levels removed from the moment in this poem in a very few lines, a remarkable accomplishment from a poet who repeatedly impresses with that very ability. To be precise, this "morning" is in fact concerning yesterday, wherein the speaker awakens from a dream that is not a dream. Furthermore, the morning begins in misery, and thus asserts that the origin of today's despair is yesterday's promise. One step beyond *that*, the following section of the poem concerns the *future* as it evokes the distant past.

Few lines are as dismal as those the speaker then reveals: "on my bed the shadow of the future fell, and on the liquid ruins / Of the sea outside, and on the shells of buildings at the water's edge" (7–8). When he concludes, we are taken back to a Strand we have not seen in almost 40 years, the Strand of his first collection of poetry. Then, the "Moonhandled" speaker talked of "sleeping with one eye open, / Hoping / That nothing, nothing will happen" ("Sleeping with One Eye Open" 35–37). Here, he "stayed in bed, / Hoping it would pass" (9–10). That Strand would reach so far back to his immediate precursor's past is surprising, for his speakers have not cowered for a very long time. Either the choice to return to that poetry is a reflection of the desperation of this poet—pulling out all stops, as it were, to resurrect a poetry that will suffice—or a conscious going back to the beginning to start again.

This new poem, "Morning, Noon, and Night," goes further than merely re-creating the former. When re-reading the former to reexamine its precise language, one has the distinct—shall we say, "uncanny"—sense that "Sleeping with One Eye Open" was, in fact, a recreation of "Morning," and not the other way around. That poem ends with the cowering poet, trapped in inbetweenness. This one, despite its gyrating between assertions of hope and surrender, leaves some promise: "What might have been still waited for its chance" (10). This line, like so many others in Strand, seems to eschew attention; it *seems* to say all it needs to say for itself. Closer analysis, however, does reveal that the line is more than a cliché. After all, something that *might have been* is grammatically locked in the past; it is something that did not happen. For it to be *waiting for a chance*, then, implies hope for the future, even if the chance has not yet come.

By twisting logic in this subtle way, Strand presents a metaphysical hope that is even more potent than a rational hope could be. One gets the sense that the speaker is being torn apart by these dueling emotions, and it is revealed in the acutely commonplace tone within which these fluctuations are uttered. The strong desire to keep those emotions veiled is further revealed by the complete break in tone and sentiment between Parts I and II. The middle part of the poem adds a second personage, very likely the now-lost lover of whom we have heard much in *Blizzard of One*. It begins with the recollection that, despite seeking help from mysticism and topography, neither of them was up to the monumental task that awaited them: "Whatever the star charts told us to watch for or the maps / Said we would find, nothing prepared us for what we discovered" (1–2).

What follows is one of the more lifeless descriptions of noontime one might find: "We toiled away in the shadowless depths of noon, / While an alien wind slept in the branches, and dead leaves / Turned to dust in the streets" (3–5). Turning what one would expect of noonday on its head, Strand provides a vision of death and sterility. The irony, of course, is that at the peak of the day, death surrounds the lovers. Strand finds himself here at the nadir of vacuity. As in "The Next Time," he is uncharacteristically concerned with the space between intention and result.

While Strand's work often *considered* past events, the poetry almost always was determined to take those events and reorder them, re-create them in imaginatively useful ways. In *Blizzard of One*, the one is himself, and he is the Emersonian snowflake turning in all directions, in any way it can, to create an effect that will suffice. No matter which attempt at turning—i.e., troping—he makes, he seems to return to this latest loss. He reconsiders that loss from divergent positions, different eras in its development or dissolution, and rarely finds satisfaction. Whether he tries to change events from the middle, alter the ending, or recreate the intended outcome from the start, all attempts seem to fail, for he keeps returning to that same place with a pathetically hopeful *what if* or a self-indulgent *what we never had*. This noontime, it is the latter:

> Cities of light, long summers
> Of leisure were not to be ours; for to come as we had, long after
> It mattered, to live among tombs, great as they are,
> Was to be no nearer the end, no farther from where we began.
>   (5–8)

Part II thus ends in a futility rarely surpassed in Strand's work. As discussed, redemption comes in an infinitesimally narrow moment. Strand's sun previously *has* shown "compassion as it disappears," and he notes "something *is* always / About to happen just at the moment it serves no purpose at all" (italics mine). Here, however, the tombs are buried within an appositional phrase "great as they are" as a throwaway gesture to their magnitude. This overwhelming liminality is a place Strand is unable to escape. Ten poems into the collection, he is "no nearer the end, no farther from where we began." For a poet who has been obsessed with capturing the all-too-fleeting moment, this enduring voidlessness is alarmingly suffocating.

When Strand begins the "Night" portion of the poem with "These nights of pinks and purples vanishing, of freakish heat / That strokes our skin until we fall asleep," he continues the theme of alienation and barrenness (1–2). The violet family is once again the colors of imaginative projection, now fading from view as the "real" world takes over. Heat once again serves not to warm but to sterilize. The sleep that comes is not an inspired one, but an all-consuming one—the perfectly dark sleep of death. When Strand says that he and his companion "stray to places / We hoped would always be beyond our reach" (2–3), it evokes such themes as encompassed within poems such as "The Idea." There, he expressed this thought as "Something beyond the world we knew, beyond ourselves, / Beyond our power to imagine, something nevertheless / In which we might see ourselves" (2–4). There, the cabin he projected needed to be unoccupied for it to remain transcendent. Here, they "stray" to such a place, and it is terrifying. "We sweat and plead to be released / Into the coming day on time, and panic at the thought / Of never getting there" is stunning in three respects (5–7).

First, there is probably nowhere in the Strand corpus where one could find a Strand speaker resorting to, let alone admitting, panic. Second, this speaker is "pleading" to be "released" back into morning, but since when does Strand recognize a benevolent force that would listen to such a request? Third, and most astounding, is the fact that the speaker is desperately searching to get back to morning, where he previously "stayed in bed, / Hoping it would pass." This of course would lead to the lifeless liminality of noon, and right back into the nighttime where he would once again plead to get away. Certainly, Strand has expressed the concept of moving to "keep things whole" much earlier in his career. Here, he has provided perhaps the antithesis to that theory. After all, he *desires* to keep moving here, yet he is, in fact, immobilized by some force greater than himself. Only a poet of magnificent strength could provide such monumental obstacles to overcome in his work. Lesser poets—the "advocates of awfulness and sorrow"—would succumb to these forces, or revel in their misery, "Pushing their dripping barge up and down the beach." Poets such as Strand confront their adversaries and actively contend with the hindrances to artistic invention.

When Strand bemoans being forgotten in a place where he will be like "a drowned swimmer whose imagination has outlived his fate," it is a revealing personal statement (9). After all, this is the poet who has created a magnum opus, found a harbor away from the world's whirlwinds, niched out a place in the poetic pantheon. Now he is a dinosaur of sorts, abandoned to the relic heap of history: he is someone whose own definition of self causes his own death; whether it is a swimmer who drowns, or a poet who is smothered by his past poems, he is overwhelmed. When he "swims / To prove, to no one in particular, how false his life had been" it stands in direct contrast to previous hopes that he had not been speaking to no one, or to the satisfaction that at least he was speaking to and for himself (9–10). Now, he swims—i.e., writes—for reasons as yet unknown to him. This poet is searching to create himself anew, to get out from under precursor Strand, and yet does not have any notion as to what reason there would be to do that very thing.

One such attempt at a new beginning comes in the form of the promising "A Piece of the Storm." Audibly, little in Strand has prepared us for the Coleridgian opening, "From the shadow of domes in the city of domes, / A snowflake . . ." (1–2). The repetition of the long "o" sound initiates what the reader might hope to be a new sound to the Strand poem. When the verse continues, it reinforces that hope: "a blizzard of one, weightless, entered your room / And made its way to the arm of the chair" (2–3). Perhaps there will be an innovative effort to map out new territory here, one thinks. At least the poem *sounds* divergent. And perhaps it remains so, for the "you" addressed in this poem seems genuinely an other, unlike so many previous poems where Strand seems to be addressing the general reader or himself as such. Nonetheless, the poem returns to a Strandian tone before the sentence ends. That is, the sentence *fails* to end, in characteristic style, until the end of the fourth line, and in doing so, reminds us of the perpetual theme of mutability. That mutability here is couched within a sense of the sublime, however. Strand's addressee, "looking up / From [her] book, saw it the moment it landed. That's all / There was to it" (3–5). This temporary consciousness, this "solemn waking / To brevity" (5–6), is captured with a sense of reverence, both by the watcher and the speaker. One gets the peculiar sense that this armchair poet has been a witness to a spiritual occurrence, and Strand honors her here for her own recognition that it was a supernal event. It is a sublime passage in Strand's corpus.

In his essay, "Illusions," Emerson speaks of each god "sitting in his sphere" when a young mortal enters. "On the instant, and incessantly, fall snow-storms of illusions" (405). From this point, the mortal then "fancies himself" amid a crowd that tells him what to do, which way to move. He also "fancies himself poor, orphaned, insignificant" (405). The crowd becomes increasingly powerful and seductive, to the point where the thought of disobeying the crowd does not even occur to him; he has accepted the snowstorm crowd as reality, which baffles him at every turn. However, on occasion "the air clears, and the cloud lifts a little, there are the gods still sitting around him on their thrones,—they alone with him alone" (405). This moment of clarity is the forerunner of Strand's woman's "solemn waking / To brevity."

As Emerson's young mortal occasionally realizes he is alone with the gods, he abandons the belief that the crowd is real. He then understands that in this knowledge, he himself becomes a god—"he alone with them alone . . . they alone with him alone"—creator of his own reality. Indeed, each of us is an individual, our own god, when we *see* ourselves as such. When we get lost in the snowstorm of *appearances*, the search for some eternal truth inside the eggshell, we gods seem to ourselves and each other as a "mad crowd," a mob that "drives hither and thither" (405).

"Illusions" offers the notion that the only undeviating fact of nature is that nature itself is deviant and unknowable. But, instead of lamenting the nonexistence of a universal reality, Emerson celebrates the solipsistic empowerment of subjectivity—that *daemonic* power of creating a world for oneself. In conforming to the illusions that we believe are fixed, we delude ourselves, and lose touch with the Oversoul. The more we try to connect with the universe as something "out there," the further we get from our goal. Conversely, the more we look inward, *away* from those illusions, the more we come in contact with the universe—in that the Universe *is* ourselves.

The minute attention to the minutest of things—the life of a snowflake as it becomes captured by time—is something Strand has made his reputation on, and in "A Piece of the Storm," he is able to sustain his own interest long enough to pay homage to the *Cogito* once more. He, his "you," and his readers are momentarily rejuvenated by such keen recognition of "A time between times" (7). Certainly here, he introduces the theme with a vague sense of sadness for the death of the snowflake. In words, he calls it "a flowerless funeral" (7); but he also recognizes that—while Strand would never have the hubris to claim he has immortalized the snowflake—in writing this poem, he has provided the flowers for its funeral. And though his poem is nearly as evanescent as the eye's capturing the snowflake in its stationery position on the chair's arm, it does memorialize the latter. It also places the snowflake within the larger context—i.e., within the "piece of the storm" (8)—in a metaphoric parallel to his own chiseling of a place within the fraternity of visionary poets in *Dark Harbor*.

Certainly, on a quick first reading, Strand would have us believe the event is insignificant. He does repeat the phrase "No more than" two times in the heart of the poem. The "Except" that begins the poem's *volta*, however, forms the apotheosis of the poem:

> Except for the feeling that this piece of the storm,
> Which turned into nothing before your eyes, would come back,
> That someone years hence, sitting as you are now, might say:
> "It's time. The air is ready. The sky has an opening."
>
> (8–11)

In essence, these last four lines negate any *faux* sense of meaninglessness in this event suggested by Strand's *No more thans*. First and foremost, as discussed, this snowflake has been enhanced by Strand's associating it with some greater whole—i.e., the "piece of the storm." Despite its "turn[ing] into nothing"—a clever trope for the ineffectuality of troping, where here it remains "the thing itself"—the snowflake is given even greater prominence by having been granted— again, by the poet—lastingness. After all, the woman is imbued with this "feeling" that the snowflake—and all the inherent authority of its short indoor existence—will "come back." Furthermore, the poetic tradition will continue as a result of this minuscule event, for it is not the speaker who will utter the final line of the poem, nor the woman sitting in the armchair. It is the "someone years hence" that picks up the gauntlet, as it were, in the same way that Whitman picked it up from Emerson, Stevens from Whitman, Strand from Stevens. When this latest person recognizes that the "sky has an opening," he will be beginning again his own *Dark Harbor*. In that work, the Proem describes "a stark sea over which / The turbulent sky would drop the shadowy shapes / Of its song" (7–9). That man is "sure [of] the great space [that] would open before him" (6–7). In *Blizzard*, the sky will make space for him, but now there is less than a sureness, less than a confidence that things will go the speaker's way. Now, there is but a limited opportunity, the "sky has an opening" standing in contrast to "the great space" of the Proem. Strand is providing his own echo, yet remarkably magnifying Strand the precursor in doing so. A *daemonization* thus seems to be occurring at this point in that, as Bloom describes it:

> The later poet opens himself to what he believes to be a power in the parent-poem that does not belong to the parent proper, but to a range of being just beyond that precursor. He does this, in his poem, by so stationing its relation to the parent-poem as to generalize away the uniqueness of the earlier work. (*Anxiety* 15)

That Strand will become the inspiration for some future poet who will have to utilize the snowflake in a way that this Strand claims he is unable to do. Of course, in the doing so, this Strand *is* effectively troping, *is making* his own opening in the sky. In fact, he is making it for three poetic generations: the Strand of *Dark Harbor*, whom he is valiantly rewriting; the armchair poet within this poem; and "That someone years hence." Near the center of this collection, Strand seems to have found a voice, one that may suffice to speak out over the voice of Strand the precursor. It is a voice that *faces* ineffectuality head-on, and, though it claims to be self-denigrating, it is a voice that continues the poetic tradition in significant ways.

The poems that make up "A Suite of Appearances" build upon the nascent confidence exhibited in "A Piece of the Storm." They echo the Strandian motif of moments and try to build upon the poet's belief, however unsteady, that small things are worth celebrating. Part I opens with a question—in fact, the entire poem is comprised of two long interrogatives—of what comes from the darkness, but there is some small conviction that *something* will always emerge: "Out of what dark or lack has he come to wait / At the edge of your gaze for the moment when you / Would look up and see through the trembling leaves / His shadow suddenly there?" (1–4). As though unsatisfied with the first attempt, Strand starts again, but this time, the scenario is bleaker: "Out of what place has he come / To enter *the light that remains*" (4–5, italics mine). When "he" speaks—and one must never forget to value that gesture—he tells of his maritime passage through storms that have battered him. He is correct to note only in passing that he has crossed "over the Sea of Something" (7). Indeed, the name of any such sea would be immaterial; the voyage and arrival on this new land make the story.

The "he" is Strand, emerging on the other side of this no-man's land with a voice to at least ask questions, to try to map out new ground and try to swerve away from his precursor-self and trope "what remains." *Blizzard of One* has presented numerous examples of the Strandian speaker being "[left] where you have never been" (10). And the speaker here sounds as sincere as any we will find in Strand. Yes, this is Strand, himself, battered by love's and poetry's "opens and closes, breaks and flashes" (8), but still in possession of a voice, or at least "all that is left of his voice" (11). In fact, the poem is one of several in this collection that are almost disconcertingly personal, telling us in no uncertain terms that "this is his / Story, which continues wherever the end is happening" (11–12). Such emotional vulnerability reveals a slightly more unfamiliar Strand to replace the one now lost on the other side of the Sea of Something. The story is still about darknesses and absences, but Strand's use of the word "continues" is an exciting word choice: it represents the slightest but still reassuring sense of hope. The poetry will continue; the final, privative darkness of death will prevail, but Strand still will attempt to portion out the darkness, present small moments between the bookends of darkness. Though the outlook seemed bleak, one must not overlook that Strand reveals that this "he" *has* entered "the light that remains" (5), and though there is "only a gleam to follow," there still *is* a gleam. As Bloom reminds us, poets write to "rally everything that remains, and not to sanctify nor propound" (*Anxiety* 22). This is no false attempt to create a completely new self, or to claim in a bout of self-pity that one has thrown up one's hands in surrender to the darkness. Instead, it is one small *daemonization* for the poet, one giant leap for poetrykind. By placing himself in the position of recognizing increasingly greater challenges, Strand positions himself better to deal with such challenges.

Part II begins with a somewhat rambling exhibition that picks up thematically, and tonally—as if to deceive the reader into not recognizing that the poem is syntactically divergent—where part I left off: "No wonder—since things come into view then drop from sight —/ We clear a space for ourselves, a stillness where nothing / Is blurred" (1–2). "No wonder," is the speaker's refrain in this poem, but one *does* wonder if the speaker is sincere in his nonchalance.

As "A Suite of Appearances" unfolds, and as part II more than hints at, Strand seems to be writing a poetical autobiography of the more recent chapters of his life. Here, Strand has reached a certain calm via the imagination, and he divulges the methodology of his latest travail through watery storms. He reveals the selection of his tropes: "a common palm, an oasis in which to rest, to sit / For hours beside the pool while the moonlight builds its palaces" (3–4). Once again, however, Strand pushes aside the details of the trials, yet instead of naming them the Sea of Something as he did in part I, here he states: "no wonder what happened / Before tonight, the history of ourselves, leaves us cold" (8–9). In refusing to discuss "the history of ourselves," of course Strand does just that. He may claim that it leaves him cold, but it does burn inside him, hence the need to discuss it by not discussing it. That "the evening paper lies unread" does not state that the news is not desired; it reveals that yesterday is too painful to read. For now, however, Strand seems able to remain in the moment, and as tenuously as he hangs on to today and its small successes, he *is* hanging on, in much the same way the conclusion of part I displayed him as having *something* left of his voice.

Perhaps the hub of *Blizzard of One* is the luminary, if Stevensian, "A Suite of Appearances" part III:

> How it comes forward, and deposits itself like wind
> In the ear which hears only the humming at first, the first
> Suggestion of what is to come, how it grows out of itself,
>
> Out of the humming because if it didn't it would die
> In the graveyard of sound without being known, and then
> Nothing would happen for days or weeks until something like it
>
> Came back, a sound announcing itself as your own, a voice
> That is yours, bending under the weight of desire,
> Suddenly turning your language into a field unfolding
>
> And all the while the humming can still be detected, the original
> Humming before it was yours, and you lie back and hear it,
> Surprised that what you are saying was something you meant,
>
> And you think that perhaps you are not who you thought, that henceforth
> Any idea of yourself must include a body surrounding a song.

When Strand begins part III with "How it comes forward," it is easy for readers to temporarily suspend their inclination to ask, "What is *it*?" and merely read further. A simple reference back to that looming pronoun does not come, however, and serious rumination is required before dispensing of that question, for it is the central concern of the poem.

That being said, this poem also is vital to our discussion of precursors. "[T]he original / Humming before it was yours" (10–11), echoes

Stevens' "The Idea of Order at Key West," where the song the woman sings is shown to be "beyond the genius of the sea," though:

> The song and water were not medleyed sound
> Even if what she sang was what she heard,
> Since what she sang was uttered word by word. . . .
> But it was she and not the sea we heard.
> For she was the maker of the song she sang.
>
> (9–15)

It may be the humming of the sea Stevens' woman has heard, yet it is also the humming that Strand has heard, and it is also the humming of the poets he has read and translated, and his own poetry that he has necessarily appropriated and is attempting to rewrite for himself as the new Great Dog.

This eloquent "it" is, at first, true inspiration. It does, after all, "deposit . . . itself like wind / In the ear" (2–3). Strand at his best is difficult not only to paraphrase (which is only correct), but also difficult to parse. At his best, his syntax can be maddeningly convoluted, with subjects being confounded with objects, and dependent clauses suppressing independent ones. This poem is a superior illustration of that practice. Initially, we readers are asked to consider the "it" that "comes forward," and keep that "it" in our minds while reading on. Before the second line is concluded, however, we are forced to consider the dependent clause, "the ear which hears only the humming at first." That being apprehended, we are bombarded by a third redirection, the apparent appositional statement, "the first / Suggestion of what is to come." The comma that ensues is the first significant break the reader gets before continuing.

So, we return to the beginning to piece together the descriptive progression of this inspirational force. At the outset, the "it" arrives as an outside force, a seed, if you will, that enters the ear of the listener perhaps accidentally, but certainly uninvited. The ear then immediately picks up the gauntlet, both conceptually and syntactically, in a masterful equilibrium of form and function. It is almost as though the nearly instantaneous presentation of this force is happening to us as readers, as well. For before we can pause to consider the wind's deposit, we are now conscious of the humming in our ear, which automatically triggers a suggestion that more is to come. It is almost natural that we would expect some growing "out of itself" to follow.

But when Strand picks up with—remember, we are still in the first *three-line* stanza—with "how it grows out of itself," the reader is likely to read the phrase too quickly as a restatement of the *first* words of the poem. Though appearing as an appositive itself, "how it grows out of itself" serves more as a correction of the initial "How it comes forward." That being accepted, we are thus being asked to (1) keep in mind the coming forward, depositing, the humming, and the suggestion of what is to come; while, (2) *at the same time* consider that it may be an inaccurate, or at least an insufficient, description.

Subsequently, we confront another rapid-fire presentation of the aural phenomenon in stanza two. As we were likely to misread the "growing out of itself" in line three, we are also likely to misapprehend the *next* in the series of apparent appositives: "Out of the humming." After all, this humming was earlier described as merely the *first* thing the ear hears, "the first / Suggestion of what is to come," and certainly not the entire phenomenon. Now the humming itself is the seed within the seed. But before we can get our minds around the concept securely, the conceptualization progresses, and the speaker tells us that "if it didn't it would die / In the graveyard of sound without being known." In a remarkable turn, Strand transforms potential fertile ground immediately into burial ground.

Before one concretizes the concept that the fate of the unheeded inspiration is eternal death—i.e., opportunity only knocks once—Strand's continuation merely says, "Nothing would happen for *days or weeks*" (italics mine). Then follows a second repetition. If the first "it" came forward and deposited itself in the ear, and the second grows out of itself, then the third is "something like it [that] / Came back," and this time it comes from within. In very much the same way Emerson has identified books as a source of wisdom but the real spirit of genius in the self, this inspiration has been transformed into "a sound announcing itself as your own." It is important to remark that the sound is not identified as *being* one's own, but merely as *announcing itself* as such. And, as such, this easily reminds us of Bloom's term *kenosis*, wherein Strand's "stance *appears* to be that of his precursor . . . but the meaning of the stance is undone; the stance is *emptied* of its priority, which is a kind of godhood, and the poet holding it becomes more isolated" (*Anxiety* 90).

But Strand goes further here, and his poem of *kenosis* may in fact be a poem of *daemonization*. The sound that previously was identified as being external to the listener has, after its third recurrence, become something like his own by now. In fact, one apparent appositional phrase later "—a voice / That is yours"— the sound *is* his own. This poem is a brilliant illumination of the anxiety of influence, or at least of poetic inspiration. After all, as Bloom has said, "The daemons make by breaking. . . . When the ephebe is daemonized, his precursor necessarily is humanized, and a new Atlantic floods outward from the new poet's transformed being" (*Anxiety* 100). Strand relates how his process occurs only after "bending under the weight of desire," before "Suddenly turning your language into a field unfolding." Few places can one find a poet's self-expression better depicted than as a "turning [of] language into a field unfolding."

Strand's poem then dutifully returns to its premise—the recognition of what has been borrowed as becoming one's own: "[A]ll the while the humming can still be detected, the original / Humming before it was yours." Make no mistake about it, the humming *is* now his, transformed from what it was—even if what it was *was* one's own—to what it is. As Stevens has said of his singer in "The Idea of Order at Key West":

> She was the single artificer of the world
> In which she sang. And when she sang, the sea,
> Whatever self it had, became the self
> That was her song, for she was the maker.
>   (37–40)

Strand then reveals his *own* artificing of the world by bringing back the language and motif previously expressed in "The Next Time": "you lie back and hear it, / Surprised that what you are saying was something you meant." Informed by the previous considerations of this theme of sounds-intentions-outcomes in "The Next Time," this line exhibits Strand as having successfully rewritten his precursor. But it also reveals that success—and more—in that it is a startlingly hopeful revelation on the part of the poem's *you*. *Success at last*, Strand may have written here, with sarcasm or sincerity. And with that breathtaking revelation, sunlight appears on the horizon, and all that comes after must now be informed by *this* poem, *this* strong poet, not the one of *Dark Harbor*, for, now "perhaps you are not who you thought . . . [and] / Any idea of yourself must include a body surrounding a song." This astonishing conclusion of course ties back into Stevens yet again. There, "The water never formed to mind or voice, / Like a body wholly body, fluttering / Its empty sleeves" (2–4). Here, the body *is* wholly body, its formerly empty sleeves in Stevens now filled by song. Thus, Strand has created a tremendous work of inclusion, a marvelous paean to the capability of poetry!

Part IV of "A Suite of Appearances" is perhaps the most loosely connected of the six poems, at least in terms of sentiment, if not sound. Like the first three parts, it too begins twice. Here the refrain is "In another time." Of note is the fact that the Strand speaker here includes himself in the future he speaks of: "In another time, we will want to know how the earth looked / Then, and were people the way we are now" (1–2). Also of note is the fact that that selfsame speaker absents himself from the present even as he speaks of the future to which he does not yet belong: "The records *they* left will convince *us* that *we* are unchanged" (3, italics mine). That said, the poem out-wardly seems to be merely the display of a well-used tool in Strand's belt—the erasure of self to make one's present more palpable.

What distances this poem from most previous Strandian exercises of absence, however, is the possibility of continuity. After all, here the speaker is confident that he "could be at ease in the past, and not alone in the present" (4). It is a far cry from the speaker of "Keeping Things Whole," who was alone and uneasy in the field. Then, only in the past—after having left the field—could he be at ease with nature, and that at the expense of the "new" present, where he would have to move to keep *that* present whole. In part IV of "A Suite of Appearances," he leaves the reader shocked by the plainly stated "And we shall be pleased" (5). Again, this is an extraordinary statement for a poet so consciously running downhill, trying to capture the moment as it races by him. The third time he repeats "In another time," he refines his own age-old philosophy:

> What cannot be seen will define us, and we shall be prompted
>
> To say that language is error, and all things are wronged
> By representation. The self, we shall say, can never be
> Seen with a disguise, and never been seen without one.
>
> (9–12)

Of course, this is Stevens' stand, too. Any attempt to reach pure being is doomed to fail, yet the desire to attempt it is too great to ignore attempting. The more the poem tries to reenact a scene, or re-create an image or object, the more that poetic action, that new creation takes the place of the image, object, or scene. Pack well states Stevensian thinking when he discusses "The Snow Man": "Stevens dramatizes the action of a mind as it becomes one with the scene it perceives, and at that instant, the mind having ceased to bring something of itself to the scene, the scene then ceases to exist fully" ("Wallace Stevens"). In Strand, the mind attempts to keep itself from entering the scene it per-ceives, for once it commences to bring something of itself to the scene, the scene ceases to be *the scene it was* and instead becomes *the scene transformed by the act of the mind engaging the scene.* Of course, as Spiegelman recognizes, "the evasions of metaphor are unavoidable; poetry, as a thing of tropes, sounds, and semantic structures, must always retain part of its mystery in order to remain itself" (134).

Part V reveals Strand relying on simile to promote his motifs, and when he does, he is often less extraordinary. At the heart of this initially engaging revision of "A Piece of the Storm" is the description of the falling snowflakes: "In their descent / They are like stars overtaken by light, or like thoughts / That drift before the long, blank windows facing the future" (4–6). The double-take simile does not work as effectively as his apparent appositives did in the previous installments of "A Suite of Appearances." They come across as mere retractions, rather than any metacognitive doubling back.

The poem continues the philosophical stop-and-think consideration of part IV, but for the first time in the suite, the poem does not repeat its opening words. Instead, it returns to the Strand motifs of absence and darkness. Its opening is hardly new or breathtaking: "To sit in this chair and wonder where is endlessness / Born, where does it go, how close has it come" strikes the experienced Strand reader as a bit of a cliché (1–2). Considering how often Strand has *engaged* the theme of endlessness—by way of its antithesis, transience—to state that one is sitting in a chair merely *considering* the theme provides little excitement. Certainly lines and phrases crop up to provide some engagement: "the flakes enlarging whatever they touch," for example (3), is in the Dante tradition by way of Stevens.

The poem's only expression of potency comes in its final four lines, where Strand discusses the snowflakes' resting place. "Where nothing is needed or said because it is already known" (9) again echoes Stevens in its concern to reach perfect absence: the desire for perfect poetry is the desire for no poem at all, for to reach a place where one's words are furthest from metaphor and closest to the thing described is to attempt to say no thing at all.

The last stanza brings us to a familiar place with an unfamiliar approach: "And when it is over, and the deep, unspeakable reaches of white / Melt into memory, how will the warmth of the fire, / So long in coming, keep us from mourning the loss?" (10–12). Few times in his corpus does Strand allow us to see past the melting moment and into the negating, privative darkness that supervenes. This poem wallows in it, and perhaps this is one explanation for the poem's lethargy. The snowflakes reach the culmination of disappearance in line four. Their final fleeting moments are recreated in the middle two stanzas, and the ultimate apogee of their existence is in the aforementioned place "[w]here nothing is needed or said because it is already known." The final stanza, then, presents the pathos of their absence. Of course, the flakes echo in "memory," but Strand has allowed a thing's existence to echo in better ends to finer poems. Finally, the last line-and-a-half is spent considering the absence that is *to come* even before the flakes have disappeared from memory. Thus, the sense of Strand's "mourning the loss" is multiplied, for these are the words that echo at the poem's end, not the words or images of the thing itself. Indeed, the thing itself here is replaced by the mournful feelings *about* the thing itself after it is no longer here. As in earlier passages of *Blizzard of One*, Strand has presented a kind of negative version of his own attempts to save what is worth saving, and instead saves what replaces the thing that was worth saving.

One would expect, then, that the concluding poem of the suite would be an attempt to amend that "mistake," and bring the thing itself back to its rightful place, at the forefront of memory, in the spotlight of the moment. Part VI is another prosaic example of Strand apparently trying to explain much of his poetic philosophy in less uncertain words. Metaphorically insubstantial lines such as "There is a limit to what we can picture / And to how much of a good thing is a good thing" come to the fore and seem to take control of the poem (5–6). To be fair, the poem does not attempt to be difficult. After all, accounting for syntax, the speaker is "tired": "Of occasions flounced with rose and gold in which the sun / Sinks deep and drowns in a blackening sea, of those, and more" (1–2). He seems to trail off, tired of the harvest he himself desired.

What to do with a poem that expresses fatigue at writing poetry? Indeed, Strand has labored in this collection. Here, he apparently has written himself into a corner. The first half of the poem contains a fatalistic sense that, while present in various doses throughout Strand's career, here seems to dominate the poem. At other moments, Strand might have used the phrase "when it goes as it must" to different ends. Here, he uses it to convince the listener—and himself?—to abandon all hope, "So, when it goes as it must, no sense of loss springs in its wake" (9).

When he returns to the ostensible waters of childhood in the second half of the poem, it evokes tones of such mid-career poems as "Pot Roast," "Shooting Whales" or those in *The Story of Our Lives*. In those efforts, Strand's "untelling" of them made them larger by their absence. Here, he seems to desire to make them simply absent: "The houses, the gardens, the roaming dogs, let them become / The factors of absence, an incantation of the ineffable" (10–11). The role of metaphor in Strand's poetry has been a central concern in his career. Here, instead of trying to capture the very slippery thing itself, Strand appears to trumpet the notion of leaving the thing be. "I seem to have stopped falling; now I am *fallen*," Strand may have quoted Bloom at this point, "consequently, I lie here in Hell" (*Anxiety* 45). But, as Bloom reminds, the strong poet "is thinking, as he says this, 'As I fell, *I swerved*, consequently I lie here in a Hell improved by my own making' " (*Anxiety* 45). Strand recalls a few sights and sounds in the poem, but without attempting to flesh them out with detail—which of course would be transforming them further from themselves—he states merely, "What more is there?" Instead of providing any sense of nobility at leaving them unaltered, undisturbed in memory, Strand flicks them away with the back of his hand: "What more is there? The odors of food, / The last traces of dinner, are gone. The glasses are washed" (13–14). Tonally, he could have stopped there, but the litany continues with a surprising positive backward glance: "The neighborhood sleeps. / Will the same day ever come back, and with it / Our amazement at having been in it[?]" (14–16).

Of course, he knows the question is rhetorical: the same day will not return. But in most previous poems, Strand may have left room for another day to take its place, or at least tried to sweep this past day from memory. Here, as in the penultimate poem of the "Suite," Strand allows not the day to echo, but the erasure. At the same time, he looks back on this day with some wistfulness. His fear: "will only a dark haze / Spread at the back of the mind, erasing events, one after / The other, so brief they may have been lost to begin with?" (16–18). Strand has reduced desires in "Suite of Appearances" to such infinitesimally small moments that they are not moments at all, but mere "appearances" of moments.

"Here" immediately strikes the reader as being a pacific poem of drought, the very antithesis to part VI of "A Suite of Appearances." The sense of losing events that "may have been lost to begin with" is replaced here by the tiniest shred of hope. That it is small, however, does not detract from its power. After all, it is the difference between poetic suicide—deciding never to write because one can never capture what has been lost to begin with—and to write in the face of the fear that one can never capture what has been lost to begin with. This is a colossal turnabout, and Strand magnificently presents that within a nihilistic, postapocalyptic framework.

From the opening, we do not recognize that this place from which the speaker speaks is suffering from unrelenting heat. We understand the opening image to be fairly maleficent: "The sun that silvers all the buildings here / Has slid behind a cloud, and left the once bright air / Something less than blue" (1–3). The sun, in its "silvering" of the buildings, initially sounds like a positive force. However, its absence does leave the formerly "*bright* air/ Something *less than* blue" (italics mine). Though we recognize some sadness in these phrases, the tenor of the words is pleasing, and, as the speaker says, after the sun's temporary absence, "Yet everything is clear" (3). This is Strand at his best, push-pulling the reader toward a horrific landscape with prepossessing language.

The first hints at the sterility of this world follow: "Across the road, some dead plants dangle down from rooms / Unoccupied for months" (4–5). Here Strand's language echoes Stevens' "Of Mere Being," wherein a singing, gold-feathered bird's "fire-fangled feathers dangle down" at its conclusion (12). That poem presented a peaceful—dare one actually say happy—tone concerning Stevens' first idea. This one's stance seems antithetical. It is no gorgeous bird whose singing delights; it is dead foliage that droops. It does not take long before the reader learns to recognize this as a poem about the death of poetry. For Strand, of course, this is a common occurrence. As he has said, "I believe that the anxiety of self-imitation is the great anxiety of the poet." Once again, Strand is facing the creative abyss, and, because dark is often a fruitful metaphor, this poem is submerged in an appalling light.

This apocalyptic world does its best, then, to include another magnificent poet, Emily Dickinson. When Strand writes, "on a nearby hill some tombs, / Half buried in a drift of wild grass, appear to merge / With houses at the edge of town," one can only be reminded of Dickinson's #712. Strand's dedicated reference to poetry and poets in this sad, sad poem, continues with its best moments, at the center of itself:

> A breeze
> Stirs up some dust, turns up a page or two, then dies.
> All the boulevards are lined with leafless trees.
> There are no dogs nosing around, no birds, no buzzing flies.
> Dust gathers everywhere— . . .
> (8–12)

Of course we recognize breath as the central creative force, from as far back as Genesis, and frequently in Strand's corpus. This breeze that stirs up some dust, is certainly the attempt to create that plagues Strand in this collection. It echoes Eliot's "Prufrock" in sound and sentiment. That poem struggled with its own starts and stops, its own attempts to get out from under the precursors, Shakespeare and Michelangelo. Here, the creative breath is but a breeze, and it can but blow only "a page or two, then dies." The boulevards "lined with leaf-less trees" are of course, unwritten poems, from a Whitmanian tradition. The dogs that are absent are Strandian dogs, and as the poet has said, "Of course, I always equated dogs with the poet" (Interview, Jan. 26, 2002). The birds and buzzing flies that would sail on the winds of song are also absent. Hence, with no breath to create life in this dead city, all that can congregate in the normal places of life—in bars, stores, and cars—is dust. Visually, this place also is evocative of Hemingway's *The Sun Also Rises.*

Strand goes further now, to take one of his infrequent stabs at organized religion. The church's primary metonymic device here is its "massive, rotting doors," not an altar or statue (15). Meanwhile, inside, the visitor is given the *opportunity* to "kneel and pray" (17), but Strand makes it clear that more likely the visitor will only:

> . . . watch the dirty light pour through the baldachin,
> Or think about the heat outside that does not go away,
> Which might be why there are no people there—who knows—
> Or about the dragon that he saw when he arrived,
> Curled up before its cave in saurian repose,
> And about how good it is to be survived.
>
> (18–23)

In this way, the poem brings to mind Stevens' "A High-Toned Old Christian Woman." There, Stevens unravels religious symbolism by proposing "The conscience is converted into palms, / Like windy citherns hankering for hymns" (4–5), and "our bawdiness . . . / Is equally converted into palms, / Squiggling like saxophones" (9–12). Here, Strand's church is desanctified by references to "massive, rotting doors" and "dirty light" pouring in through the stained-glass windows. Since stained glass is a visual narrative, the dirty light thus taints the message of the story—the fate of the "intended story" of "The Next Time" and "Morning, Noon, and Night."

Initially, the reader recognizes this church as the place where perhaps the visitor would go to seek an end to the relentless heat. But what happens with the visitor, and with the reader, is that, perhaps not unlike King Claudius from Hamlet, his mind wanders from its prayerful task. Instead, he watches "the dirty light pour through the baldachin," or his mind cannot become unfocused from the oppressive heat.

Then, pursuing that thought, he considers the heat as the reason "why there are no people there—who knows." In an unsettling paean to the fantastic, the visitor then turns his mind to "the dragon that he saw when he arrived, / Curled up before its cave in saurian repose" which vaguely feels like Yeats' "rough beast [that] slouches towards Bethlehem" ("The Second Coming" 21–22). The last line, read ironically or not, is one of the more frightening in Strand. Is it indeed "good . . . to be survived" by the saurian beast? Whether or not the speaker truly feels glad to be survived is debatable. Nonetheless, there is a passing of the torch, so to speak, from poetry to stagnancy, from Christianity to paganism—but this is not to equate poetry with Christianity, of which certainly Strand would not approve. Though reminiscent of so many others, this is one of Strand's more startlingly original, visionary poems.

The final irony in this mourning of the death of poetry involves the typically Strandian title. Strand's speaker is usually quite intent, focused on capturing the *Cogito*—the quintessence of a moment or a place. In "Here," the speaker ends up ruminating about anything *but* where he is. This speaker is unfocused, his mind wandering from one image to the next, even to the point of giving himself up—to the dragon, perhaps?

By the time Strand commences Part III, "Five Dogs" seems as much a summation as an expansion of the drama provided in the earlier efforts. The drama of loss and recovery has played itself out in the first two parts. Part III may be recognized as a précis of the travails. Emerging on the other side of the liminal zone—after all, this is someone who has celebrated primitive absences recently having had a more enduring privative absence become the prevalent theme of his life—the Strandian speaker provides five stages of existence, five possible scenarios.[7]

Part IV of *Blizzard of One* continues to unravel, from one particular perspective. That is to say, any sense of continuity established in parts I, the first half of part II and part III, is interrupted here. Or, more precisely, with the clever yet emotionally resonant "The Delirium Waltz" and its interlaced lines as the centerpiece of section IV, any repeatable motif one might desire to find would be eminently interrupted by this poem. "In Memory of Joseph Brodsky," however, would be worth exploring in light of previous discussions of remaking the self. At first glance, it is an unremarkable and almost clumsy poem. The abundant references to unwinding and absences the speaker provides seem to present their case with unnecessary overstatement. So many motifs for the same idea initially appear to lapse into clichés.

Okay, we get it already, one might be inclined to say were one not to read along carefully and see that Strand is not merely declaring a string of appositives.

From the outset, we expect that this poem has at its heart some elegiac intent. It begins with a properly—in the face of death, of course—passive proclamation, "It could be said." What follows is a remarkably omnipresent losing of the self that never ultimately reaches complete silence. By my count, Strand provides a string of 12 separate unwindings—or erasures or silencings—of the self in the first sentence of the poem. There is the initial *unwinding* of the "remains of the self / . . . into a *vanishing* light" (1–2, italics mine). The third silencing is the self, which "thins like dust," before it then, in a tripartite erasure, "heads / To a place where knowing and nothing pass into each other, and through" (2–3). The seventh movement toward oblivion is a mere "That it moves, unwinding still" (4), but again where it moves is to a place that itself is defined as a silencing, erasure, or darkness: "beyond the vault of brightness ended" (4). Ultimately, the self "continues to a place which may never be found" (5), and *that* place is defined as one "where the unsayable, / Finally, once more is uttered" (5–6). Still, that utterance, which one might expect to be the final sentence of the self, is uttered "lightly, quickly, like random rain" (6). Strand has thus removed the self even further from the poem by turning it into a simile—rain—which itself then moves further into silence and darkness, for it "passes in sleep" (7). Before that seven-line sentence ends, Strand provides a last, twelfth passing in the apparently appositional but actually oppositional correction of the rain that passes in sleep: "that one imagines passes in sleep" (7). If one's head begins to spin while calculating the levels of detachment Strand is providing, that is because Strand *wants* the reader to see how far the self unwinds, yet also that the journey is so long that it approaches infinity.

Strand then recommences with his second sentence, one that is much less figurative, much more plainspoken: "What remains of the self unwinds and unwinds," he says, perhaps unnecessarily, for the tangents of the first sentence has made that point clear (8). Neither does he need to say, "none / Of the boundaries holds," yet he makes clearer the poem's intent when he explains what boundaries he means: "neither the shapeless one between us, / Nor the one that falls between your body and your voice" (9–10). In this second part of the poem, Strand more obviously signifies the poet's power by attributing to Brodsky "the places / And times whose greatest life was the one you gave them" (11–12). When Strand likens those places and times to "ghosts in your wake," it is a surprising simile. After all, one might expect to hear someone say that one's memories of the deceased friend return "as clearly as if they happened yesterday." But Strand's ghost trope is no insult here; it is instead a reminder of the ever-present evanescence of the poet's life. Strand is not likely to resort to outlandish hyperbole that does not ring true. Instead, he allows Brodsky to echo infinitely, approaching infinity.

The ultimate unwinding of the self comes in a surprising last sentence that dismantles itself in a Cummings-esque burst: "What remains of the self unwinds / Beyond us, for whom time is only a measure of meanwhile / And the future no more than et cetera et cetera . . . but fast and forever" (13–15). When we reach this concluding unwinding, we realize the poem too has unwound—or rather is unwinding immeasurably *toward* silence while ostensibly never reaching total silence. This is a reversal—or more precisely an attenuated extension—of Strandian poetics, though one Strand has indulged in such places as "The Untelling" and "Elegy for my Father." Despite the desire to reach immortality, Strand is deeply conscious of temporal limitations upon the poem—and the poet. That is, a poem is performing its sole role of *being* a poem only while being read. Here, Brodsky is dead, but he—and the poem—is in a continual stage of *dying*, and is thus perpetually *not* dead. Through poetic manipulation, the poem does not end with the final words, but rather whispers itself infinitely quieter, yet infinitely present. Bloom is certainly correct when he reminds us that

> all major elegies for poets, do not express grief but center upon their composers' own creative anxieties. They offer therefore as consolation their own ambitions . . . or if they are beyond ambition then they offer oblivion. . . . [T]he later poets, confronting the imminence of death, work to subvert the immortality of their precursors, as though any one poet's afterlife could be metaphorically prolonged at the expense of another's. (*Anxiety* 151)

As such the Brodsky elegy may, in fact, be the strongest revisionary movement Strand makes in this collection away from his own *The Story of Our Lives*. Again, the apparent clarity of the poem masks a magnificent complexity. But another strong poem follows.

"What It Was" revisits "The Idea," from *The Continuous Life*. That poem celebrated the imagination in a way that most of the early parts of *Blizzard of One* seem incapable of even contemplating; such is the weight of "the weather of leavetaking." There Strand had discussed the desire to reach "beyond the world we knew, beyond ourselves, / Beyond our power to imagine, something nevertheless / In which we might see ourselves" (2–4). Here, the dilemma is more of an enigma: "It was impossible to imagine, impossible / Not to imagine" (1–2). One might say that while the theme of both poems is identical, the opening tone marks the divergence in the poems. The first poem's speaker expresses a far-reaching idealism. The second's has provided himself a no-win situation: he desires to imagine something that is impossible to imagine, then, having failed at that, desires to *not* imagine that same something that is now impossible *not* to imagine. As Bloom says, for the poet "rebelling more strongly against the consciousness of death's necessity than all other men and women do . . . from his start as a poet he quests for an impossible object" (*Anxiety* 10).

Nonetheless, it is there, in its remarkable "blueness," which is expected to fill "the dark with the chill of itself" (2–3). In "The Idea," Strand let the idea speak of and for itself. It was and contained only an "it." Here, Strand's "it" has its "blueness." This poem's attempt to capture a smallness of infinite proportions is much like what Strand does in his Brodsky elegy. The duplication of darkness here attempts in one way to cancel out darkness while at the same time helping it to endure indefinitely. It begins with its blueness, but Strand further distances us from it—or it from itself—by having its "shadow," not its "self" do the "[f]alling downward" (3). Furthermore, it is its shadow which fills the dark—another duplicate darkness—but what it fills the darkness with is "the chill of itself," and not the shadow of itself which had fallen downward. Furthermore, when Strand continues the monumental unfinished sentence that is this poem, he no longer discusses the blueness of itself, or its shadow, or the chill of itself, but rather "[t]he cold of it," which then falls "out of itself" (4). But to make it even more protean, Strand corrects himself in an apparent appositional statement, and says not that the cold of it was falling out of itself but rather, "out of whatever *idea* / Of itself it described as it fell" (4–5, italics mine). Indeed, Strand has so convoluted our idea of the imaginatively unimaginable that it is its own idea of itself that is being described as it falls. This illuminates Bloom's revisionary ratio of *daemonization*, in that he "opens himself to what he believes to be a power in ['The Idea'] that does not belong to ['The Idea'], but to a range of being just beyond that [poem]. He does this [in 'What it Was'] by so stationing its relation to ['The Idea'] as to generalize away the uniqueness of the earlier work." Here, the self that this cold blue thing is, exists only *because* it describes an idea of itself even as it falls—swerves, one is inclined to think.

Strand seems to begin again after the second semicolon in line five, as though the attempt to capture the uncapturable needed a new trope. Now the "it" is "a something, a smallness, / A dot, a speck, a speck within a speck, an endless depth / Of smallness" (5–7). Again, as in his elegy to Joseph Brodsky, Strand allows his speaker to be perceived as floundering in his description. He may as well have culled from Eliot: "And this, and so much more?—/ It is impossible to say just what I mean!" ("The Love Song of J. Alfred Prufrock" 103–4). He does not do that, but rather he allows for the speaker to ramble in his attempt to define infinite smallness—which, of course, once described, would no longer be infinitely small, because it would become static, cease shrinking. This place might be recognizable as Poulet's *Cogito*, "reduction of all to a central point" (Miller 484). This central point, Miller says, is the "source of all, and at various places within consciousness all the objects of consciousness are located in a moving totality which sometimes expands to infinity and sometimes contracts to a point, but always remains enclosed in itself" (484). Strand writes the same idea as: "the last of it, the blank of it, / The tender small blank of it filling its echo, and falling, / And riding unnoticed, and falling again, and always thus . . ." (9–11).

After the next semicolon, in line 7, we recognize the pattern: the speaker starts anew. Color did not work, nor heat, nor size. Now he will try sound: "What it was" was "a song, but less than a song, something drowning / Into itself, something going, a flood of sound, but less / Than a sound" (7–9). The first attempt described a falling out of itself; here the something is described as a drowning into itself. One attempt is a birthing, the second a dying, but in either case the active *process* of becoming is evidenced by the repeated use of the present participial form of verbs—drowning, going, and so on. Once the action ceases, the subject of the poem becomes stagnant and describable, and thus less than what it was. In a revision of "Keeping Things Whole," Strand describes this "what it was" as a perpetually moving object, every bit as mobile as the earlier poem's speaker, but far more slippery.

The speaker of the former poem claims that he is anomalous in the natural world. Just as the Stevens' jar gives order to the slovenly wilderness in "Anecdote of a Jar," so too does this human projection of self "part the air" (9), disturbing the world's perfect slovenliness. The speaker and the world are estranged; there is a dichotomous nature between the poet's identification of self and his understanding of the world: "Wherever I am / I am what is missing" (6–7). He is, in other words, a perpetual outsider in every situation, so long as he is conscious of that situation. Of course, the converse would be as follows: if one is *not* conscious of oneself in any given environment, then one becomes one with that environment—e.g., while imaginatively engrossed in a momentary experience. However, once one becomes conscious of the self, the delicate equipoise is disturbed, and one immediately returns to outsider status.

In "What It Was," Strand's attempt to state with certainty what "it" is turns out to be as elusive a proposition as placing oneself within nature and defining that. In his final attempts, Strand returns to visual representation of the thing itself by referring to "the last of it, the blank of it" (9). With those words, Strand seems to allow it to pass into nonexistence, but his final three lines then deny *that* possibility, allowing—as we might have expected from an earlier Strand than the one in this collection—the absence of the thing itself to represent the thing itself in as strong a way as the presence of it ever could: "The tender small blank of it filling its echo, and falling, / And rising unnoticed, and falling again, and always thus, / And always because, and only because, once having been, it was . . ." (9–12). At first glance, this is one of the more remarkable conclusions to a Strand poem one has ever seen. After all, as Strand has said, "I don't believe in any kind of afterlife or anything of that sort. When we are gone, we are gone" (Interview, Jan. 26, 2002). But here, Strand propounds an eternal life of some type. After all, the concluding words "it was . . ." refer us back to the opening words, "It was." Thus, we necessarily read that the thing continues to exist as an *idea* of what it was. It "exists" not as itself but as something transformed by memory, *this* thing, this *poem*. Thus Strand returns importance to *this* thing and not the *that* thing it was. Few times does Strand exhibit such transformative capacities, and as such provides one of his more astonishing poems.

If part I of "What It Was" is a poem of privative darkness, the going away of things, the absenting of self, the returning to nothingness that speaks louder than the presence does, then part II is a scattered attempt to recreate from the abyss. If part I is a poem of privative darknesses, part II begins in the place that ensues: a primitive darkness. From just such a place Strand is able to paint a picture, one brushstroke at a time, filling in the blank spaces created by privative erasures. "It was the beginning of a chair," Strand begins, and the poem thus immediately echoes "A Piece of the Storm," within which the subject sat in a chair and watched as the single snowflake landed. Here, Strand marks the first image as but "the beginning" of a chair, and not as an entire chair. This forces the reader to ask then, *Just what is the beginning of a chair?* Of course, it is an *idea* of a chair, is the answer, and not a chair at all. From here, Strand builds upon his ideas, advancing in outward attempts to describe rather than reduce to a smallest blank as he did in part I. Nonetheless, this second part still may be identified as an echo of Poulet's *Cogito*. As Miller reminds us, "The other possibility [of the development of the *Cogito*] is an expansive diffusion of that point until it includes everything as . . . a stone dropped in water will start a series of concentric circles radiating outward to infinity" (484).

As in part I, Strand uses semicolons to separate each attempt to, in this case, paint; in the former case, to describe a picture that will suffice. When Strand proceeds to render the portraiture of "the way / The ruined moonlight fell across her hair," it demonstrates a different tack than the first part of "What It Was" (3–4). After all, now there is immediate connotation to this image. Furthermore, Strand adulterates pure portrayal by providing the pathetic fallacy of "ruined moonlight," which is very much akin to his "dirty light" of "Here." Perhaps he allows his speaker to begin to indulge in self-pity at this point, to recognize that he fails in his attempt to capture the moment with unadorned integrity. Hence, the period, followed by the Prufrockian "And this, and so much more" admission: "It was that, and it was more" (5). So, recognizing the failed attempt, the speaker begins again: "It was the wind that tore / At the trees;" he says, but stops with a semicolon, recognizing the undesired personification of "tore" (5). Then he attributes "fuss and clutter" to clouds, before describing the shore as being "[l]ittered with stars" (6–7). It is almost a clinical Poetry 101 lesson: the speaker is having a bad day, and thus all things in nature are "ruined."

Strand continues after the second sentence to lapse into personification and abstraction, rather than hold steadfast in his attempt to capture an image precisely *as it is.* Or perhaps one might say that Strand has attempted to capture the *essence* of emotion. By the time Strand makes his eighth attempt at defining "What it was," in attributing speaking powers to "the hour" (7), readers should recognize that this is a very different poem from part I's attempt to pinpoint "it." Here he repeatedly attempts to attribute accurate metaphors to "it," providing movement increasingly upward and outward away from the subject itself toward Pouletian infinity, rather than trying to strip abstraction down to its very essence.

Midway through the poem, then, Strand personifies nature (in the form of "the hour") in a lukewarm attempt to bring about some fear of death—and of imposed guilt for having ignored death's power—on the speaker's part. "[I]f you knew what time it really was, you would not / Ask for anything again" (8–9), he echoes from "The Next Time." Of course, it is important to note that the hour did not in fact say these words, but only "seemed to say" them. Again, the onus of the ruined night—the ruined life?—is on the speaker, not nature itself. When Strand ends the ninth line with "It was that. It was certainly that," he seems to be giving only lip service to the initial nine-line stanza. In other words, it sounds as if he is saying, "Okay, I'll grant you that."

But line ten seems to mark a *volta* in this enlarged sonnet. When Strand says, "It was also what never happened," he is making more of a correction than an addendum (10). What he means to say is, "It was more of what never happened than what did happen." And thus his description of what never happened then requires more attention: "a moment so full / That when it went, as it had to, no grief was large enough / To contain it" (10–12). Here again, there are two possible readings. First, one might say that *the moment*—the one that was so full, and then went—"never happened." On the other hand—and the experienced Strand reader will subscribe to this reading: nothing happened, and *that nothingness* was so full that "no grief was large enough to contain it."

Strand has made a career of absenting absences to leave monumental presences in their wake. Strand asserts here that *it is* what it *isn't*. This perhaps appears as a correction of what Strand has said earlier in *Blizzard*, "So, when it goes as it must, no sense of loss springs in its wake." Strand of course recognizes that moments pass, and this time not even grief can take its place. This moment appears to be the kind of catharsis of self that Bloom identifies as *askesis*: "a way of purgation intending solitude as its proximate goal. . . . [T]he strong poet in his daemonic elevation is empowered to turn his energy upon himself, and achieves, at terrible cost, his clearest victory in wrestling with the mighty dead" (*Anxiety* 116).

Strand's purgation continues by returning, ostensibly, to the previously sketched room of chair, gray couch, and walls. Now he speaks with more certainty. Replacing the first nine lines' "It was that, and it was more" is a less equivocal: "It was the room that appeared unchanged / After so many years. It was that" (12–13). Remarkably, "the hat / She'd forgotten to take, the pen she left on the table" have remained in the room even after "so many years" (13–14). Strand then ends the poem with a sense of debilitation, as he dumbfoundedly explains, "It was the sun on my hand. It was the sun's heat. It was the way / I sat, the way I waited for hours, for days. It was that. Just that" (15–16).

So, surprisingly, a poem that attempts to build in brushstrokes, growing in inclusiveness, finds itself correcting its movement outward (with its sense of "it was that, and more"), ending with a mere "Just that." The room that "appeared unchanged" of course probably had, in fact, changed. Nonetheless, the room has returned the speaker to another negative spot of time, one might say. All the images that come flooding into the speaker's mind at the sight of other incidental images *take the place* of those now subordinate images. What *was*— i.e., "what time it really was"—is nothing compared with what "appeared" to be. As such, all the speaker can do is feel the sun's heat on his hand and wait as he must have those many years before.

"The Delirium Waltz" is a delightfully inclusive Strandian auto-biography of sorts. It begins with a prose paragraph that seems to celebrate action in the face of loss. Or at least it *attempts* to erase details and replace them with the dance—i.e., the poem. "I cannot remember when it began," Strand begins. This opening itself is an erasure, for it is unlikely that the poet would not remember the beginning; the poet—or at least *this* poet—creates the beginnings. More than likely, this speaker chooses not to define when the dance began. He then creates the dance from this primitive darkness: "The lights were low. We were walking across the floor, over pol-ished wood and inlaid marble, through shallow water, through dustings of snow, through cloudy figures of fallen light. I cannot remember but I think you were there—whoever you were."

Strand's details could be analyzed indefinitely, but it is more important to recognize the motifs Strand wants to remind us of: it is in a darkness that the imaginative act begins; snow has provided the backdrop to this particular collection; the "cloudy figures of fallen light" are likely past people and events that have been erased by the privative darkness that occurs before one can begin the new dance. "The Delirium Waltz" can be a metaphor for life, or against impending death, but in either case it is also a metaphor for the creation of poetry. This con-tention is that—since the creation of poetry *is* in fact the poet's life— the poem is a metaphor for life in that it is primarily a metaphor for the imaginative act. When Strand says, at the poem's outset, "Shapes assembled themselves and dissolved," he explains exactly what hap-pens in poetry. At the outset, of course, "The hall to the ballroom seemed endless," for there is no limit to the potential of the poem just at the moment of its inception (47). As the poem proceeds, then, it necessarily retains its own temporal existence, out of step with the nat-ural world: "We moved in the drift of sound, and whether we went towards the future or back to the past we weren't able to tell." Furthermore, once one has temporarily conquered the anxiety of influence—even if it is the influence of one's own poetry—the poem takes over: "Anxiety has its inflections—wasteful, sad, tragic at times—but here it had none. In its harmless hovering it was merely fantastic, so we kept dancing." Then, as the poem begins to attain its rhythm, the speaker becomes fully engrossed in the imaginative act,

> so much so that it was clear that we had always been dancing, always been eager to give ourselves to the rapture of music. Even the simplest movement, from the wafting of clouds to the wink of an eye, could catch and hold our attention. The rooms became larger and finally dimensionless. (46)

Ultimately, all that remains is the glorious troping: "we kept gliding, gliding and turning" (46).

The first verse poem within "The Delirium Waltz" describes the music of the poem about which the whole of "The Delirium Waltz" speaks. When the second prose-poem-interruption begins, Strand describes another effect of the imaginative act: how the poetry alters the natural landscape: "And our shadows floated away towards sunset and darkened the backs of birds, and blackened the sea. . . . Soon the air was soiled with dust and purple clouds" (49). The second verse poem then moves the imagination outside to exhibit the effect of poetry on nature.

The third prose discussion then exhibits the speaker becoming lost in a whirlwind of poetic movement until, ultimately, not unlike a dervish, he breaks free of earth in imaginative boundlessness: "I was dancing alone in the absence of all that I knew and was bound by. And here was the sea—the blur, the erasure of difference, the end of self, the end of whatever surrounds the self. And I kept going. The breakers flashed and fell under the moon's gaze" (51). The speaker soon returns to the others in this massive yet intimate dance to watch them and their progeny dance some more, ad infinitum.

When Strand returns in the conclusion to the words he used in the opening, he defines more clearly that the importance of the poem is not what is inside it, but that one erases what has come before. The poem's structure—four prose poems interspersed by three similarly interlocked verse poems—makes clear that the participation in the dance is vital. The ensuing delirium waltz that comes will be different, certainly. The characters may change, the actions within may vary. But so long as the gliding, gliding and turning remain, there is value to the dance for Strand. Or, more precisely, the dance is everything that can be, and transports all who participate into a frenzy.

After "The Delirium Waltz," Strand returns to an established pattern of providing a pensive, quietly resonant poem at the conclusion of his collection. In *Blizzard of One*, it is "The View" that reverberates. The poem begins with a striking, three-sentence, nearly monosyllabic, end-stopped first line that gives the reader plenty of pause: "This is the place. The chairs are white. The table shines." This poem packs its punch in the reaffirmation of poetry's place, while at the same time declares that the poet himself has adequately overcome the anxiety of his own influence. The speaker of "The View" can be understood as a revision of the speaker of *Dark Harbor*. There, the speaker of "Proem"

> watched
> For the great space that he felt sure
>
> Would open before him, a stark sea over which
> The turbulent sky would drop the shadowy shapes
> Of its song.

Here, with equal aplomb, the speaker exhibits confidence that there is a place for him. We recall chapter 9 of Strand's *The Monument*, where he says, "It has been necessary to submit to vacancy in order to begin again, to clear ground, to make space" (9). And of course let us not forget Bloom's quintessential assertion: "[S]trong poets make that history by misreading one another, so as to clear imaginative space for themselves" (*Anxiety* 5).

That much fertile ground having been tilled, we recognize that, as the wind—the poet's breath—"moves the air around," the speaker recognizes the place opened up as "A space for me" (4). It is the poem that creates the poet, then, in much the same way for Stevens' beach-walker:

> She was the single artificer of the world
> In which she sang. And when she sang, the sea,
> Whatever self it had, became the self
> That was her song, for she was the maker.

Again, poetry's power takes prominence, even if all that can achieved in the imaginative creation results in "a mild version / Of the story that is told just once if true, and always too late" (9–10).

One of the most honest passages in Strand's corpus comes when he says, as usual thinly veiling himself with a third person reference, "He's always been drawn to the weather of leavetaking, / Arranging itself so that grief—even the most intimate— / Might be read from a distance" (5–7). Strand had been undergoing his second divorce at the time most of the poems from *Blizzard* were written. Few griefs can be more intimate than the negation of love. And we have seen too many references to the solitary figure enduring the loss of "the dust of a passion," mentions of "And she was beautiful," "the hat / She'd forgotten to take, the pen she left on the table" or "the lavender [that] turns to ash. . . . Where / Is she now?" Yet, Strand *is* honest enough to reveal to us that it is the *weather* of leavetaking he is drawn to, make no mistake, *not* the leavetaking itself. And of course, the weather of leavetaking is anything *but* the leavetaking; it is the presence that replaces the absence or, if you will, the troping that allows the speaker to put distance between himself and the pain.

Strand then provides one of the more astonishing images to remind the diligent reader of how necessary it is to replace the natural world with an artificial one:

> The waitress brings his drink, which he holds
> Against the waning light, but just for a moment.
> Its red reflection tints his shirt. Slowly the sky becomes darker,
> The wind relents, the view sublimes. The violent sweep of it
> Seems, in this effortless nightfall, more than a reason
> For being there, for seeing it, seems itself a kind
> Of happiness, as if that plain fact were enough and would last.
>
> (11–17)

The drink—a sanguine red wine to replace the white Beaune from "Our Masterpiece is the Private Life"—is held up against the light of a sunset, itself already a filtered and buffered light, not the sun itself. Even though this action is performed "just for a moment," that moment is enough to achieve sublimity. Just as his looking through the red glass transforms the sun—a much more fertile motif than mere rose-colored glasses—the sun's light "looks through" the glass in the other direction and "tints his shirt." The trope is effective in both directions then. This is not the light of the sun, but the light of the sun doubly transformed by an artifice—atmospheric interference naturally transforming its light, and the glass of wine. Likewise, this is also not the man, but the synecdochal *shirt* of the man transformed by a light made artificial by said glass of wine. In a remarkable juxtaposition, the speaker is transformed—swept away, to use the words of the poem—by a "violent sweep" which is yet contained within "this effortless nightfall." And during this cinematic spot of time—if—there is a "more than a reason / For being there," and a sudden "kind / Of happiness."

This is a virtual outpouring of emotion for a poet such as Mark Strand. The mere juxtaposition of artificial and natural has brought about a momentary impulse of comfort, if not joy. Even if "that plain fact" were *not* enough and will *not* last, which is what Strand's final syntactical arrangement suggests, there is a final pulse of meaningfulness, a final burst of sufficiency to stave off the otherwise unremitting existential crisis that is life.

Sarah Manguso makes the assertion, with some merit, that the subjects of *Blizzard of One* are missing. She recognizes the enormous multiplicities that make unifying the works under a coherent critical umbrella unachievable, but also identifies that, ultimately, the focus should be on Strand's emphasis on the poetic cosmos erected within the poem:

> The act of living in a moment, after all, carries value in itself, however little sense we can make of it, and a moment's ability or inability to last in the world bears no relevance to its "kind of happiness." In these poems it is not up to us to capture the subject. . . . What the poems do capture, whether the subject is "there" or not, is what we must turn our attention to. Keats's "heard melodies" *are* the subject of this collection, and they are the moment, and they are all.   (171)

In *Blizzard of One*, Mark Strand revives the notion that "even the green trees can be saved / For a moment and look bejeweled" (*Dark Harbor* XV 2–3), even if now we are no longer sure if "we feel better for trying" (*Dark Harbor* XXVIII 18). Bloom contends that "[T]he covert subject of most poetry for the last three centuries has been the anxiety of influence, each poet's fear that no proper work remains for him to perform" (*Anxiety* 148). Strand does not entirely disagree when he admits, "[T]he anxiety of self-imitation is the great anxiety of the poet." Eschewing Bloomian terminology, we recognize Strand addressing the consideration of what to do "Now that the great dog I worshipped for years / Has become none other than myself." His answer is to take the molds created by the Mark Strand who wrote poetry before him and "rally everything that remains." He must recognize that in the poet's distress he shall find the potency to create— not anew, but askew. Such a poet will find "a sound announcing itself as your own, a voice / That is yours, bending under the weight of desire, / Suddenly turning your language into a field unfolding." Though further challenged in this collection, Strand exhibits the ability to imagine his way out from under the oppressing forces of nature and society, and once again find fertile ground for erecting a temporary monument to poetry.

CHAPTER 5

SUPPLEMENT

ANGEL BECOMES DOG BECOMES CAMEL: *MAN AND CAMEL*

As this monograph was being prepared for publication, Mark Strand was readying for release his most surprising collection to date, one that might shock some of his readership into believing he had made a substantial departure in style and philosophy. From a mere glance at the playful cover of *Man and Camel*—which received more than one quizzical comment from listeners at a reading early in 2006—one would recognize the prevalent place humor would have in the collection, for indeed the title alone is hard to read with utter seriousness. Yet, while humor does weave its way more deeply in many of these poems, Strand also is somewhat more biting in his treatment of established subjects, as well. He is less tongue-in-cheek on both levels, thus, though certainly not at the expense of his characteristic subtlety. Ultimately, while there is playfulness and wit in the poetry, the alterations in these poems are primarily tonal, substantive in style, but familiar in theme and philosophy. Still, the remaking of the self that was undertaken in *Blizzard of One*, must not stop at any one moment in the poet's career, but continue throughout that career, and this collection is no different in its mapping out new territory within which the Strand poem can flourish.

Recent readings by, and personal meetings with, Mark Strand have revealed a poet undergoing a revision of himself that is remarkable in its unabashedness. As Lydialyle Gibson says of a Strand reading in 2004,

"At once cool and distant, yet intimate and emotional, Strand is working a kind of magic. He spends more than one stanza poking fun at himself and others, puncturing one absurdity or another—or creating a few of his own—with an almost invisible twist of understatement." While Strand is not attempting to remake himself entirely, what does appear to occur in his latest poetry is, generally, a more fearless approach to previous concerns. In some ways, Strand continues to step out from the shadows of his forebears Stevens, Bishop, Borges et al. More remarkably, for a poet so death-haunted as Strand, it seems that he has reached a stage where, after years of fighting death, he has grown so intimate with the subject that he has become desensitized to it. While previous humorous stabs at death rightly might be called whistling in the dark, Strand seems somewhat reconciled to it. His humor now seems genuine rather than grasping.

See most particularly his poem "2002."[1] One of the most humorous poems Strand has written, "2002" is not *merely* a humorous poem. While Strand often has exhibited stretches of levity that mask fears of some sort, or presented humorous poems that had no goal other than comedy, this one utilizes its wit to exhibit a definitive confidence in the face of death. Strand here does not just whistle in the dark, but personifies death in order to extract pity for Death, and seems to have fun throughout the endeavor. Strand has said of the poem, "Clearly it's just a fantasy about my own value to Death," but the fantasy does, in fact, reveal a certain poise within the poetic endeavor (Gibson).

"I am not thinking of death now, but death is thinking of me," the poem begins, and the humor is up front, unavoidable, and effective. Of course, the line is ironic: no poet can *write* such lines without thinking of death, and yet to turn the Strandian not-me into the personification of Death here immediately diminishes Death. In fact, as the poem progresses, Strand makes death laughable, and whatever ironic twist one can assign to the poem's ultimate death theme, the disempowerment of death is absolute. Poetic power in *Man and Camel* reveals itself in Strand as a poet in open antagonism toward death, toward the natural world, and toward social institutions. The Strand persona's latest evolution is someone who is tired of tolerating his apprehensions and is in outward revolt against them. His revolt may take the form of humor or may take the form of bluntness. That being said, Strand does not abandon his poetic voice, nor his philosophy. He uses familiar motifs to make his latest contentions, a word I choose carefully here, for contentions they are. In exercising these declarations within the framework of the Strandian poem, however, he proves that his typical poetic verse form can, in fact, contain multitudinous affirmations, and thus he stretches his own poem's boundaries even further. Thus, to the uninitiated reader, this still sounds like Strand, but to the carefully trained ear, what is happening is quite remarkable. Early exposure to the works that will be *Man and Camel* reveal that Strand's latest endeavors certainly stand up to the rest of his fine corpus.

While Strand has argued on more than one occasion, "I've always thought of myself as a humorous poet," the statement may be worth challenging (Gibson). Like Stevens, Strand's humorous verse usually is not his finest. That is to say, the poems that one would immediately label "funny," might be labeled as nothing *but* humorous verse. Strand's best uses of humor, on the other hand, always mask more disturbing concepts, or are used to soften the verbal blows of otherwise off-putting concepts. In "2002," Strand seems to be straightforwardly playing with the concept of death, and legitimately having fun doing so. Furthermore, this poem, as with each of the poems Strand has shared with me for the forthcoming *Man and Camel*, exhibits a humor that is integral to the poem, and helps produce something more than merely a laugh. More importantly, only a poet of still-increasing confidence can write lighthearted poetry that is also vital poetry.

Strand's "2002" is such vital poetry. When Death fantasizes about the poet as appearing "In a jacket and tie, and together under the boulevards' / Leafless trees we'll stroll into the city of souls," one is almost inclined to pity poor death. *I am not afraid*, Strand now says, and the humor he uses is not to avoid the fear but rather to illustrate the reduction of it. Although typically Strand's wit intentionally wanes at the poem's end, here it is not to be replaced by the "somber moment" that has been trailing behind humor's veil. Here, when Death and Strand are strolling under the "Leafless trees," it sounds like a pacific death that Strand will indulge in. Or at least from Death's point of view, it will be. The "leafless trees" of this afterlife, of course, represent the absence of poetry, that time after which Strand will be silenced forever. The poet will be like those *Dark Harbor* angels who were "unable to say / Words whose absence had been the silence of love, / Of pain, and even of pleasure." This privative stripping away of poetry then is not a promising darkness. Nonetheless, Strand is not moved to tears, nor frightened into inaction. The fact remains that that time is not here, and there is nothing Death can do to bring it near as yet. So, Strand seems to say, *As long as it is not here, I shall soldier on, smiling all the way.* But before one can revel fully in the assonant phrasings that populate this poem, Strand needs to return us to humor, with Death imploring, "O let it be soon. Let it be soon" (12). Thus, he cements both the assertion that humor is the primary mode of the poem while at the same time denying the reader any sense of lasting peacefulness evoked by an image of two old friends strolling into eternity forever. Indeed, Strand strips the poignancy of death away from both mortality and the reader. The primary motif here is longing, but from a reversed perspective. That is, not unlike in several Woody Allen stories, Death is a pathetic figure who cannot fulfill his duties, and must wait for his and Strand's triumphant return to the underworld and concomitant reward.

Strand's "2032," then, returns to this same Death character, and continues in the vein of pity. Is the death-haunted poet now reversing the terms on the second of the two great darks? Indeed, the poem may be viewed as being 30 years in the future from "2002," and while the speaker's humor prevails, Death has grown weary of waiting: "It is evening in the town of X / where Death, who used to love me, sits / in a limo" (1–3). Death is now an old man, eerily reminiscent of Strand in his whiteness, and topically related to "The Great Poet Returns." While Strand physically maintains a towering, striking, and impressive presence, Death, however, is shrinking (literally here to mimic the metaphorical): "His hair / is white, his eyes have gotten small, his cheeks / have lost their luster" (4–6). A virtual invalid, Death now needs a driver to propel him; he has not culled a soul in years, nor even checked his hourglass. Though he still daydreams, this time it is not of Strand, who will vault him his lost prominence, but of "the Blue Hotel, the ultimate resort, / where an endless silence fills the lilac-scented air" (8–9). That endless silence that he desires: his own death, which, remarkably enough, is one where the imagination reigns in perpetuity, hence the reference to the characteristically Strandian "lilac-scented air." Indeed, now Strand has turned the tables completely on Death, who is now life-haunted, if you will. More than merely an amusing poem, "2032" approaches hilarity with cleverness and apparent ease.

In "Black Sea," Strand opens with one of his lovelier portraits of nature. Though the poem is tonally familiar, Strand surprisingly juxtaposes some beautiful language against the backdrop of what would otherwise be a threatening sea: it is, after all, a "clear night" (1), and though the wind is whipping across the surface of the sea, Strand likens the foam to "bits of lace tossed in the air" (5). When he writes of "waiting for something, a sign, the approach / of a distant light," it evokes his own "The Continuous Life" (6–7). In that poem, the parents waited for "a piece of the dark that might have been [theirs]."

"Black Sea" is more a revision of Dark Harbor's "Proem," however. Like the speaker of *Dark Harbor* who was "sure [of] the great space [that] would open before him," and who would "whip [passages of greater and lesser worth] into shape," this speaker evokes just what he claims to evoke. Though he appears less confident than his counterpart in the "Proem," his "waiting for something" quickly evolves into "I imagined you coming closer, / the dark waves of your hair mingling with the sea, / and the dark became desire, and desire the arriving light" (7–9). That very imagining manifests itself in a "nearness, the momentary warmth of you" (10). Strand thus again reveals to his reader the realization of the imaginative process. First he "waits" for an appropriate symbol; then it arrives in the form of the sea; he incorporates the symbol into his desire for "you"; and the result is a functional trope that brings "nearness" and "warmth" in the middle of a cold, dark ocean. And of course, it is "momentary"—for it lasts only as long as the speaker remains imaginatively engrossed in the creative act.

The poem seems to turn on its head in *la volta* of the final two lines, when the subject becomes thought *about* rather than thought, thus severing the imaginative link. There it *appears* as though Strand is chastising himself for believing in what could not be, but in fact, the tone belies the truth of the poetic incarnation. That is, while one is likely to read, "Why did I believe you would come out of nowhere? Why with all / that the world offers would you come only because I was here?" as though the speaker were kicking himself over a futile attempt to conjure "you," he in fact *has* done so. The concluding couplet serves then, not to inform us that the you—who may be a woman, the reader, or both—does not arrive, but serves more as a questioning of poetic eminence. That is, the hubris that *seems* to be a self-reprimand is really a recognition of his own creative capacity. It is not a "why me?" of self-pity, but a "why me?" of humility. As such, it is one of the rare instances in Strand's latest poems where he approaches previous considerations with a humbler attitude. In fact, the poem resonates with "The End" from *The Continuous Life*. In the former poem, also set in a maritime environment, Strand is also watching the sea from the shore, listening to its Arnoldian roaring. In that poem also, the imagination transforms the movement of the sea into momentary flashes of motionlessness, where "birds are suspended in flight" (10). At the conclusion of "The End," Strand claimed, "Not every man knows what is waiting for him, or what he shall sing / . . . there at the end," with the understanding that he knew what he was singing at the end of that collection of poems. The poet of "Black Sea" knows that he too has been able to conjure something from the sea—itself a fertile motif from ancient mythology—and exhibits some mystification as to why he does have that capacity.

If levity plays a big role in Strand's latest collection, poems like "Cake" also reveal the poet actually having fun. In fact, during readings from *Man and Camel*, Strand not only exhibits amusement, but also professes to be enjoying himself in these latest endeavors. Making a fiction of himself, Strand returns to his age-old theme of identity-switching in having a man "leave . . . for the next town to pick up a cake" (1), only to never actually complete the task, but show up on a beach "Years later" (3) where he plans to leave town to, yes, pick up a cake. Again, the sound and sentiment here are lighthearted and delightful; this surely is the work of a poet truly at the top of his game. Within the wittiness, not beneath it, is the enjoyable puzzle of discovering why the man never picks up the first cake, how and why he arrives at the sea, and then ultimately why he decides to leave the second town to pick up a second (or is it still the initial?) cake. It is Strandian riddling at its finest here, which can intentionally obfuscate the obvious. In this case, the fundamental depiction here is the man who gets lost in the woods and never picks up the cake the first time around. In the middle of the poem, he is *lost in thought* near the ocean and ostensibly does not/will not pick up the cake. Initially, in each case, there is a *desire* to pick up a cake. However mundane the task, it sets in motion a series of events, in each case, involving getting lost. The pattern, ostensibly, has the potential to repeat itself indefinitely, adding a new element each time a cake-seeking trip occurs. The central thrust of the poem, however, is that the man ends up in a more dynamic place than the place he set out for. Thus, even the most routine desire results in some appreciable imaginative gain, this one resulting in a transformation of the sea.

A second example of a tremendously unassuming poem of repetition is the seemingly offhanded lyric, "Elevator." In it, Strand presents two identical three-line stanzas of a man descending in an elevator when the doors open for another passenger. The first time Strand has his speaker state, "I'm going down . . . I won't be going up," a palpable humor is evoked (3). By the time he repeats the line a second time, the humor is infused with a certain poignancy. At two separate readings, audiences immediately were moved from laughter to sadness within a span of seconds, which illustrates the kind of effective juxtaposition of comedy and pathos that Strand employs in such apparently simple strokes in these latest poems.

Strand's facile use of humor continues in the title poem, and once again the infusion of humor allows the poem to succeed on several levels. In "Man and Camel," Strand rewrites his quasi-translation, "Leopardi," and makes it truly his own. The poem opens with the speaker at age 40, ostensibly Strand himself, "on the porch having a smoke / when out of the blue a man and a camel / happened by" (2–4). The juxtaposition of cigarette and camel immediately strikes a chord in the reader, and establishes a lightheartedness and absurdity amid the nostalgia. When the pair begins to sing, "their voices / rose as one above the sifting sound / or windblown sand" (10–12), and this immediately echoes Stevens. Strand thus revises Stevens' "The Idea of Order at Key West," here as well, and when he brings humor back into the mix, he seems to leave Stevens far behind in terms of Bloomian influenza: "The wonder of their singing, / its elusive blend of man and camel seemed / an ideal image for all uncommon couples" (12–14). His "uncommon couples" here is a strange innovation for Strand, but it reveals an uncanny pride in his own ability to conjure "an ideal image." Reversing the humility of "Black Sea," now the poet is again impressed—however slightly and however temporarily—with his capacities here.

At line 15, Strand performs another characteristic *volta*, a turn in the direction of the poem, usually marked by a tonal shift and intro-spective narrative thrust. He considers, "Was this the night that I had waited for / so long?" (14–15). At this juncture, there is wonderment in the pair's singing—a lucid metaphor for poetry—and it achieves the Platonic "ideal" state. Were the poem to end here, it would have achieved lasting perfection, ending, as it were, in the perfect moment. However, when the speaker steps out of the subjective indulgence of the moment to objectively analyze it: "Was this the night that I had waited for / so long?" he severs the imaginative indulgence. To reit-erate Stevens, "As long as we ourselves are caught up in the process of creation, we neither see nor understand; indeed we ought not to understand, for nothing is more injurious to immediate experience than cognition." The speaker and reader are not the only ones who experience this disconnection of the imagination with its creation. In another deft stroke of humor Strand allows the unified man and camel metaphor to realize the break as well. They return from their apparent stroll into the sunset, stare at the speaker in disgusted disapproval, and rebuke, "You ruined it. You ruined it forever" (21).[2]

There is, certainly, more than humor to be acquired from *Man and Camel*. In fact, the poignancy Strand elicits in poems such as "Mother and Son," "Mirror" and "Poem After the Seven Last Words" is com-parable to anything in his corpus. Strand makes some of his more nihilistic statements to date in these works, and in granting almost complete indeterminacy to the world, he clears the way for his humorous poems to fill the gaps of meaninglessness. Nietzsche has asserted that, once humankind realizes that the process of becoming starts from nothing and leads to nothing, we are freed to select any personally fulfilling moment and value that instead.

While "Mirror" seems to be the latest incarnation of the quintessential Strand poem, "Mother and Son" resonates with nihilistic energy. It is one of Strand's saddest poems, focusing as it does on a maternal deathbed scene. That backdrop, however, is merely the catalyst for the downward spiral that ensues. In the second line, the desire for familial communion is presented as the son "stands by the bed where the mother lies. / The son believes that she wants to tell him / what he longs to hear—that he is her boy" (2–4). Of course, that wish will not be fulfilled, and the declension continues. When the son attempts to kiss his mother, he finds "her lips are cold" (6). In another poignant example of Strand's ability to enjamb his most emotionally provocative lines, he pronounces directly, "The burial of feelings has begun" (7). It is a stunning line in its poetic resonance: at this most traumatic moment, the death of his mother, the son is not grieving openly, but commencing instead an anti-exhumation of sorts.

When the son reaches for his mother's hands and "then turns and sees the moon's full face" (9), one expects to find the poet troping the moon to fill the space left by the mother's death. Instead, "An ashen light falls across the floor" (10), which is in its own right the commencement of an imaginative troping. However, just as in "Man and Camel," any creative progress is halted here, as the speaker intercedes with an editorializing of sorts. This stunts both the emotional progression and the poetic progression: "If the moon could speak, what would it say?" (11). One might view this intercession on the poet's part as a monologue with the self, as if he is thinking on the fly, "What should I have the moon say in the subsequent line?" One barely needs to wait, for Strand's immediate answer to the proposed question is unequivocal: "If the moon could speak, it would say nothing" (12). Stunning in the absoluteness of the defeat, this poem surprises in its growing pessimism from one moment to the next, ultimately ending in a doubly defeatist testimony. First, the question itself only supposes a hypothetical hope: "If the moon could speak" in fact asserts that the moon cannot speak. Second, the answer cancels the hypothetical hope, removing hope to the second degree: it cannot speak, and would not if it could. There is no guiding force in the world, Strand reasserts here—just in case one would believe he was transformed into an idealist—and if there was a force, it would not concern itself in human affairs. It is blunt, and it is unequivocal, and it is thus Strand at his most unambiguous.

"Mirror," on the other hand, is full of the ambiguity that Strand's best work contains. Such works compel the reader repeatedly to return to them to plumb further; they are fertile enough to allow for repeated readings without the experience becoming commonplace. "Mirror" reveals Strand again refining his craft, bringing his brilliance to yet greater heights. Though the poem will not surprise any readers thematically or lexicographically, it revises one of the poet's primary themes with such aplomb that it immediately becomes one of Strand's "must-read" poems. While it is *one* of his finer poems, it is perhaps his most quintessential one, a poem that a great majority of anthologists will select for inclusion in their future projects. In its uncanny Strandness, it incorporates much of what Strand does imaginatively, thematically, and tonally. For that it merits attention here.

The poem's opening is reminiscent of the social scenes presented in "Luminism" from *The Continuous Life*. Here, again, the speaker and his fellow partygoers are intent on describing the natural scene that surrounds them. In the former poem, the attempts were modest at best, usually reverting to the nondescript adjective, "great." Now, the attempts seem to satisfy the speaker enough for him to at least take part in the communal effort to describe "what precise shade of yellow / the setting sun turned our drinks" (9–10). This is a task similar to one that Strand undertook in *Blizzard of One*, where the speaker's shirt was the subject of sunlight's reflection through a glass of red wine. Here, the drink of choice is whiskey, but when the speaker closes his eyes in a gesture that evokes an escape into the self, he becomes characteristically distanced from the other partygoers, and retreats to a dialogue within his own mind. He opens his mind to look into a mirror, wherein he sees, as one might expect after reading so many of Strand's poems, a woman. What ensues is a series of doubling or mirroring that obfuscates identity in ways heretofore unseen in Strand's work.

The woman in the mirror is "distracted" in much the same way the speaker is (15). Though she—who in fact is not herself but the reflection of herself—is also looking into the mirror (where she would see not the speaker, but the *image* of the speaker), she does not look at the speaker at all. Surprisingly, she looks past him, into a fictional space "that *might* be filled by someone / yet to arrive" (20–21, italics mine). At this point, the veteran Strand reader will recognize him/herself becoming increasingly distanced from the narrative thread, and from any dependable, consistent, and steadfast sense of the speaker. As such, the reader also will acknowledge that the further Strand distances the speaker from himself, the more intimate the association becomes. Thus, the intimacy shared between the man in the mirror and the woman looking past his reflection becomes palpable. But what worsens the experience is that she is looking, in the speaker's imagination, toward someone else:

> into a space
> that might be filled by someone
> yet to arrive, who at that moment
> could be starting the journey
> which would lead eventually to her.
>   (19–23)

When the speaker's friends bring him to another party, the consummation of that imaginative moment of desire in the mirror already is complete, in a negative marriage of sorts. Like "Man and Camel" and "Mother and Son," the imaginative event is completed before the poem is, hence the fact that though all details of the actual event have been forgotten by the speaker, "I still recall that moment of looking up / and seeing the woman stare past me / into a place I could only imagine" (30–32).

That Strand mentions the word "moment" twice is significant; here he is mourning the event that he and this woman do not share. Also significant is the fact that the place the woman looks into is one the *speaker imagines*. That is, the failure of unity is ensured by the success of the imaginative act that is produced by the speaker himself: two mirror images of people will not meet because the speaker allows the double of the woman to miss his own double's gaze in a mirror. Thus, the speaker is doomed to fail to achieve lasting communion here just as he was doomed to fail to unify with the joint song of man and camel. Likewise, he experiences the same pain of loss that he does when he fails to unite with the song of the drunken man in "Leopardi." His last lines then recall the wistful nostalgic moments of each of the above moments, tied in with the language of "Untitled" from *Blizzard of One*. There he stated that "something is always / About to happen just at the moment it serves no purpose at all." Here he is brought back to that lost moment, "only to discover too late / that she is not there" (37–38).

There are other poems in this collection that are bound to receive due attention from readers and critics: the delightful "Webern Variations," perhaps the best intertextual poem Strand has yet conceived is one; the challenging experiment called "Marsyas" another. The poem "Poem After the Seven Last Words" that is set at the conclusion of *Man and Camel* should be noted here, as well, for it is striking in its uncharacteristic theme and in its very approach to that theme. It is only with several dozen readings that the richness of the poem begins to reveal itself, and only after thorough research does it begin to truly impress itself on the reader as being a masterful work. It very well might become Strand's most considered work, should other critics be willing to undertake the formidable task of sounding its depths.

Although "Poem After the Seven Last Words" was a commissioned work and was motivated by a suggestion from Harold Bloom, it is Strand's most provocative poem, and may prove a challenge to conservative religious groups. Unconcerned about the reception his latest work may garner, Strand seems unafraid to seek out certain topics— popular and confessionalist poetry and religion—that may prompt criticism. Here, in "Seven Last Words," Strand avoids the safe path while presenting a compelling poem that reinterprets Christ's suffering on the cross. Occasionally criticized for what some perceive as wrongs of omission, Strand lays himself open to criticism by attempting to think originally about one of the world's most revered stories.

"Poem After the Seven Last Words" begins by terming the crucifixion as "The story of the end, of the last word / of the end, when told, is a story that never ends" (1–2). Immediately, this sounds more like a Strandian story than a biblical one, and if pursued as such—as very much a Strand translation of an ancient text—one will discover that the poem follows a course that pursues a human Jesus as much as the divine one. Or rather, that the divinity that Strand assigns to Jesus originates in his humanity. Therefore, depending upon one's inclinations, it is either an exciting poem indeed, or a shocking one. Not unlike Martin Scorcese's *The Last Temptation of Christ*, Strand's poem—written to accompany a performance of Haydn's *op. 51*— reconsiders Jesus as a human entity, someone whose words contain a miraculous power more than any physical actions. It also vacillates between honoring Jesus and utilizing him as a poetic trope. This is not to say that Strand attempts heresy; he rather attempts to intimately understand Jesus and—perhaps more centrally—his effect on humanity, from a secular viewpoint.

In the first two cantos of these seven "words"—statements uttered by Christ on the cross—the poet is entrusted with telling the greatest story ever told, and Strand resourcefully returns to his early Hopkinsesque sensibilities in the implementation of sprung rhythm and replication of a solemn tone. Here, Strand exemplifies that the veneer of reality proves stronger than one would expect. Strand is left with a story populated by "silken / remains of something they were but cannot recall," which, as a depiction both ghostly and echolike (2.5–6), effectively revises Strand's *Dark Harbor*, wherein his speaker "would move his arms / And begin to mark . . . / The passages of greater and lesser worth, the silken / Tropes and calls to this or that . . ." Using his synesthetic sensibilities in phrases like "They move to the sound of the stars" (2.7), Strand reveals the transformation of the original story into, in fact, a revision of several stories, including and especially his own. He thus creates an echo life within the first few cantos. In this place, all beings live in the imagination, and belief is the operative word here. So long as those who believe are engaging in the imaginative projection of their faith, they are satisfied within that imaginative creation. This is a new iteration of Strand's familiar theme: what *is* does not matter when what one *perceives* suffices. The poet works with intangibles, echoes of things that are. He manipulates a nothingness to create a something to convey the greatest story ever told to people who may not see how he put the building blocks of nothingness together. Yet all he has is the ability to put words together. And, Christlike himself, the writer thinks he is the Whitmanian high priest who transmutes words with alchemy, manipulating shadowy images of nothingness to create a great story that people might think is substanceless. When Strand invokes Jesus' words to one of the thieves being crucified with him, he indeed reveals that this is much more a story about a poet than about a deity. Or, that the Deity status was achieved by His poetry. Or, the poet is the deity, for "the leaves will turn and never fall" is about as substantial a trope for poetic omnipotence as can be created (2.15). Or, perhaps, all of the above is filtered into the experience of this poem.

In part three, the alchemy gets away from the writer. The story he has created develops its own life, for the characters have a secret that the writer does not know. The writer has to put down the pen and in doing so, he also allows his characters to go on their own. Like Yeats here, the center does not hold, and it challenges the poet. The fourth canto brings more palpably into play Whitman's "When Lilacs Last in the Dooryard Bloom'd," as well as revisits Yeats' "The Second Coming." It is also perhaps the most irreverent of the sections in this poem. Calling Jesus, "the man who saved others, and believed / he was the chosen one" (4.13–14) alone should get Strand in sufficient hot water, but more remarkable is his reference to God himself as "master of the weather" (4.9), and a power who may or may not wish to eradicate His entire creation. Nonetheless, the poem's ability to stand up to the huge historical presence of such a figure as Jesus Christ is noteworthy.

Arguably, the most powerful passage in this challenging poem is canto five, wherein Strand invokes a series of infinitive verbs to describe the pain and humility suffered by Christ on the cross. Strand utilized this motif in another of his strong poems, "A.M.," and while it feels vaguely borrowed to a reader who has experienced the former poem, the method does justice to the theme here. After all, Strand's desire to be in the present yet everlasting can be no better expressed than by invoking, literally and etymologically, the *infinitive*. Equally evocative in this passage is the power given to the logos. Furthermore, when the poet—again, meaning Jesus, other poets or Strand himself—constructs new worlds, the act arises from a *closing* of eyes and imagination of one's own *death*. In making dark and not light the generative force, the poet enacts a reversal of Genesis to suit his own purposes (for, after all, the poet is making the greatest story ever told his *own* story). When Strand reconsiders his own and Stevens' quest for the nature of nothingness at the conclusion of the fifth canto, one begins to realize that this poem has achieved transcendence in its revelation of the theory of poetry as evidenced through the life of Christ. It is a remarkable act to many, but impious to others perhaps.

In canto six, Strand presents a central dialectical model that further captivates the reader. This section of the poem is a challenge, both philosophically and poetically, for Strand issues some of his more candid imaginative statements in this poem, and in his secular description of the importance of Christ presents an alternative view of history. The miracle of Jesus that Strand recognizes and values is the duality of Jesus' life, he who encapsulated largeness and smallness, peace and power, God and man, nothing and everything.

Concluding this secular passage, part seven achieves the unimaginable in that it transforms the reader's secular experience into a spiritual journey. Reverting to the sounds and sentiment of Hopkins' "Spring and Fall," Strand addresses the seventh and final word of Christ. "Father, into your hands I commend my spirit" is the Seventh word on the cross—the last meditation of the stations of the cross. Strand ends his poem with his own version of one of the prayers of the meditations on the stations. The effect is powerful and humbling at the same time. Strand has erected the appearance of a paean to—or at least meditation on—Jesus, but this ultimately is also a projection to disguise the fact that he is mourning his own poetic mortality, yet is willing to enter that place. Thus, this canto is also an homage to the purposes of spring and fall, life and death.

When Strand completes the seventh and final segment of the poem, it involves a transformation from an active scene to a passive one. This, too, represents a reversal of traditional motifs about Christ's death, which almost always inaugurates a religious invitation to future salvation. Strand instead posits a place of absolute peace, of complete conclusion, a Stevensian place of perfect nothingness, where all words and all thought no longer need be breathed into existence. Ultimately, the poem converts itself more into a statement about the poet himself, though it began as a majestic subject. When Strand's more distant precursor, Whitman, wrote his "When Lilacs Last in the Dooryard Bloom'd," he ostensibly addressed the death of an enormous legend, Abraham Lincoln. However, ultimately, his poem concerned itself more with his own poetic death. Here, Strand addresses the colossal figure of Jesus Christ, but evokes instead and as well the worry of his own poetic finality. Were Strand to never write again, one would look to this poem's last words, "To that place, to the keeper of that place, I commit myself" as evidence that Strand himself was succumbing to poetic finality. "Poem After the Seven Last Words" is a poem bound to be misperceived. However, it should astound readers and critics with the richness of its metaphors and allusions, its thorough command of the Christian traditions regarding Jesus' death on the cross, and its ability to unify one massively catholic story with one intimately personal one. In due course, it reveals that the universal story of Jesus is primarily a very personal one, and the personal story of the poet is quite a universal one. That may be, in fact, what Strand has been saying all along.

Mark Strand's latest works, contained within the mostly delightful, sporadically demanding collection *Man and Camel*, reveal a poet who is unwilling to concede to fate, death, accepted views, or bad poetry. Though the Strand of 2006 is vastly enhanced from the Strand of 1966, incremental evolutionary changes do not reveal him altered in substantial ways. That said, innovation continues in the career of this visionary poet, but in such inconspicuous ways as to appear unnoticeable. In his newest work, Strand seems as determined a poet as ever. If there is resonant anxiety, it is masterfully subsumed beneath a forceful speaker's voice that asserts itself frequently, is unafraid to laugh at himself and Death, and takes on specific issues in less uncertain terms than in most previous efforts. That Strand continues to clear new territory for his imaginative creations is a witness to the depth of his poetic power. Few poets who have written in the English idiom have been able to produce such consistently engaging work as his that maintains its voice and vision. For that alone, Mark Strand's career is worth pursuing as a testament to writing—and reading—poetry.

CODA

BETWEEN TWO GREAT DARKS

Strandian poetics has revealed itself through the course of the poet's corpus, and a revisitation of his entire work here should attend to the transformations Strand has undergone in the latest part of his career. If Strand is to be viewed as a strong poet, careful study of the influence of his earlier work on his later work should be undertaken to understand how in the latter the refinement of his poetic philosophy and technique exhibit a poet at the pinnacle of his craft.

The world is a nightmare of storms, we learn from Strand's earliest poems. That is what the poet perpetually confronts in each of his poetic endeavors. As Deborah Garrison adeptly says, "One of the most interesting things about his work is what meets his Olympian searchlight when it sweeps across the plains: an essentially godless vista. His poems have always evoked a universe that returns our eager gaze with a blank stare." Strand engages in an ongoing attempt to deal with an indeterminate world as it is, and to find redemption in the transcendent act of imagination. To begin, Strand advises, we must achieve a blank—a nothingness described most frequently as a darkness, later in his career often as a whiteness, but consistently as an absence. Strand is not a fatalist—a nihilist perhaps—not one resigned to a life of inaction in the face of unalterable fate. Absence is, instead, a state of being likened in many poems "to a place beyond, / beyond love, / where nothing, / everything, / wants to be born." Georges Poulet and J. Hillis Miller recognize this imaginative procreative capacity inside the individual as the *Cogito*. Strand knows that to attain this state, one must strip away the multitudinous horrors of the world, hence Miller's description of the *Cogito* as "reduction of all to a central point." Later in his career, Strand occasionally provides an alternative Pouletian approach: "an expansive diffusion of that point until it includes everything as . . . a stone dropped in water will start a series of concentric circles radiating outward to infinity." While the natural world presents a privative darkness representing the removal of what was once there, Strand's transforms it into a primitive one, that original state before things were. From this primal state arises the poem, and thus the poet, disconnected from the cosmos, becomes the creative force in the absence of a God-force. Instead of God breathing life into the world, it is the poet who breathes life into the poem—into a new genesis in which we, as readers, also participate.

Once initiated, one must fully engage in the poetic process—whether as reader or writer. When one does so, it is as Stevens says, "The house was quiet and the world was calm. / The reader became the book" ("The House was Quiet" 1–2). In "Eating Poetry," Strand indulges in the ancient ritual of eating poetry and becomes canine in his primal joy. Poetry is thus consistently expressed as a participatory action, a private compulsion that must be engaged in completely and unselfconsciously, as a dog eats. Strand's poetic theory is that each poem must be written—and read—in one sitting, in the complete immersion of the imagination.

Many significant gestures in Strand's poems, therefore, take place in the present tense, ostensibly during the writing of the poem. This can account for his frequent use of present participles. By subtracting "real-world" items—the items in the room one is sitting in, the sounds outside the window—before one begins (a privative action), all possibilities exist (a primitive condition). We as Strand's readers are not limited by our physical or emotional selves, our past, present, or future. When Strand helps us achieve that privative darkness, our imagination is free to construct what it wishes. Once we are relieved of our burdens and return to a near tabula rasa state, we can go toward wherever our imagination takes us. While our imagination is so engaged in the writing or reading of the poem, we effectively erase the items in the room and silence the sounds outside the window, thus affirming the virtues of the poetic endeavor, "between two great darks, the first / With an ending, the second without one."

As Garrison has said of *Blizzard of One*:

> In these haunted outcroppings Strand sets the purity of his language against the dusty, purposeless vagueness of so much of life—indeed, against the specter of death, which is often his true subject. In answer to its insidious whisper he offers up small consolations . . . and, once in a while, the promise of poetic epiphany. But he constantly reminds us of the limits of his enterprise. . . .

The limits of which Garrison speaks are several, but none more restrictive than the temporal ones. That is, moments are a quintessentially important qualification in Strand's poetry: a poem is frequently the precise moment where the personal universe is erected to replace the grim torments or mere monotony of life. As Strand notes vividly in *Dark Harbor*, "There is a luminousness, a convergence of enchantments, / And the world is altered for the better as trees, / Rivers, mountains, animals, all find their true place, / But only while Orpheus sings." The poem frequently is, for writer and reader, the perfect moment of existence. Still, this moment of clarity, safety, enjoyment, or redemption is fleeting. In the early stages of Strand's career, his speaker cannot summon up the power of the imagination at will, and several poems confront the challenge of summoning the regenerative power of poetry. Even at its most capable, however, at the very moment the poetic indulgence ends—with the final words of the poem—we return to a privative darkness. And again, there are occasions when Strand is acquiescent to that darkness—when he is confident of the ability to transform privative darkness to primitive darkness and create anew— and occasions when he responds with mournfulness—over the passing of the previous poem, or over his anxiety about his ability to summon up another poem.

PLACING STRAND IN THE CANON

The delights of reading Strand are also the difficulties, and critics often revolve around his poetry without attempting to confront it intimately. Many seem to be secure in their knowledge, but confronting any three will reveal at least two oppositional readings. Several critics argue over whether Strand's *materia poetica* is found in minute observation of the world or abstract revelation of dreamlike existence. Benfey identifies Strand's visions as borrowed and indistinct: "He is neither a minute observer of present things nor a hoarder of things past. . . . The props in his poems are abstract and secondhand: valleys, clouds, darkness, silence, the sea, the mountains" ("Enigma" 34). Meanwhile, Spiegelman says his poetry "mingles the particularity of observation that Strand shares with Elizabeth Bishop" (136). To some, Strand is a confessionalist; to others—properly—the antithesis of a confessionalist. Some enlist him as a postmodernist; others choose to identify him with the long history of the Romantic tradition.

Mark Strand's career eludes easy classification, even if individual poems seem to be easily classifiable. This fact does not preclude the knowing of a Mark Strand poem. His latest work continues to reveal a poet whose fear of and dissatisfaction with the world results in the creation of an alternate cosmos called the poem. Within the poem, natural-world elements are selected and imaginatively reintegrated with one another, and thus breathed into a new existence by the Creator—the Strand speaker. This speaker is more concerned in the items of the world as tropes than as the things themselves. As themselves, they are but forbidding mountains, trees, and clouds, doing little more than obstructing light. Imaginative readers and writers must borrow from the natural world the items they need to fashion "better" worlds, or as Strand describes it, "urging the harsh syllables / Of disaster into music."

Indeed, the world as itself is old and sad, and needs reinvigoration. While each Strand poem exists as a personal triumph of reconfigurations of the world into serviceable imaginative indulgences, each "masterpiece" of the private life is its own world. From poem to poem, Strand creates new tropes, new trials, alters previous ones, and reverses the rules, if necessary. From poem to poem, then, we may find a more or less contemplative speaker, a varied tone, a slightly altered set of values, and a reclassification of familiar metaphors. Nonetheless, in seeing Strand's motifs in light of his poetry's previous statements about the world, and in bracketing what his poems are saying with what his poems *have said*, the subjective worlds of the poem can be known. They are escapes from the world while at the same time existing within the world. Whether they are caves within a mountain, harbors within a city, breaks in a cloud, silences within a din or darknesses within blinding reality, or, yes, dogs among humans, the Strand poem presents alternatives to modern existence.

How do we recognize a poet's evolution into mastery? How can we assess a poetic career in the midst of its happening? Intriguing stylistics, uniqueness of vision, and resonance with a master poet alone do not qualify a poet for greatness, though they may earn him great attention. Strand says as much when he mournfully reports of those weak poets who "do nothing but count the trees, the clouds, / The few birds left." The strong poet must do more than generate a compendium of images as he compellingly presents the world as it appears to him. He must chart new territory, do something productive in the face of the perpetual annihilation, say something to the page that eats up his words, and leave the reader with a sense of having encountered something generative. He provides an alternative within the poem to the malfeasance of the world external to the poem. The strong poet encompasses the reader also in his imaginative creation.

By the time Strand evolves into the master that he is in his magnificent *Dark Harbor*, the poetry contained therein is no longer fragile but capable, no longer helpless but effectual. It is informed by something greater than abstract fears—the weight of personal survival and the ideas of the past virtuosos, which enable him to chisel his niche within the community of poets. The progression of Strand from the world's victim to citizen of his own imaginative world, from champion of indeterminacy to director of his artistic fate, is the process by which we recognize the poet of accomplishment.

After *Dark Harbor*'s achievement of community with the great angel-poets, Strand confronts what to do once he has become "the great dog . . . myself." In *Blizzard of One*, he faces the anxiety of influence of the self; his success has led him to become his own precursor. His achievement in *Blizzard* helps identify an important stage in the ongoing evolution of a luminary poet. Strand looks deeper into the abyss, so to speak, and in confronting keener demons, he proves that the poet of capable imagination can continue to expand his own wings, propel himself further, and still emerge on the other side of the poetic darkness as a dynamic creator. Ultimately, a poet of such astonishing capacities continues to face stronger challenges as he outperforms his previous self. The sustaining of such a career is, perhaps, the most impressive feat Strand can achieve, for he writes on the graveyard of masters, who were unable to do just what he has done, that is, to continue to maintain his poetic voice and occasionally exceed his own greatest accomplishments.

Poets in the vein of Whitman, Stevens, and Bishop, from whose lineage Strand descends, necessarily hold back something of the self in their presentation of persona. One of Strand's finest achievements is that he does not remain distanced from the poem as he did in his early career. As this monograph suggests, the more Strand opens up the lyric to the personal, to the natural world, to the specifics of loss, and to Death, the stronger his poetry becomes. This is not to say that the result is *inevitably* better poetry than that of his earlier years, though many of his later poems are his strongest. What it does say is that a poet must continually remake himself in order to sustain his artistic integrity. That remaking involves allowing the lyric to confront not only new challenges but more intricate ones. "The anxiety of self-imitation is the great anxiety of the poet," Strand has said, and he is a qualified source, for his poetry greets the increasingly taxing predicament of having to write something that he has not already written, and encounter artistic obstacles with a sense of originality and innovation.

From his earliest work to his most recent, the voice of Strand's speaker and its capacity to call forth an imaginative vision generally grow stronger. This statement allows for exceptions. Evolutionary changes in the Strand corpus are recognizable only within the context of those poems that come before and after those of the present. Transformations in his poetic philosophy and practice have occurred in increments throughout his career. From collection to collection, much of what appears is familiar, but some poems, or parts of poems, exhibit a new challenge to established Strandian poetics. These changes ultimately become integrated into subsequent poetry, thus continuously renewing a corpus while remaining faithful to Strand's poetic sensibilities. Strand therefore, to take a broad view, repeatedly appears both familiar and challenging, never surprising us, but always surprising us.

This monograph has not endeavored to put together a reductive study of Strand's work, nor to merely summarize the poems, noting the landscape as we pass by. As Strand has warned:

> Understanding a poem is often reductive. . . . It is more important to experience the poem. Many poems are not paraphrasable—you must read it again and again and again. . . . Poetry speaks to parts of ourselves, levels of experience that nothing else does—what it's like to be alive, to live in time, about loss and mortal life. It's almost narcotic. Rhyme and meter are so delicious that you want to do it again and again. There is retrieval in the poetry of loss. And poetry keeps time. It provides what we are denied—time.   (Quoted in Gibson)

By paying close attention to what Mark Strand's poems do and how they do it, and using a phenomenological approach that ascertains the effect of the Strand poem during the reading of it, we have endeavored to achieve what Henri Cole rightly calls "the cumulative effect" of Strand's vision. As such, we have tried to recognize the refinements that Mark Strand has achieved throughout his career: the subtle and deliberate movements toward inclusion in the community of poets; the revisionary attempts toward other poets but most vitally the reconsiderations of self; the recognition of poetry's place in the writer's and reader's life; and the continual reformulation of his poetic vision. For all his ambiguity, complexity and removals, projections and mirrorings of self, Strand does not make a mystery of the imaginative process. He quite lucidly shares his requirements for poetic engagement, and is quite willing to include his readers in the experience of the poem.

The poem's power to sustain itself is always in question for the contemporary poet. Strand undoubtedly has not exhausted his voice, and to put a capstone on his career now would prove to be short-sighted. Strand continues to feel that he is "no nearer the end, no farther from where we began," and protests "the advocates of awful-ness and sorrow [who] / Push their drooping barge up and down the beach." He seems increasingly motivated to oppose such awfulness and to outshout such advocates. While his past successes led to a new dilemma, the anxiety of self-influence, in *Blizzard of One*, he also continues to recognize that he, like Sisyphus walking down back up the hill to retrieve his rock, can always laugh in the face of the gods and say, "So what. We like it here. . . . why live / For anything else? Our masterpiece is the private life."

NOTES

INTRODUCTION

1. Although I understand and respect the number of critics' deploring the use of the word "world," in this sense, I defend, my use of the word by referring to Emerson in *Nature:* "Build, therefore, your own world" (36). No, I do not believe a poet creates an entire, full-of-actual-living-breathing-sentient-beings "world," as it were, in a poem. However, what I do contend is that, for me, there is no more suitable word. Strand himself repeatedly uses the term "world" freely, not the least unequivocal of which was in a January 26, 2002, interview: "I propose a metaphorical world, and not a metonymic world." In a PBS interview with Elizabeth Farnsworth, Strand defines the solipsistic nature of the self-enclosed poetic world by saying, "It's still your world, it's not a world of other people." In that same interview with Farnsworth, he differentiates between the "imaginary world" and the "real world." Such terminologies are thus sufficient for my needs, as well.

2. "My Son" appears in *The Late Hour*. All Strand selections other than *The Monument, The Continuous Life, Dark Harbor, Blizzard of One* and *The Weather of Words* are culled from *Selected Poems,* unless otherwise noted.

3. Strand has said of Frost: "There's a certain kind of moral smugness that obtains there, and I just don't like it. It lacks color . . . and dimension" (Interview 26 January 2002). The distinction Strand makes about Frost's smugness seems to identify precisely how the two poets share worldviews but part company in their poetry's response to the natural world. They share ambivalence, but Frost has a far more cocksure attitude than the whimsically cynical Strand. As such, Strand is unequivocal about Frost's approach to the perennial problems that poetry confronts.

Chapter 2 "Still We Feel Better for Trying," or Why Write a Poem?

1. Strand reveals that the poem is in fact a response to Archibald Macleish's "You, Andrew Marvell" (Author's interview Nov. 2, 2002).

Chapter 3 Earning One's Wings

1. Spiegelman suggests that the poem does move linearly—in reverse narrative fashion. "Only at the end of this book do we realize that its journey moves backward in time," he says. This study, as has been discussed, contends that the narrative progression is loosely built in circular fashion, with the center sections representing the portions furthest removed from the Strandian darknesses, and thus furthest removed from poetic strength.

2. Frequent lines such as these challenges Spiegelman's contention that "Strand writes in a clear, uncomplicated syntax" (139):

> He merely stands
> And stares as if in the severity
>
> Of his motionlessness he were a stand-in
> For somebody or something, an idea
> Of withdrawal or silence, for instance,
>
> Or for the perfection of watchfulness, how
> It entraps by casting an invisible net
> Around the watched, paralyzing him,
>
> Turning him into a watcher as well,
> A watcher who sees and must say what he sees,
> Must carve a figure out of blankness,
>
> Invent it in other words so that it has meaning,
> Which is the burden of invention, its
> Awkward weight, which must fit the man's
>
> Appearance, the way he raises a hand
> And extends it at arm's length, holding within it
> A small gun, which he points at the one who assumed
>
> The responsibility of watching, and now he squeezes
> The trigger and the gun goes off and something falls,
> A fragment, a piece of a larger intention, that is all.

Although few lines reach these proportions, the level of subordination exhibited here is as close to a norm as an exception. Undoubtedly, in the past, Strand has exhibited "the syntactic clarity of Bishop [to] strengthen his own emotional uncertainties" (Spiegelman 139).

Progressively throughout his career, Strand has enriched the mix to include various syntactical puzzles.

Chapter 4   Reinventing the Self

1. If we were to apply Bloom more vigorously, one might assert that this single poem progresses through all of the revisionary stages of Bloom's poetic theory. The poem does seem to "complete" Part XLV of *Dark Harbor*, a requirement of Bloom's *kenosis* (14). This later Strand then appears to "empty himself of his own afflatus, his imaginative godhood, seem[ing] to humble himself as though he were ceasing to be a poet" (*Anxiety* 14–15), in the concluding lines. Ultimately, the poem "The Adorable One"—also known as Part XLV of *Dark Harbor*—also may reveal the apophrades, the "uncanny effect is that the new poem's achievement makes it seem to us, not as though the precursor were writing it, but as though the later poet himself had written the precursor's characteristic work" (16). Of course, it requires a bit of verbal gymnastics to first explain how the Strand of *Dark Harbor* and the Strand of *Blizzard* are two separate poets, yet then contend that the fact that the first seems to have been written by the second should be "uncanny." Such contentions are better left for the body of this paper, and not its notes. So we will cease here.
2. Strand's only alterations from its originally published form are a single contraction, several stanzas, and line breaks.
3. Originally, as "Great Dog Poem No. 1," the lines read in more celebratory fashion: "the music of dogs / Fills up the air" (6–7). In fact, the original poem contains many vital alterations:

   > Before the tremendous dogs are unleashed,
   > Let's get the little ones inside, let's drag
   >
   > The big bones onto the lawn and clean the Royal Dog Hotel.
   > You lied when you said the world was secretly glad
   >
   > This would happen, that the end of the century
   > Called for no less. Even now, the music of dogs
   >
   > Fills up the air. And look at that man on all fours
   > Dancing under the moon's dumbfounded gaze,
   >
   > And look at that woman doing the same. The wave
   > Of the future has gotten to them, and they have responded
   >
   > With all they have, O heavenly bodies that sway in the dark.
   > O bodies of time unfolding. O golden bodies of lasting fire.

4. The publication dates of these poems places "The Great Poet Returns" ahead of "Five Dogs" #2 and #4 by a little less than two months.
5. The poem's overtness perhaps was the reason for its omission from *Dark Harbor*. It was published during the time Strand had been

preparing that collection; it is presented in tercets, as each of the parts of *Dark Harbor* is; and its theme of the private creation is in line with everything *Dark Harbor* suggests. The fact that this poem pronounces what Strand usually would intimate, however, prevents it from being as compelling a Strand poem as his most others are.

6. The original publication of this poem printed the phrase as "Star Emaculate."

7. One theory worth mentioning is that of Elizabeth Kübler-Ross' seminal discussion of the stages of loss. Ross acknowledges five stages in the process of coming to grips with loss: (1) denial; (2) anger; (3) bargaining; (4) depression; (5) and acceptance. I do not contend that Great Dog poems one through five necessarily directly correspond to the five stages, but should one wish to pursue the precise development of this process, one may meet with success. In any case, when Strand ends the quintet of poems with the words "goodbye all, goodbye dog," perhaps he is saying goodbye to, and accepting the loss of, the Mark Strand who had been, thus putting his precursor behind him.

CHAPTER 5 SUPPLEMENT

1. Because *Man and Camel* was not released before this monograph was readied for press, here we have referenced versions of the poems that were shared by Mark Strand personally with the author or, when possible, published in journals. The author thus does not account for any alterations of the poems, including potential titles, made for the final printing of *Man and Camel*. All attempts to provide accuracy of the versions discussed have been made.

2. Attending one of Strand's readings is perhaps the most valuable act a regular reader of Strand can make. While much has been said of his compelling clear and understated tone of voice, the responses of Strand's audience also adds to the experience. Their responses to the twists and turns of a Strand poem assist in the recognition of the complexity of his poetic movement. In "Man and Camel," for example, his audience properly laughed heartily at the opening; reflected seriously on the poem's philosophical underpinnings ("their voices / rose as one above the sifting sound / or windblown sand"); giggled, still thoughtfully, at "The wonder of their singing, / its elusive blend of man and camel seemed / an ideal image for all uncommon couples"; grew seriously silent at the Leopardian "Was this the night that I had waited for / so long?"; and laughed thoroughly at the closing, "You ruined it. You ruined it forever," before finally pausing contemplatively. Few poets have the ability to evoke such a range of emotions in such a small amount of lines of lyrics, yet Strand does, in fact, have people in tears of laughter and sadness within minutes of each other. While this monograph has not attempted to chart Strand's emotional range in his poetry, it is magnificent, and should be experienced firsthand to be truly comprehended.

BIBLIOGRAPHY

Aaron, Jonathan. "About Mark Strand." *Ploughshares* 21.4 (Winter 1995): 202–5.

"A Conversation with Mark Strand." *Ohio Review* 13.2 (1972): 54–71.

Alexander, Bobby C. *Victor Turner Revisited: Ritual as Social Change.* Atlanta: Scholars, 1991.

Ashley, Kathleen M., ed. *Victor Turner and the Construction of Cultural Criticism: Between Literature and Anthropology.* Bloomington: Indiana University Press, 1990.

Bacchilega, Cristina. "An Interview with Mark Strand." *The Missouri Review* 4.3 (1981): 51–64.

Barry, Elaine. "Robert Frost on Writing: The Scope of Frost's Criticism." The Frost Free Library. FrostFriends.org. www.frostfriends.org/FFL/Frost%20on%20writing%20-%20Barry/barryessay1.html (accessed December 4, 2006).

Bayley, John. "The Way We Write Now." *New York Review of Books* 45.12 (July 16, 2008): 41–43.

Benfey, Christopher. "Books Considered: *Dark Harbor.*" *The New Republic* 209.4 (December 14, 1993): 37–39.

———. "The Enigma of Arrival." *The New Republic* 208.10 (March 8, 1993): 34–37.

Bensko, John. "Reflexive Narration in Contemporary American Poetry: Some Examples from Mark Strand, John Ashbery, Norman Dubie, and Louis Simpson." *Journal of Narrative Technique* 16.2 (1986): 81–96.

Berger, Charles. "Poetry Chronicle: Amy Clampitt, Louise Gluck, Mark Strand." *Raritan: A Quarterly Review* 10.3 (1991): 119–33.

———. "Reading As Poets Read: Following Mark Strand." *Philosophy and Literature* 20.1 (1996): 177–88.

Birkerts, Sven. "The Art of Absence." *The New Republic* 203.25 (December 17, 1990): 36–38.

Bishop, Elizabeth. *The Complete Poems, 1927–1979.* New York: Farrar, Straus, and Giroux, 1984.

Bloom, Harold. *The Anxiety of Influence: A Theory of Poetry.* New York: Oxford University Press, 1973.

———. "Books Considered: 'The Monument' and 'The Late Hour.' " *The New Republic* 179.5 (July 29, 1978): 29–30.

———. *Figures of Capable Imagination.* New York: Continuum, 1976.

———. *How to Read and Why.* New York: Scribner, 2000.

Bloom, Harold. "Mark Strand." *The Gettysburg Review* 4 (1991): 247–48.

———. *Wallace Stevens: The Poems of Our Climate*. Ithaca: Cornell University Press, 1977.

Bradley, George. "Lush and Lean." *Partisan Review* 58.3 (1991): 562–65.

Brennan, Matthew. "Mark Strand's 'For Her.' " *Notes on Contemporary Literature* 13 (1983): 11–12.

Brooks, David. "A Conversation with Mark Strand." *Ontario Review: A North American Journal of the Arts* 8 (1978): 23–33.

Cavalieri, Grace. "Mark Strand: An Interview by Grace Cavalieri." *American Poetry Review* 23.4 (July/August 1994): 39–41.

Cole, Henri. "The Continuous Life." *Poetry* 58 (1991): 54–57.

Coleman, Jane Candia. "The Continuous Life." *Western American Literature* 26 (1991): 178–79.

Coles, Katharine. "In Presence of America: A Conversation with Mark Strand." *Weber Studies: An Interdisciplinary Humanities Journal* 9.3 (1992): 8–28.

Cooper, Philip. "The Waiting Dark: Talking to Mark Strand." *The Hollins Critic* 21.4 (1984): 1–7.

Corn, Alfred. "Plural Perspectives, Heightened Perceptions." *The New York Times Book Review* (March 24, 1991): 26–27.

"Dark Harbor." *Virginia Quarterly Review* 69.4 (1993): 136.

Dodd, Wayne, and Stanley Plumly. "A Conversation with Mark Strand." *Ohio Review* 64/65 (2001): 369–94.

Donaldson, Jeffery. "Mark Strand." *American Writers Supplement* IV. Part 2. Ed. A. Walton Litz and Molly Weigel. New York: Scribner, 1996. 1417–71.

———. "The Still Life of Mark Strand's Darkening Harbor." *Dalhousie Review* 74.1 (1994): 110–25.

Donoghue, Denis. "Waiting for the End." *The New York Review of Books* 16.8 (May 6, 1971): 28–29.

Ehrenpreis, Irvin. "Digging In." *The New York Review of Books* 28.15 (October 8, 1981): 45–47.

Eliot, T. S. *The Waste Land and Other Poems*. New York: Harcourt, 1962.

Emerson, Ralph Waldo. *Ralph Waldo Emerson*. Ed. Richard Poirier. New York: Oxford University Press, 1990.

Farrell, John P. "'The Scholar-Gipsy' and the Continuous Life of Victorian Poetry." *Victorian Poetry* 43.3 (2005): 277–96.

Flint, R. W. "Strong Intuitions and Lurking Wit." *The New York Times Book Review* January 18, 1981: 13.

Freibert, Stuart. "All We Can Do." *Field: Contemporary Poetry and Poetics* 44 (1991): 58–66.

French, Roberts W. "Eating Poetry: The Poems of Mark Strand." *Far Point* 5 (1970): 61–66.

Frost, Robert. *The Poetry of Robert Frost: The Collected Poems, Complete and Unabridged*. Ed. Edward Connery Lathem. New York: Holt, 1979.

Garrison, Deborah. "The Universe Stares Back: The Poet Mark Strand Confronts the Infinite, Which Sometimes Returns His Gaze." *The New York Times Book Review*, September 13, 1998. http:// ww.nytimes.com/ books/98/09/13/reviews/980913.13garrist.html

Gibson, Lydialyle. "Killing Time with the Grim Reaper: A Self-Described 'Humorous Poet,' Mark Strand is Serious, Spellbinding, Heartbreaking— and Outright Funny." *A Chicago Journal Poetry Center Event Review* April 22, 2004. http:// www.poetrycenter.org/involved/news/strand-journal.html (accessed December 4, 2006).

Gregerson, Linda. "Negative Capability." *Parnassus: Poetry in Review* 9.2 (1981): 90–114.

Gullette, David. "Mark Strand: Nervous in His Own Kingdom." *New Boston Review* 4.2 (1978): 15–16+.

Haft, Adele J. "The Poet as Map-Maker: The Cartographic Inspiration and Influence of Elizabeth Bishop's 'The Map.' " *Cartographic Perspectives* 38 (Winter 2001): 37–65.

Hamilton, Craig A. "Strand's 'The History of Poetry.' " *Explicator* 60.3 (Spring 2002): 177–79.

Hamilton, Ian., ed. *The Oxford Companion to Twentieth-Century Poetry in English.* New York: Oxford University Press, 1994.

"Holism." *American Heritage Dictionary.* 3rd ed. 3.5″ diskette. Macintosh Version. Novato: Star, 1993.

Hollander, John. "Summary of the Spoken Responses by the Poets to Their Critics." *Philosophy and Literature* 20.1 (1996) 189–92.

Howard, Richard. *Alone with America: Essays on the Art of Poetry in the United States since 1950.* Enlarged ed. New York: Atheneum, 1980. 589–602.

———. "(Mark Strand: The Story of Our Lives)." *Ohio Review* 15.3 (1974): 104–7.

Jackson, Richard. "Charles Simic and Mark Strand: The Presence of Absence." *Contemporary Literature* 21 (1980): 136–45.

Jenkins, Nicholas. "Joy in the Bookish Dark." *Times Literary Supplement* (May 17, 1996): 25.

Jurado, Mario. "Mark Strand: Dejar el mundo fuera." *Cuadernos Hispanoamericanos* 664 (October 2005): 123–27.

Kardokas, Laima. "The Twilight Zone of Experience Uncannily Shared by Mark Strand and Edward Hopper." *Mosaic: A Journal for the Interdisciplinary Study of Literature* 38.2 (June 2005): 111–28.

Kelen, Leslie. "Finding Room in the Myth: An Interview with Mark Strand." *Boulevard* 5–6 (Spring 1991): 61–82.

Kinzie, Mary. "Books: Collected and Selected." *The American Poetry Review* 10.6 (1981): 35–45.

Kirby, David K. *Mark Strand and the Poet's Place in Contemporary Culture.* Columbia: University of Missouri Press, 1990.

Klein, Norman. "A Conversation (Interview with Mark Strand)." *Ploughshares* 2.3 (1975): 6. http://www.pshares.org/issues/article.cfm? prmarticleID=283 (accessed August 1, 2002).

Leopardi, Giacomo. *Leopardi: Selected Poems.* Trans. Eamon Grennan. Princeton: Princeton University Press, 1997.

Lesser, Wendy. "Metamorphoses." *The New York Times Book Review* (March 17, 1985): 16.

Leithauser, Brad. "The Hard Life of the Lyric." *The New Republic* 198.21 (May 23, 1988): 30–35.

Lieberman, Laurence. "Mark Strand." *Poetry* 128.5 (1974): 280–87.

Logan, William. "Sins & Sensibility." *New Criterion* 17.4 (December 1998): 69–76.

López Ortega, Antonio. "La traducción como transfiguración (Juan Sánchez Peláez traduce a Mark Strand)." *Hispamérica: Revista de Literatura* 27 (1998): 217–27.

Macksey, Richard. "The Consciousness of the Critic: Georges Poulet and the Reader's Share." *Velocities of Change: Critical Essays from MLN.* Ed. Richard Macksey. Baltimore: Johns Hopkins University Press, 1974. 304–40.

Manguso, Sarah. "Where Is That Boy?" *Iowa Review* 29.2 (Fall 1999): 168–71.

Martz, Louis L. "Recent Poetry: Visions and Revisions." *The Yale Review* 60 (1971): 403–17.

McMichael, James. "Borges and Strand, Weak Henry, Philip Levine." *Southern Review* 8 (1972): 213–24.

Miklitsch, Robert. "Beginnings and Endings: Mark Strand's 'The Untelling.' " *Literary Review: An International Journal of Contemporary Writing* 21 (1978): 357–73.

Miller, Christopher R. "Mark Strand's Inventions of Farewell." *Wallace Stevens Journal: A Publication of the Wallace Stevens Society* 24.2 (Fall 2000): 135–50.

Miller, J. Hillis. "The Literary Criticism of Georges Poulet." *Modern Language Notes* 79.5 (1963): 471–88.

Miller, Nolan. "Books." *The Antioch Review* 54 (1996): 245–46.

———. "The Education of a Poet: A Conversation between Mark Strand and Nolan Miller." *The Antioch Review* 39 (1981): 106–18; 181–193.

Mitova, Katia. "On the Ease of Writing Lists." *Denver Quarterly* 36.3–4 (Fall–Winter 2002/2003): 94–97.

Moore, Marianne. *Complete Poems.* New York: Penguin, 1994.

Oakes, Elizabeth. "To 'Hold Them in Solution, Unsolved': The Ethics of Wholeness in Four Contemporary Poems." *The Journal of Liberal Arts* 25 (2000): 49–59.

Olsen, Lance. "The Country Nobody Visits: Varieties of Fantasy in Strand's Poetry." *The Shape of the Fantastic.* Ed. Olena H. Saciuk: Westport: Greenwood Press, 1990. 3–14.

———. "Entry to the Unaccounted For: Mark Strand's Fantastic Autism." In *The Poetic Fantastic: Studies in an Evolving Genre.* Ed. Patrick D.

Murphy and Vernon Ross Hyles. Westport: Greenwood Press, 1989. 89–96.

Pack, Robert. "Wallace Stevens: On 'The Snow Man.' " *Modern American Poetry: An Online Journal and Multimedia Companion to Anthology of Modern American Poetry.* Ed. Cary Nelson. 2000. New York: Oxford U P. http://www.english.uiuc.edu/maps/poets/s_z/stevens/ snowman.htm (accessed January 22, 2002).

———. "To Be Loved for Its Voice." *Saturday Review* 51.34 (August 24, 1968): 39–40.

Pernik, Cornelia A. "Mark Strand." *Literature Resource Center.* Version 3.1. Contemporary Authors Online. The Gale Group. http://galenet.gale-group.com/servlet/LitRC?c=1&ai=85825&ste=6&docNum=H1000 095816&bConts=16047&tab=1&vrsn=3&ca=1&tbst=arp&ST= mark+strand&srchtp=athr&n=10&locID=oakl38377&OP=contains (accessed August, 2006).

Pettingell, Phoebe. "Lyrics in Periods of Crisis." *New Leader* 84.6 (November/December 2001): 40–42.

Pinsky, Robert. "More of the Story." *Poetry* 132.5 (August 1978): 293–302.

Poulet, Georges. "Criticism and the Experience of Interiority." Trans. Catherine Macksey and Richard Macksey. In *Reader-Response Criticism: From Formalism to Post-Structuralism.* Ed. Jane P. Tompkins. Baltimore: Johns Hopkins University Press, 1980. 41–49.

———. "The Phenomenology of Reading." *New Literary History* 1 (1969): 53–68.

"The Pulitzer Poet." Online NewsHour: A NewsHour with Jim Lehrer Transcript. http://www.pbs.org/newshour/bb/entertainment/jan-june99/ pulitzer_4–15.html (accessed April 15, 2006).

Russo, John Paul. "The Great Forgetting: From the Library to the Media Center." *Bulletin of Science, Technology & Society* 21.1 (February 2001): 20–25.

Sampson, Dennis. "The Continuous Life." *The Hudson Review* 44 (1991): 333–42.

Sanders, Seth. "Strand to Share Results of Challenge He Undertook for 'Seven Last Words.'" *The University of Chicago Chronicle* 21.9 (February 7, 2002). http://chronicle.uchicago.edu/ 020207/strand.shtml

Shaw, Robert B. "Quartet." *Poetry* 139 (1981): 171–77.

Shawn, Wallace. "Mark Strand." *Paris Review* 40.148 (Fall 1998): 146–78.

Spiegelman, Willard. "Poetry in Review." *The Yale Review* 81.3 (July 1993): 134–51.

Stevens, Wallace. *The Palm at the End of the Mind: Selected Poems and a Play.* New York: Vintage, 1989.

———. *The Necessary Angel: Essays on Reality and the Imagination.* New York: Vintage, 1951.

Stitt, Peter. "Book Reviews: *The Late Hour.*" *The Georgia Review* 33 (1979): 466–67.

———. "Engagements with Reality." *The Georgia Review* 35 (1981): 874–82.

Stitt, Peter. "Stages of Reality: The Mind/Body Problem in Contemporary Poetry." *The Georgia Review* 37 (1983): 201–10.

Strand, Mark. *Blizzard of One.* New York: Knopf, 1998.

———. *Chicken, Shadow, Moon and More.* New York: Turtle Point Press, 2000.

———. *The Continuous Life.* New York: Knopf, 1990.

———. *Dark Harbor: A Poem.* New York: Knopf, 1994.

———. "Great Dog Poem No. 1." *The New Yorker* (January 15, 1996): 38.

———. "Great Dog Poem No. 2." *The New Yorker* (January 15, 1996): 53.

———. "The Great Poet Returns." *The New Yorker* (November 20, 1995): 62.

———. Telephone interview. January 26, 2002.

———. Telephone interview. November 2, 2002.

———. *The Late Hour.* New York: Atheneum, 1978.

———. *Man and Camel.* New York: Knopf, 2006.

———. "Mark Strand: The Art of Poetry: LXXVII." *The Paris Review* 148 (Fall 1998): 146–78.

———. "Our Masterpiece Is the Private Life." *The New Yorker* (November 2, 1992): 66.

———. *The Monument.* New York: Ecco, 1978.

———. *Poems: Reasons for Moving, Darker and The Sargentville Notebook.* New York: Knopf, 1992.

———. *Selected Poems.* New York: Knopf, 1991.

———. *Sleeping with One Eye Open.* New York: Atheneum, 1964.

———. "Slow Down for Poetry." *The New York Times Book Review* (September 15, 1991): 1+.

———. *The Story of Our Lives.* New York: Atheneum, 1973.

———. *The Weather of Words: Poetic Invention.* New York: Knopf, 2000.

Tillinghast, Richard. "Stars & Departures, Hummingbirds & Statues." *Poetry* 166.5 (1995): 292–95.

Trikha, Manorama. "Searching 'The Artifice of Artlessness' of His Poetry: A Conversation with Mark Strand." *Indian Journal of American Studies* 22.2 (Summer 1992): 119–25.

Turner, Victor. *The Ritual Process: Structure and Anti-Structure.* Ithaca: Cornell University Press, 1991.

Vine, Richard. "A Conversation with Mark Strand." *Chicago Review* 28.4 (1977): 130–40.

Ward, David C. "Holding the Line." *Sewanee Review* 109.1 (Winter 2001): 147–51.

Wood, Michael. "Experience's Ghosts." *New York Review of Books* 50.10 (June 12, 2003): 71–73.

Woodland, Malcolm. " 'Pursuit of Unsayables': Repetition in Kristeva's Black Sun and Strand's 'Two de Chiricos.' " *Mosaic: A Journal for the Interdisciplinary Study of Literature* 37.3 (2004): 121–38.

Yeats, W. B. *Selected Poems and Three Plays of William Butler Yeats.* Ed. Macha L. Rosenthal. New York: Macmillan, 1986.

INDEX